CONCUSSION IS BRAIN INJURY

CONCUSSION IS BRAIN INJURY
Revised Edition

Treating the Neurons and Me

Shireen Jeejeebhoy

Copyright © 2017 Shireen Anne Jeejeebhoy

All rights reserved. No part of this publication may be reproduced, stored in a retrieval system or transmitted, in any form or by any means, electronic, mechanical, recording or otherwise (except brief passages for purposes of review) without the prior permission of the author or a licence from The Canadian Copyright Licensing Agency (Access Copyright). For an Access Copyright licence, visit www.accesscopyright.ca or call toll free to 1-800-893-5777. Medical information provided herein, in the absence of a visit with a health-care professional, must be considered as an educational service only. This book is not designed to replace a physician's independent judgement about the appropriateness or risks of a procedure or therapy for a given patient or client. The purpose of this book is to provide you with information that will help you make your own health-care decisions. The information and opinions provided here are believed to be accurate and sound, based on the best judgement available to the author, editors, and publisher, but readers who fail to consult appropriate health authorities assume the risk of any injuries. The publisher and author are not responsible for errors or omissions. The editors and publisher welcome any reader to report to the publisher any discrepancies or inaccuracies noticed.

Publisher: SA Jeejeebhoy
Editor: Pam Elise Harris
Front cover image: Provided by Shireen Jeejeebhoy
Front cover design: Daniella Postavsky
Book layout design: Suzanne Verheul

Jeejeebhoy, Shireen
    Concussion Is Brain Injury / *Shireen Jeejeebhoy.*

Issued also in electronic formats.
ISBN: 978-0-9919698-6-9

This is a revised edition of *Concussion Is Brain Injury.*

For Mum

And in memoriam

Richard Hammond aka @MyABI_byRH.

May he always be remembered for his motto, #adaptandovercome.

Other Titles by Shireen Jeejeebhoy

Lifeliner
She
Aban's Accension
Time and Space
Eleven Shorts +1
The Job Sessions
A Nibble of Chocolate

Online Presence

jeejeebhoy.ca
pario.blogspot.com
@ShireenJ
flickr.com/photos/pario
facebook.com/Jeejeebhoy
plus.google.com/+ShireenJeejeebhoy
youtube.com/ShireenJeejeebhoy

Acknowledgements

Many encouraged and pushed me to update, well, rewrite *Concussion Is Brain Injury*. It all started with my healthcare team pronouncing that I needed to get my story out. Then the PubLaunch team helped me raise funds for it. And then community care provided the practical help to write.

I want to thank all the people who buoyed me up by generously contributing funds during the PubLaunch campaign: Andrew Fogg, Liz Marshall, Amanda, Meher and Joan Jeejeebhoy, Khursheed and Olive Jeejeebhoy, Mind Alive Inc., D.M. Cain, TJ Williams, Meri Perra, Peter John Palmer, Aisha, Errol Elumir, Marlene Close, Michelle Malmberg, Rick Axon, Eleanor MacLean, Lynn Terry, Sara Joyce, Sharon and Sholem Prasow, Robert Carnell, Judy Moir, Diane Marshall, Lynda L. Ciaschini, and beautiful anonymous folk.

I want to thank Daniella at PubLaunch, who ably lead me through the foreign world of fundraising; Greg at Iguana Books for guiding me; and Kathryn for answering all my questions and reviewing my book-related posts and letters. Their kindnesses ensured this book got launched.

I first met Pam Elise Harris through Bibliocrunch when I was looking for an editor for my novel *Time and Space*. We had so much fun together creating a new English language, and I so respected her diligence and desire to use Canadian English in my books that I stuck with her. With *Concussion Is Brain Injury*, she's done two massive rounds of editing, structural, and copyediting. It's been quite an adventure! Huge props!

I'm grateful to two older and wiser women, grounded in God, who reminded me I am loved by God, as well as my neurodoc for encouraging me and my lawyer for supporting me.

Huge thanks to Deanna and Krishan who set up my writing schedule, kept me going, commanded rest breaks for my screaming brain and fed-up body, brainstormed with me, and provided a mirror for my writings. And to Ali for responding to my last-minute call for help.

The folks at the ADD Centre reminded me to focus on the book whenever life threatened to derail me. Without them, this book would not be possible.

And finally and most importantly, humongous thanks to Mum who told me, "this is your book, write your story." She gave me the courage to start, continue, and finish it.

Foreword

Patients and healthcare professionals need reliable and up-to-date information about the effects of a condition, if and how a treatment works, and how to make a reliable diagnosis. This information will be evidence-based and derived from reliable research studies. This is what people mean when they talk about evidence-based medicine or evidence-based healthcare. I say this because I conducted research in the fields of healthcare, medicine, and pharmacy for thirteen years, and so I understand the importance of research underlying healthcare. Research, and by that I mean medical and healthcare research, has largely (but not solely) had a constrained view of what "counts" as "evidence." Data has tended to be restricted to numbers that were crunched to produce a statistical output. But not all research has been like that. Neuroscience has often used what is called a single-person case study. This is where the evidence is based on studying the life of one person with a brain injury. The classic example is Henry Molaison, known by his initials, patient "HM," who suffered amnesia after surgery to stop him from suffering epileptic seizures that damaged some of the parts of the brain that function for memory.

These case studies were, however, written up in a way that would be difficult for many people in similar circumstances to recognize, if they ever had access to the journal articles. They would tell the story of the life of someone who was living with a brain insult, but it was one driven by and for research and written in an Academicy way that would be uninterpretable to many. The unfortunate upshot of this was that for a long time the story of the patient was not heard as often as it should have been. It seems bizarre that I feel the need to have to say that the patient is the true expert when it comes to their condition, but even in our supposed enlightened times, the adage that the doctor knows best is still held by some. Therefore, I see Shireen's book to be a welcome throwing open the windows in the rather stuffy house of medical knowledge.

Shireen's book presents not just her own devastating story, but also an opportunity for researchers and healthcare professionals to better appreciate the impact that an insult to the brain had on her through her own words. I am confident that the story that Shireen tells is not just something that is personal to her but will add to our knowledge and understanding of concussion. To use the key word in research, the knowledge that she shares could then be transferred into a better way for doctors and other healthcare professionals to approach people with concussion.

Like Shireen, I am now a writer, and I too have had a brain insult. So, this book is something that I can read and in places feel that in some small way I can relate to. I will never say to Shireen, "I know how you feel," and no one should because any condition is personal to that person and can never be truly experienced by the other. But that does not mean we cannot try to understand a little better. And this book can help people to do so.

Donald J. Nicolson, Ph.D.

Dr. Nicolson has recently returned to research, working for NHS Fife in Scotland as a Health Services Researcher.

Table of Contents

Introduction 1

The Honeymoon 5

    CHAPTER 1: Y2K 7
    CHAPTER 2: WHAT ABOUT BOOKS 19
    CHAPTER 3: JOURNALING 36
    CHAPTER 4: STAYCATION TO VACATION 46

The Honeymoon Learnings 59

    CHAPTER A: THE DETAILS 61
        Diagnosis 63
        Observation 64
        My Brain Injury 64
        Diffuse Axonal Injury 67
    CHAPTER B: ANGER AND PERCEPTION 69
    CHAPTER C: TRADITIONAL STRATEGIES AND THERAPIES 73
        Pacing 73
        Deep Breathing 74
        SMART Goals 74
        Reading Strategies 74
        Decision-Making Strategies 75
        Cognitive-Behavioural Therapy 76
        Talk Therapy 76
    CHAPTER D: TECHNOLOGY ASSISTANTS 77

Abandonment 81

    CHAPTER 5: MY FORTIETH YEAR 83
    CHAPTER 6: YEAR OF HELL 89
    CHAPTER 7: SHATTERED 104

Abandonment Learnings 111

    CHAPTER E: EVIDENCE-BASED MEDICINE FAILS 113
    CHAPTER F: MEDICAL TEAM, SOCIAL SUPPORT 115
        Medical Team Support 115
        Social Support 116
    CHAPTER G: REMARKABLE RECOVERY 118

Chapter H: Insurance Principles 120

Salvation 123

Chapter 8: Brainwave 125
Chapter 9: Brain on Training Wheels 134
Chapter 10: Biofeedback Begins and Lifeliner Ends 138
Chapter 11: Becoming Me 154
Chapter 12: Open a Window.. 161

Salvation Learnings 167

Chapter I: Neurons and Brainwaves 169
    Delta Brainwaves 169
    Theta 170
    Alpha 170
    SMR 170
    Beta 171
    Busy Brain.. 171
    Gamma.. 171
    EMG... 172
Chapter J: Audiovisual Entrainment 173
    SMR 14 Hz 174
    SMR/Beta L13.5/R18 Hz 174
    Alpha 10 Hz 175
    Brain Booster/ADD L14-10/R19-10 Hz 175
    0.5–1 Hz, Sub-Delta 176
Chapter K: Attention 177
Chapter L: Fatigue 180

Fear 183

Chapter 13: Terror and Erebus 185
Chapter 14: Humans Aren't Tigers but Elephants 192
Chapter 15: I Need a Therapist 203

Fear Learnings 211

Chapter M: Thermoregulation.. 213
Chapter N: Stress.. 216
Chapter O: Treat the Person 218

Stall 221

Chapter 16: The Law Settles 223
Chapter 17: The Promise of Recovery 230

CHAPTER 18: NANOWRIMO 2009 237
CHAPTER 19: I CLICKED PUBLISH 239

Stall Learnings **243**

CHAPTER P: COMMUNITY SERVICES 245

Hope **247**

CHAPTER 20: CRUELTY WITH INTENT 249
CHAPTER 21: NEURODOC 255
CHAPTER 22: THE DREAM WAS WITHIN REACH 260
CHAPTER 23: HAPPY GAMMA 270
CHAPTER 24: THREADING NEW NETWORKS 279

Hope Learnings **287**

CHAPTER Q: HYPOTHALAMUS FIX 289
   Hypothesis *295*
   Method *296*
   Results *297*
   Unexpected Results *299*
CHAPTER R: GAMMA 303
   Introduction *303*
   Hypothesis *306*
   Method *308*
   Training *310*
   Data *312*
   Results after Forty-Four Sessions *313*
   IVA *313*
   TOVA *315*
   Single-Electrode EEG Gamma Brainwave Ranges *315*
   Functional Changes *315*
   Conclusion *317*
   Discussion *318*

Shock **323**

CHAPTER 25: ALONE IN THE CITY 325
CHAPTER 26: NOT A READER 335

Shock Learnings **345**

FLASHBACKS 351
GRIEF 352

Now What? **355**

CHAPTER 27: LABYRINTHINE RECOVERY 357
CHAPTER 28: YOU'RE NOT ALONE 366

Now What? Learnings 373

CHAPTER S: SOCIAL ISOLATION 375
Remedy to Social Isolation 375
CHAPTER T: WHEN TO TREAT 380
Theory 381
Assessment 382
Passive Treatment 383
Passive-Active Treatment 386
Reassessment 387
Active Treatment 388
Intensive Treatment 391
Maintenance 392
CHAPTER U: READING REHAB 394
Assessment 396
Passive-Active Treatment in Phase with Passive of "When to Treat" Chapter 399
Active Treatment 401
Intensive Treatment 404
Maintenance 405

Introduction

I'm not going to quote statistics at you; you already know brain injury a.k.a. concussion is a hidden epidemic. You want to know more about it and how to get better. In a weird way, I was set up to find answers to my brain injury. I studied neurophysiology as part of my psychology degree at the University of Toronto.

Dr. Norman Doidge of the University of Toronto said at the May 2017 Healing the Brain conference, "The brain's basic function is to change its structure and function in response to mental experience and mental activity and its dynamic assemblies constantly reorganize themselves in real time, especially during conscious activity." At the same conference, Dr. Lynda Thompson called these networks "interconnected, functionally related, groups of neurons." The brain comprises neural networks, structures are named locations on those networks, and functions are the networks' outputs. The brain changes its networks every second of every minute of every hour of every day of your life in response to everything you see, hear, smell, touch, taste, do, and is done to you. So if you watch TV, the brain's networks change so that you can watch TV easier. The more TV you watch, the more TV you will watch because your brain will make itself cool with that. When you read, the brain sprouts new neurons into new networks in order to learn how to do this new activity. The more you read, the more the brain reinforces those networks and in doing so allows you to enjoy and desire reading.

Conversely, if you stop reading or an injury stops you, the brain unplugs neurons from your reading network. The less you read, the harder it becomes to read and the less enjoyable. You then read even less, creating what Doidge calls "learned nonuse."

The brain learns not to use the reading network you spent your childhood wiring up. You wake up in your fifties and go, "What just happened? Why is it so hard to read those paperbacks I read all the time in university?"

Brain injury is like a massive plough that trenches through your established networks. Sheared axons blink useless electrical signals into voids of pooling blood and biochemical chaos. Interrupted networks with nowhere to send their signals feed noise into your brain. Since the basic function of the brain is to change, the brain changes itself to accommodate this injury while some cells begin the sloth-like process of regeneration. But it's tough bringing order into chaos. It would be like you with the worst case of laryngitis standing between two armies telling them to stop shooting at each other. They wouldn't hear you over the volley of bullets and bombs, whistling missiles and lobbing grenades.

In my opinion, the part that's missing from Doidge's definition is that we humans are biologically social animals, social meaning relationships with professionals, local baristas, your bus driver, not simply family and close friends. Riffing off of Doidge, I theorize the brain's function is to change its neural networks in response to mental and physical experience and activity within a web of relationships.

Standard brain injury treatment keeps you stuck between the grenade-lobbing armies with not even a bullhorn to amplify your futile requests for peace. It relabels the armies as mysterious aliens and still doesn't toss you a lozenge. It may even label you as someone with a personality disorder or depression who should stop screaming. That'll help your throat.

The brain controls everything. Medical doctors seem to be unaware that no brain, no expression of you, no pulse, no breath, no metabolism, no sight, no hearing, no muscle function. Of course, you can have cardiac problems from brain injury. Other problems, too. And if a broken bone cannot mend to exactly like it was before the break, why would the brain? No wonder people with brain injury swear up a storm. Not only are swear words located more persistently and separately from regular vocabulary so that they're more accessible in speech, but also trying to get people to understand and provide effective treatment is a Texas-sized tornado of frustration.

"Lifelong learning and Continuing Professional Development (CPD) are fundamental components of a physician's commitment to practise medicine competently and ethically." (CPSO, Continuing Professional Development)[1]

Unfortunately, most healthcare practitioners are welded to the old model of the brain as a rigid anatomical structure with no regenerating capacity. They open up the DSM, the Diagnostic and Statistical Manual of Mental Disorders, the bible of psychiatric illnesses, as if that has anything useful to say about an injury. Or they tell you to get on with your life as if short-circuiting neurons and neural networks leading nowhere are capable of allowing you to function.

My journey was about quieting down the armies. The narrative sections tell my story. The Learnings sections summarize what I've learnt about the brain, the injury, and treatments that actually heal injured neurons and restore function.

I've set up blog pages with references and further thoughts for some of the chapters. Any updates will appear in them. They can be accessed with password HoneyABC. I use fake names except for the ADD Centre and Mind Alive to protect identities.

---

[1] College of Physicians and Surgeons. http://www.cpso.on.ca/CPSO-Members/Continuing-Professional-Development

The Honeymoon

I got this.

Chapter 1

Y2K

I laughed and laughed. My friend said, a grin lighting up her voice, that it was the happiest she'd ever heard me. I nodded. After years of research, I was finally writing *Lifeliner*! I was living my dream, writing a book about Judy Taylor, a Canadian woman and the first person in the world to live on artificial feeding without eating. On top of that, my husband was home more. He had a knack for making me fall off the couch, clutching my stomach, gasping for air, gasping out, "Stop. Stop. I gotta stop laughing." Of course, that egged him on, so I'd return the compliment till we were both on the floor telling each other to stop while our dog sniffed and licked our faces.

I had come a long way since the summer before my first year of university.

I had walked unsteadily between the throngs of people laughing and talking and eating cotton candy as they tasted the new wonders of Canada's Wonderland one Saturday afternoon in 1981. The cold rain of the morning had steamed away under the June sun's blasting heat. There was no shade in sight. The theme park was too new for trees to have leafed out great shadows to shelter under. Buildings provided meagre side panels of shade. I put one foot in front of the other under the sun as I willed my dizzy head up, set my eyes ahead, and put my mind on my purpose: find Dad. There was shade where he was, too. The pale bricks underneath my running shoes were soaked in the sun's rays and billowed up heat into my legs and into my body. My heart couldn't take it. Halfway across the wide, wide path I stopped walking.

My eyes dropped.

My view narrowed to the bricks.

Fear clutched my chest as my head plummeted down toward the relentlessly hot solid surface. Somehow, I stopped myself from falling.

People swirled around me as I stood there bent at the waist, watching the path beneath me to ensure it didn't come any closer while I talked to myself. *I have to stand up. I can't make it to Dad. I have to return to Mum. I have to stand up. I can't stand up. I must stand up. I can't walk back to Mum and Gracious bent over like this.* I waited for the familiar black strands of mist to clear from my vision. Low blood pressure had dogged me for a few years, although never like this. The sun beat on my back while the people walked around me like I was an obstacle between them and their next ride. Finally, millimetre by millimetre I cautiously straightened myself. I waited to ensure that I wouldn't keel over, and then I walked very, very carefully back to my mother and Gracious, who took one look at my white face and cold body and sounded the alarm. Minutes later ambulance attendants were futilely trying to measure my blood pressure. It had dropped to unreadable.

Decades later, I asked God why He didn't let me die that day. I was a teenager on the way to her first year at the University of Toronto. I was a young woman full of potential, determined to study psychology and enter med school. I was the first girl on my father's side who had survived in three generations, and I was following in my dad's footsteps. If I had died that day, I would have been remembered as a person who had a bright future. I would have been mourned and missed. I wouldn't have become a failure, a fuck-up, an embarrassment with a destroyed life, shunned and left in the solitary confinement of brain injury.

Job spoke for all of us who have been flung into the abyss of brain injury when he said, "May the day of my birth perish."

The day of my birth, snow flung itself around the maternity hospital as the doctor dragged me out of my mother's womb with forceps. The night of my second birth—the day of my brain injury—was cold, too.

But the sky was clear, the wind still, the road dry in the middle. No snow, no drink nor drugs nor sleep obscured the vision of the sober drivers zooming at us at sixty kilometres per hour as we sat stopped behind a steep downhill snaky line of cars.

Bang.

The old sedan slammed into our bumper. Shocked at the violence of being hit, I raised my left hand up to protect my neck as the force of that old sedan rammed us into the trunk of the red car in front of us.

Bang!

Another car crashed into and underneath the trunk of the one behind us, which again flung itself against our bumper.

Silence.

Stunned silence.

And then...

A car flew by us on the damp right shoulder, unknowingly saving my brain enough for it to save me.

And then...

I keeled over and sobbed like Job, like I had lost everything: my loved ones, my job, myself.

And then...

I sat up and felt nothing.

"Call 911," my husband instructed me as he got out of the driver's seat to assess the damage to the car.

The paramedics lead me to the back of the ambulance. The wintry air hit my bare arm, as I slipped off one sleeve of my heavy, red wool coat so that the paramedic could wind the blood pressure cuff around my skinny arm.

"120/80," he declared. "Normal." He added that my heart rate was a bit high.

That can't be right.

"Nope, you're normal," he said again. "Nothing's wrong." I knew something was off. The numbers were wrong for me. Shouldn't it be 110/70 or 90/60? But the way my blood pressure normally dropped under stress was slipping out of my memory.

Never mind. I knew what to do. I followed the paramedic's instructions, and on Monday morning, I telephoned my GP, my physiotherapist, the one I'd seen for my 1991 injuries from a car crash, my acupuncturist, and my insurance broker. By mid-week, I was seeing both the physiotherapist and acupuncturist. I was on my way to healing. My GP reviewed my X-rays and sent me to my old physiatrist—a physician who specialized in the musculoskeletal system—who referred me to a psychologist and the Toronto Rehabilitation Institute (TRI), Rumsey Centre for treatment of the fibromyalgia that the crash had flashed back into life.

Oh goody. Fatigue is here again, I thought briefly before recommencing my single goal of getting better and returning to writing in three months.

My weeks became a blur of twice weekly physiotherapist and acupuncturist appointments, psychologist appointment, GP appointment, maybe a specialist appointment to treat my neck sprain, seatbelt injury spraining my right shoulder, left shoulder sprain, impaired blood supply into the right arm (and a bit into the left), and ulnar nerve problems in the left arm, all similar to ones I'd had in 1991 but without the killer migraines. The nausea with dizziness was new, but I forgot about them when not feeling them. I kept phoning my insurance adjuster, a.k.a. the accident benefits claim representative, trying to be the organized person I always had been. Phone calls with kith became trying, feeling endless after fifteen minutes. Brief homecare to feed me and to sort of clean the house when my husband was away was a godsend. Walks with my dog felt more and more like I was shoving a square boulder (me) while attempting to keep him from pulling on any part of my shoulders, arms, or hands. My waist became my purse and leash holder. But his devoted presence comforted me. I waited for my appointment at the TRI as my life began to unravel.

On April 3, I had my first IME. That's Independent Medical Exam for those of you blessedly innocent of the medicine-through-insurance-company system. The idea is that after you are injured in a car crash, your doctor refers you to a physiotherapist, say, and the physiotherapist fills out a treatment plan for the insurer. Since naturally the GP you've been seeing for years can't be trusted to know your health, the insurer, with governmental blessing, sends you to a doctor who knows squat about you because that way they can be trusted to advise what you really need. And to ensure true independence, the insurer pays the IME doctor so that s/he has zero obligation to you.

Anxiety riddled me the night before because this IME was happening awfully early in the process. I'd been oblivious to how the year 2000 version of Ontario's insurance accident benefits was ensnaring me in its tentacles. Confident from having acquired the support and healthcare I needed from it nine years earlier, I believed it wouldn't defeat me.

But its tentacles had trapped me.

They demanded a ritual of being told the date of the IME appointment and being told to show up, even if it means cancelling the medical appointments designed to heal. It's a ritual of the IME examination ensuring its results will show you are fine. It's a ritual of pain, confusion, and fatigue that attack your honesty and your health, yet if you don't remain calm and be co-operative, you'll be black marked. That means denial of your treatment plans, the lifeline to getting better. It's a ritual of waiting weeks to months for the verdict while reports are written and the insurer decides if they'll pay the clinic or therapist to continue to heal you. It's a ritual of you begging the therapist or clinic to keep you on while everyone waits or to not interrupt your treatment if the plan is denied, for interrupted treatment means setbacks, maybe even permanent disability.

Between the severe pain in my right injured shoulder and my terror that the IME would derail me getting back to writing *Lifeliner*, I stared sightlessly at my bedroom wall. I lay on my back, praying for release from this hell.

And then...

I sensed God's presence over my head like a golden light looking down upon me. It reminded me of when I was six years old. I was sitting on the floor in Sunday school with the other children in this new land my parents had brought me to. I was probably sitting lotus style, for I hadn't yet mastered cross-legged, but I was trying to in order to fit in. One of the mothers sat on a chair in front of us, her acoustic guitar on her lap. I stared at her straight black hair shining in the sunlight while her voice sweetly trilled one of the songs I was coming to know, "Jesus Loves Me." The other kids sang along with her. All of a sudden, I felt Jesus near me as if he was a golden light around and speaking within me. I knew without a doubt that Jesus loved me. It didn't matter that I was considered a brat, bossy, stubborn, relentlessly asking questions, too dark, too light, too small. Jesus loved the whole of me. And then the presence was gone. It was back to normal in that room except that my heart sang that at least one being loved me no matter what.

I slept.

That IME approved the treatment plan.

I continued my physiotherapy and acupuncture and psychology appointments.

And I stepped further onto the thick ice of God though cracks created by doubters laced the surface.

A good thing because it wasn't long before the news worsened.

My psychologist sat down in front of me, leaned forward to look at me eye to eye, and told me what he believed, that I had a closed head injury and needed to have my physiatrist refer me for official diagnosis. I did what I was told though I couldn't comprehend his calm bombshell in any way other than intellectually and glacially at that. My emotions were shut off like a dried-up well. I followed his instructions. I told people his assessment.

But I couldn't absorb it.

And so I forgot about it.

I returned to rehabilitating my neck and shoulders. That I understood. I knew who to see and what to do. I knew about the métier of insurance companies. I knew about keeping on top of the paper trail. I knew everything.

But I didn't.

When my psychologist told me he had to teach me a visualization exercise to reach the peace deep within me, for I would need it in the months to come, I didn't understand why. I knew my injuries. I'd get better and back to writing. But I obeyed him. My certainty of who I was, my life's path, my tribe, my place in its secure web began to dissolve little wisps at a time.

One night I dreamt of boulders rising out of the water. Behind and to the left and right of me lay the land. Amorphous green trees surrounded me. The black, glistening boulders loomed out of the calm water of deceptive depths to block my escape. Every time I clambered over one, another would rise up ahead of me. Always before me were ragged rows of water-rubbed round boulders and rocks, their blackness both glistened and sucked in all the light.

I couldn't escape.

The depth of the water beyond the boulders terrified me, for I didn't know what lay beneath or if a boulder would suddenly pop up. I awoke.

By July, I admitted to myself I had trouble reading the numbers in my Day-timer. I could read them, yet I misread them. My attention hopped from eating to my pain to my husband's deep voice to my dog woofing at the door to my fatigue to trying to remember what I was supposed to be doing, all in about a minute. I had to buy a PDA. I chose a Visor. This appealed to my computer-loving heart. I hadn't yet faced up to the fact that my ability to work with computers had been severely damaged. I could still use one, but I couldn't troubleshoot them at all, me who had been everyone's personal IT department. Typing, mousing, or trying to read the screen quickly extinguished my energy.

By the time I got my Visor, my TRI assessment appointment had arrived. I was still waiting for my physiatrist appointment. You would think the possibility of a closed head injury would open doors tout de suite. Nope. I waited three months for the physiatrist, about four for the TRI appointment, and then another for the psychiatrist.

The Occupational Therapist (OT) who assessed me at TRI said I was typical for closed head injury. She recommended that I be admitted to the one-on-one outpatient neurorehab, pending official diagnosis by the psychiatrist. The logical part of my brain nodded. The coping part wept in relief that I was typical because then my experience was real and the doubting Thomases in my life would have to see my injury. The emotional part burst through briefly and decided it was having no part of this conversation.

On the second-last day of August 2000, the psychiatrist said he was positive I had a closed head injury. I was typical. He ordered a SPECT scan to see where injury had interrupted blood flow in my brain even though he said it would show normal so many months after the injury. He wanted me to have it anyway for research purposes at least.

I waited. What's a few weeks after so many months of waiting? I was so afraid. I didn't want to be this injured. I was supposed to be writing *Lifeliner*. I had committed to Judy's family and the many, many people who'd known and loved her to write this book and get it out to the world. I had already been set back once by the 1991 crash and didn't want to lose more years. I'd spent nine years interviewing dozens of people, meeting with Judy's daughters and widower several times, reading research journals, interviewing medical experts, and sitting for hours with her eldest in the Toronto General Hospital archives, transcribing the almost human-height medical records of this medical groundbreaking woman. I was so close to finishing it.

When the psychiatrist's office called me to come in a week earlier than scheduled, I told my husband in my new monotone that something was up. But I refused to face what my mind already knew. I was terrified and worried the psychiatrist would say I was just malingering. I was a neurotic hypochondriac as the independent experts and my kith and kin had made me feel. All the problems I was starting to become aware of—brain injury takes away your ability to perceive yourself—were "in my mind." *That's what he would say,* I thought.

I didn't know which was worse: to have a closed head injury or to have the people who loved me be right that I was malingering, depressed, and needed to get on with things.

Closed head injury. His diagnosis seeped around my dead neurons until live ones heard the phrase and my mind asked: *closed head injury? What's that? A concussion?* I said nothing. I couldn't respond. Mild traumatic brain injury, I heard it called later. *Mild? Why mild*, I wondered. Because you can walk and talk, I was told. I wasn't sure about that. Every word, every step was an effort. All these terms confused me: closed head injury, concussion, mild traumatic brain injury. Were they the same? They all connoted mild. Yet my life was swirling down with my ship into a dead whirlpool. Not mild.

> Concussion is a closed head injury.
> Closed head injury is a brain injury.
> Brain injuries are diffuse and focal.
> Mine is diffuse, I heard and forgot.
> Concussion is a brain injury.
> My entire brain is concussed.
> Isn't concussion supposed to be temporary?
> Concussion is brain injury.

I stopped struggling to understand and simply listened and believed because I was going to get better!

The psychiatrist read out the scan results and gave me a copy:

> *There is a moderate reduction in perfusion in the right frontoparietal area and right inferior frontal area on images 4, 5 and 6 sagittally and the left parietal area with some extension to the frontal lobe and left inferior frontal lobe seen on sagittal images 4, 5, 6, 7, 9, 10 and 11. Abnormalities are less clearly seen on transaxial image, but are partially seen on coronal images 8, 9, 10, 11 and 12. A minor reduction in perfusion in the anterior temporal lobes is also noted seen on sagittal images 3, 4, 5 and 6 as well as 10, 11 and 12.*

The diagnosing psychiatrist said that there was only one treatment, experimental yes, but the usual treatments were placebos. I had two years in which to improve. After that, wherever I was in two years, I would remain forever. But in recent studies, Aricept showed promise to ease short-term memory problems. I needed to take it. He wanted me in the research trial; it was my only chance. There was only one problem. It was contraindicated for people with asthma. And my asthma had returned with my brain injury, making me sound like a coughing dog. It freaked me out. So taking a drug that triggered it? Shudder. My husband was furious that I didn't say yes to the drug instantly. As he drove, we argued over the Aricept all the way home. He said in frustration that I was to take it and demanded to know why I wouldn't take it. He said that I didn't accept his opinion, and I should take it.

The thought that this was my only chance confounded me. Maybe I should take it. What if I didn't take it? Would I be forever injured? And anyway, how could I be injured? The scan results were definitive. The psychiatrist was adamant. My psychologist and TRI were all in agreement. I was typical for closed head injury. I had a brain injury. I needed rehab and treatment.

Later, alone in the kitchen with my dog, I called Dad up to tell him the news. He and I spoke clinically about my diagnosis, probable outcome, and the drug because that's how we talk all things medical in my family. But in my brain-injury-created, unfamiliar indecisiveness—on top of my normal way of seeing and arguing both sides first—I suggested I should take it. He huffed that I shouldn't take it, that I don't accept his opinion, but it's my decision.

What should I do? Whatever I did, someone would be mad at me. I didn't want anyone to be mad at me. I only wanted to get better. I couldn't express my angst out loud. The words wouldn't form.

I phoned my mother at work. My voice cracked. I heard my voice in disbelief. My voice didn't crack. I had mastered my emotions decades ago. When I cried, it was rare and not from zero to full blowout in an instant, and I didn't cry in front of people. Surely, hearing this strange behaviour and awful news, my mother would come right over. Surely, she could find another nurse to take over her shift on the cancer ward for a couple of hours at least. She couldn't.

She sent my sister. Then my best friend called. Relief. In her take-charge voice, she prescribed tea, some croissants I had bought on my way home from the psychiatrist, and chocolate. After work, she and her husband brought me a chocolate cake for medicine. She told me that it was not for sharing. None of us knew what to say. They all left. I took the cake into my kitchen, my dog trailing me, and ate a slice. Fatigue, confusion, and fear blanketed me like smog.

I felt very alone.

Chapter 2

What About Books

The Energizer Bunny booted me out of bed. God or the inherited will of the women in my bloodline got me to sit up then stand up against the fatigue that sat on me like an elephant resting his butt on my chest, against the pain plating my neck and shoulders, digging into my hips, and razing my right arm and hand. I stumbled into my day and to my favourite bookstore on hurting feet.

I walked through its glass doors and rode the escalator up, clinging to the germ-ridden moving rail, walking past the armchairs facing a cozy fireplace, up another escalator, feeling like I was going to fall over and down, down, down. But I made it safely off. Feeling relieved at once again foiling the gods of unbalance, I hurried at my slow pace with my right leg making its usual objections, not really noticing that I had to think to walk, think to know where to go, as I disappeared into the mystery section.

Being on my own meant being free to be in my slowed-down time. I could inhale the scent of fresh books unencumbered by anyone else misting out their impatience at me while I let my eyes slide across black and yellow and white small paperback spines until I found a name I could discern and knew.

I stuffed down the memory of the big change. I got to buy books now because of this big change. This was good. Well, OK, I didn't have the money to buy as many books as I liked. I could buy one. I had begun haunting the bookstore because I could no longer devour in two hours a mystery I'd borrowed from the library. For some reason, it took more than three weeks, and I was always getting them back late to the library. Like a child, seconds for me lasted weeks. Three weeks became amorphous. I'd check and recheck the slips, but they referred to numbers not the book titles. They were gibberish, and I couldn't match them up to the books I'd borrowed. I carried a paperback with me everywhere because I always had: on the subway, in doctors' offices, at lunch on my own. I always had borrowed three, maximum five, paperbacks in my weekly or more-than-weekly library visits. I had been on a book diet. I could've easily read one a day, but everyone around me got grumpy about it if I did. I hadn't known why. What did it matter if I read while they watched TV? I was sitting beside them. Or what did it matter if while they were at work and I was at home taking a break from my work that I flew on the words of another's imagination into a different place, a different life, enthralled by the mysteries enfolding me in their suspense?

Apparently, it had. And I acquiesced, putting myself on a diet. In 2000, I was starting to regret it.

I rationalized my pre-injury reading diet by telling myself that I had my morning start of emails and e-newsletters, my post-writing time of marketing books, my mid-afternoon stroll through different biography styles, and my post-coding late-day cool down of literary tomes to supplement. Well, the last could've dropped into the abyss of should-reads we all have and don't do. I could've gotten by with three or five paperbacks a week.

I couldn't fathom that since the car crash I was reading one book over more than three weeks. This made no sense.

I wandered on the third floor of Chapters, lost in the mystery stacks, until I found a book by an author I knew with characters I knew. I had come to buy only series familiar to me or ones so simplistically written that I could follow them. I happily headed for the cashiers, but first I had to navigate the scary escalators down. It didn't occur to me to use the elevator. I had always used the escalators.

Back outside, I willed my hand to grasp my new book tight so that it wouldn't fall away from me as I rode the subway to my acupuncturist's office, walked through her door, and into my reality of lying face down—because sitting up risked me fainting—with needles in my back to relieve my pain, alleviate my fatigue, and maybe heal my brain.

Tick. Tick. Tick. As each month slid by with *Lifeliner* on hold, a clock ticked louder and louder in my head, counting up my lost time, driving me to work harder and harder at healing faster and faster.

The penultimate day of August 2000, after I'd received the first official inkling I had a closed head injury from the diagnosing psychiatrist, I talked with a good friend and my dad on the phone when I got home. They made it clear how much my personality had changed.

Abrupt.

That was one word they used.

I didn't understand what they meant. After several months, the only changes I'd gradually perceived in myself was that anger wasn't meant to be 24/7, and I did tune out occasionally. It was frightening to completely forget some elements of my conversations. And I couldn't finish writing my outraged letters to my insurance company. My husband, Mistral, had to finish them. But I chalked that up to the deadening, endless fatigue. What my dad and friend had confessed didn't feel good. Confusion, despair, and hope vanished. My thoughts vanished, descending my emotions into an unreachable place. I rested in that blankness, staring fixedly into space and hearing and feeling my local environment but unable to respond, relieved in the rest my exhausted brain had enforced.

And then I got on with it.

Because that's what I did and was expected to do, to have a plan, to drive toward ambition, to be successful. I had a paperback in hand to keep me anchored to myself, to my life as I had planned it, to read while I waited for the acupuncturist, for the physiotherapist to call me in to stretch and manipulate my muscles gently, or for the psychologist to call me to determine what brainwaves to entrain in me. At home, I dropped the paperback wherever and switched on the TV. I flipped, flipped, flipped channels. My husband got annoyed. I walked out mid-scene, distracted by thirst. Halfway to the kitchen, I forgot my thirst and wondered why I wasn't watching the drama unfold on the TV. Back in front of the TV, my husband had forgotten the remote, and since I couldn't understand the dialogue, I picked up the black box and upped the volume to punishing levels.

The audiologist I was sent to said I had excellent hearing.

Tick. Tick. Tick.

Imeda and Vashti visited. Their small children ran in and spent alone time with us. Watching them, memory took me back to when their first was born.

The newborn that had greeted us so wide-eyed through the nursery window late the first night out in the world was sleeping in Vashti's arms as we walked in to the white-painted hospital room, me carrying my camera bag. Picture time! As I hauled out my Minolta Maxxum, Mistral cooed over the tiny infant, Vashti smiled down quietly, and Imeda talked and talked, his laughter infecting me. I shot a few frames, and then Vashti called a halt. She had a red outfit complete with hood, mitts, and booties, she wanted to dress her first-born in. Vashti laid their first-born out on the bed in front of her, one of her legs protecting her babe, as I stood on the other side clicking the shutter and Imeda opposite me watching this intriguing procedure of dressing a newborn.

Mistral was an old hand from his years of babysitting babies. He slid the tiny hood on and tied it under the fat little chin as best he could while Vashti pulled first the left little bootie up over foot and ankle then the right.

The infant screamed.

Imeda hunkered down, laying his right cheek against the tiny face reddening angrily. He squeezed his eyes tight shut, dragging his lower lip down as he feign-screamed with his progeny. I tried to hold the camera still, my laughter shaking my hands. I clicked off a good shot. And then we got serious. I only had thirty-six frames max to shoot. The tiny being hid their eyes behind clasped mittened hands as Vashti smiled down. Click. Head craned over to the left to see what that sound was. Click. The newborn snuggled under Vashti's chin, as Vashti wrapped her arms under and around the little body. I captured the moment and smiled.

And now here they were in my home and too soon leaving.

Tick. Tick. Tick.

I began to see the OT at the TRI tucked behind houses in midtown Toronto with its cream-painted block walls, its light-oak coloured wooden doors that reminded me of my childhood. Its busy yet not busy waiting room emptied into wide hallways devoid of people, filled with sunlight, a quiet contrast to Baycrest where I had met my diagnosis. The OT's smile punctured my confusion with light, and I followed her joyous presence into a large room that opened up into a smaller, darker room with a table and two chairs on either side. She told me that we would begin with a neuropsych test.

This was not my first neuropsychological test. That had been with yet another IME in his plush office. Time for me to get serious about my one-on-one neurorehab at TRI. My OT told me I would have a social worker and a speech-language pathologist (SPT).

Why? My speech was fine! Everyone said so. I could sound out words. I could put a sentence together. Why did I need an SPT?

My OT gently explained that SPTs also dealt with communication issues. Well, I did have trouble understanding English sometimes and getting out my thoughts.

"OK," I acquiesced. I'd see the SPT, too. My OT led the team I'd meet once a week. But I couldn't imagine spending one and a half hours with two therapists, never mind an additional forty-five minutes with a third and then having enough energy to get myself home and eat and attend my other appointments in the week.

And so the social worker and SPT alternated weeks.

Tick. Tick. Tick.

October 13, 2000, I walked to my OT session, the pain in my chest growing with each step. I wondered if I was having some sort of slo-mo heart attack. But I assured myself there was no such thing. My OT session was work with a capital W. My OT gave me a small, yellow pamphlet spelling out how to pace myself to conserve my energy. I felt like I knew it all. But I was dutiful. I furrowed my tight forehead to keep my attention on her, to absorb what she was telling me. "Keep a chart for three days of all your activities, read the handouts, and be ready to discuss it all next week."

Tick. Tick. Tick.

I wrote in my gratitude journal about how I was afraid conversation over dinner with my husband would lag as it often had recently. I'd been given this kind of popular journal to focus on what I should be grateful for instead of focusing on the negatives of life, like my brain injury and the losses that I had begun to experience.

But not once that night! I wrote. I asked my husband if he enjoyed the entire evening, not just the food.

"If I have to admit," he replied rather listlessly and reluctantly, "I guess so." I made a note to myself not to ask in the future. It had dampened my mood. I wrote how my energy was much better. I had written the day before how grateful I was for hugs. My psychologist as he was about to usher me out the door to my waiting husband had asked if he could hug me. I'd stood before the rotund man, perplexed. He'd said that I looked like I needed a hug. I hadn't been sure with the pain layering my body, and all my life I hadn't liked people touching me. Yet this person inside my injured body had seemed to want hugs. I'd nodded. He had gently put his arms around me in the most asexual hug ever that had calmed my soul.

Two days later, I stopped writing. I could not think. I could not feel. My husband had told me he had to leave me. My memory fled back to when we were still dating.

The best part of having a boyfriend, I'd decided, was having someone to troll the shops with on Boxing Day, holding my hand, waiting patiently while I tried on dress after dress, and helping me find the right colour, right length, and right look for me. The man had a fashionable eye. The bestest part was we were searching for a ball gown for me for our first ever Garrison Ball, coming up in February. Mistral had just become a Second Lieutenant and as a commissioned officer was entitled to attend. It took awhile, but we had found it! An indigo blue backless, rhinestone-edged dress.

Endless days later, February had dawned cold, and we entered the to-my-eyes extremely grand entrance of the Harbour Castle Hilton, a grey-block hotel squatting on the edge of the inner harbour, filled with glittering lights and glittering people. Officers in their brown kilts and red deerskin jackets and ceremonial swords and spurs on boots; their partners in flowing ball gowns or black tuxedos and stiff white shirts. Mistral had walked by my side, tall and elegant in his regimental mess dress and spit-polished boots, me in my blue silk ruffles. He'd pulled out my chair at our table in the enormous Metropolitan Ballroom, sat down, leaned over, and whispered, "You are the prettiest and most elegant one at our table." I'd preened under Mistral's warm, admiring gaze.

Now he looked at me with pained eyes and moved to sleeping on the couch.

Exhaustion crawled over me. Pain leadened my muscles and poked here and there all over me. That bunny with its powerful hind paws booted me out of bed. I kept on going to my appointments. I kept on reading. The clock in my head kept on ticking while Mistral announced that he was leaving on an airplane for a month. He said he wasn't separating from me yet, but he had to work, and this place he was going to was going to pay him. While he was in Toronto and driving me to my appointments, I was the mill around his neck stopping him from finding a job. But he had one elsewhere for a month, and he was going. And so I decided to become independent.

I did not need him.

OK, I needed him. I needed him to feed me, to look after me, to drive me even though the car was my enemy. The roads were passages of danger, spilling hurtling metal blocks toward Mistral and me. He was already waiting in the car to take me to yet another appointment. The car was running impatiently, waiting, waiting, waiting for me to get my coat on, to gather up my purse, to go over what I had forgotten, and to say good-bye to my dog. With my injured arm and shoulder, imposing my will over my hand failing in strength, I opened the door and climbed in. I slowly pulled at the seatbelt against its great force and, with frowning attention that it wouldn't stay put, clipped it in to the buckle. And then I realized I'd forgotten to brush my teeth. I used my tongue to rub at my teeth, feeling ashamed and then promptly forgetting, as Mistral pulled out onto the main road and drove toward my next appointment.

His cell phone rang.

"Don't answer it."

He ignored me and said, "Hello." Phone clamped to his ear, he drove one-handed at speed along the busy road. He braked at the last minute for the red light. I prayed. Anger rose in me and blurted out, "Get off the phone!"

He ignored me and continued to talk to the man on the other end. I steamed, trapped inside my head, fear bubbling away that his attention to the call and not to the road would drive us into the car in front of us. I prayed and prayed.

Near the end of the ride, he took the fat, dark-grey phone off his ear and pushed the top part down toward the main part with a click. "Don't interrupt me," he lectured me. He informed me that he had to take these calls, that if he didn't have to drive me places, he would be at his job. It was my fault he was not working.

My injured brain abandoned its communication networks, and I climbed out of the car stiffly, slowly, silently. *It's not my fault!* As soon as I shut the car door, he was off. I walked with an effort I was not aware of toward the building's doors and my psychologist's appointment.

I would not need him to drive me.

I had a month—the month he was away—to train myself to be independent. I watched him walk out the door, suitcase in hand, and felt nothing. Our dog was confused, but his favourite person was remaining at home: me. So, he trotted back to his bed.

Silence descended.

Tick. Tick. Tick.

I began my independence movement.

Detachment became my friend, my mentor. Self-talk, which had been with me since the earliest age I could remember, became my companion, my friend.

My mind knew what to do. It was like my mind was not my brain.

Pour cereal, my mind instructed my fuzzy brain. I reached into the cupboard with my left hand and took out the cereal box. I found a bowl. I poured the cereal and stared at it.

Put bran on top of the cereal, my mind told me. I looked around for the bran. There it was in its familiar glass container. How much? I wasn't sure. I didn't remember. An old picture in my memory showed me how high I ought to heap it. But I couldn't walk that far, over to the counter, the two steps there.

No, but you need to put the bran on top of the cereal, instructed my mind.

I obeyed, my left hand scooping out flakes and letting them fall on top of the cereal while my right arm hung listlessly by my side. I put the lid back on the container, hoping I had enough bran on the cereal, and stared at the flakes.

Get the milk, my mind instructed.

And so it went, the clock ticking the minutes away as I prepared my breakfast and sank down to eat it.

I propped the *Toronto Star* up in front of my cereal bowl and attempted to read it. (I'd read it since I was thirteen years old when I'd gotten my first job as a newspaper delivery girl.) It was strange how I couldn't seem to finish reading a comic strip. I read the first panel of *For Better or For Worse*, my favourite comic. My eyes took in the first panel. I chewed. The second panel. My eyes roved to another comic. I wondered somewhere vaguely how that day's *For Better or For Worse* strip turned out. I interrupted my reading of the next strip about two panels in to find another one. Maybe I should read Ann Landers. My hands flipped through the paper in increasing frustration, trying to spot her column in the cacophony of print and ads. With relief, I found it and folded the paper into a three-dimensional mess of a newsprint tent so that I could read it.

I slurped up the last of my cereal and left Landers midsentence to go brush my teeth. I mustn't forget my teeth today. My dog trotted behind me as I headed to the bathroom, hoping I'd given myself enough time to get to my psychologist's for what he called neurofeedback, but time meant nothing to me. I really didn't care if I was early or late until I was there. It was so far into the future, the only thing that mattered was the now.

And the now was about finding my keys and my Visor. The now was about making sure I locked the door. The now was about whether I had enough tokens on me for the TTC (Toronto Transit Commission). The now was about my mind instructing my legs to move, one after the other, in a slow walk, reminding me where I was going and in which direction to walk and to pull myself back from the curb where I'd listed to and walk in a straight line down the inside of the sidewalk. I began to list to the curb again, and my right leg shot pain into my right hip. And then my right leg was all pain, deep within, right to the bone. I gritted my jaw and told my leg to keep moving. I called out a rhythm: *one, two, one, two.* My leg screamed to stop. But I couldn't. I had to get to the subway northbound. The thought of being on that train, wondering if I would get a seat, wondering if I would be able to endure the journey joined with the pain in my right leg and almost halted me.

Self-talk increased its volume, for this was the first day of my independence movement.

I cannot depend on my husband.

I cannot depend on anyone.

People gave me rides and complained.

I will not be dependent on anyone.

The train rattled up the line toward my stop. I steeled myself. The dizziness, so unlike that of low blood pressure I was familiar with much of my life, scared me. I didn't have this kind of pain, this kind of fatigue even with the fibromyalgia. I lurched up and grabbed the pole nearest me. I walked toward the door while the train was screaming up the tunnel at a steady speed so I didn't have to fight to stay balanced against deceleration. I reached the doors. I commanded my left hand to hold the pole tightly. The train braked, pulling me down toward the floor. I tensed all my muscles. My dizzy head swam as the doors slid apart. Keeping an eye on the wall, I aimed my feet out and hoped not to trip on the small gap between train and platform.

I leaned against the wall, and the fluids in my brain stopped their whirlpool.

I closed my eyes and told myself I can walk the Mt. Everest hill to the office.

The elephant was on my chest, but the neurofeedback my psychologist provided awaited me. *Oh my God, I hope I get to have it!* I didn't have it every week. Some weeks, my psychologist decided I needed to do visualization exercises instead, and I was unable to open my mouth to ask him for the neurofeedback when it looked like I wouldn't get it. But I really, really wanted that neurofeedback, that light and sound show, as I called it. It gave me energy. It helped me think. *Please, God, let him give me the feedback.*

I weaved down the sidewalk, feeling a magnetic pull to the right, the pain mushrooming in my leg from calf to thigh to hip.

I was at the door of his building.

I was at his floor. My bladder, which had been screaming all the way up, demanded I take a detour into the bathroom. It was not that it was full or anything. It was just that my injured brain and seatbelt injuries said it was so. The lie was more powerful than the truth.

I obeyed.

At last, I was ready to see the psychologist. I had made it on time. He asked me how I was. I was articulate. I could talk. Yet...I felt like I was squinting down a barrel sight at a target far in the distance, almost invisible, needing to see his mouth and hear his words, in order to know what to say. I spoke in bursts of sudden volubility as the target morphed into a massively familiar object, only to shrink back down to its infinitesimal state. But everything else...

Day one of thirty of my independence movement accomplished, I had to get myself home. I had to repeat this exercise to acupuncture, physiotherapy, and TRI. And when my husband returned, I had to stick my ground and tell him that I would get there on my own. He did not need to drive me, and I would make him believe it.

I can do this.
I am strong.
I can do this.
I have to.
Tick. Tick. Tick.

About two months later, my OT said, "You can't read." Facing me across a table, in a gentle, compassionate voice, she pointed to my ubiquitous paperback and dropped the devastating news that I was not actually reading it. I was going through the motions, but I was absorbing nothing. I sat there, the stone of her news rippling its honesty into my mind.

No!

What do you mean I cannot read? I know my alphabet. I can read words. Yeah, I make mistakes all the time, misreading words so that sentences make no sense. I have to read and reread over and over again until I understand that sentence or paragraph. Yeah, I don't remember characters, I lose track of the plot, and I can no longer solve mysteries I used to solve halfway through the book. But I'm still reading the same newspaper I have read since I was thirteen years old. Well, OK, I'm skimming it, bouncing from the beginning of an article to the end to the middle back to the beginning and on to the next, absorbing very little but the headlines. I've given up reading three newspapers per week, sticking only with the Toronto Star. *Yet I'm reading my Bible every night!* I had set myself that task in early January 2000 before my injury to read a few verses every night from the beginning to the end. I thought, *Yeah, OK, I've read the entire Bible before, and I know most of the stories quite well. And yeah the boring bits go in one eyeball and out the other, but that's true for everyone, even scholars and writers like me, isn't it? They can't learn and remember either, right?*

No. Wrong.

I'm so tired.

She said she would help me relearn how to read. She said the SPT would also work with me to bring my reading back. But now, I had to accept that...

I paused my hearing. I didn't want to think further.

I cannot believe that this is true. OK, I'll do the homework because she asked me to. I have to get better and get back to writing Lifeliner *and get back to my life.*

I was to pick a book I'd read before my brain injury. That was the book we would work with in bringing my reading back. I was to put away my paperbacks.

"What will I do?" I asked, flummoxed at the thought of not reading on the subway, on the bus, on the streetcar, waiting to be called in to one of my appointments, at lunch, or breakfast.

"Try audiobooks," she suggested.

Glenda had given me the MP3 player attachment for my Visor. I loaded an audiobook onto it. Swaying on the train, packed around by people, I attempted to listen to a story. Words entered my ears and floated away. I didn't know how to rewind the story to where my attention had gone walkabout. I tried to just enjoy it. But it was worse than reading with my eyes. At least when my mind realized I had stopped taking in the words on a page, I could flip back and restart.

Tick. Tick. Tick.

I chose a biography I'd read for *Lifeliner*. The OT explained to me how I was going to relearn a skill I couldn't remember learning the first time because I'd been so young. I nodded dutifully and ensured I understood my homework: read one page per day of the familiar biography and use the reading strategies my OT had gone over with me.

I struggled to grasp these compensating strategies. *I'm supposed to read like I'm studying for a neurophysiology exam?* Highlight key words, she had said. Write notes in the margins. Write summary notes in a notebook. Cover off text I wasn't reading. Well, that last was not something I had done before. It sounded intriguing, but the rest?

I hate exams! I can't read like I'm studying for an exam, my mind screamed as my OT reviewed the lesson and my homework: read one page using the strategies.

One page.

That was insane.

I read pages and pages in one sitting. I read two-hundred-page paperbacks in two hours. *A page will take me a minute*, I scoffed. *I can read!*

This is surreal.

This can't be real.

I hate exams.

I can't read Agatha Christie like I'm sitting for a test! I balked at the idea.

My mind blanked. I returned home. I rested. The next day, in the new obedient way I had become, I followed my OT's instructions. I searched my bookcase for the book bristling with multi-hued Post-it flags. I opened it to the first page. Since it was the first page of a chapter, it was actually half a page. I carefully noted all the things I was supposed to do and began to read one paragraph. Five minutes. I closed the book and laid myself down for a nap. I had no thoughts, no emotions. Tomorrow, I would read page two. The idea daunted me.

I learnt that only covering off the text helped me focus long enough to read one page in five minutes.

I remembered the paragraph only because I had read this book before and had paid especial attention to it because it was research for *Lifeliner*.

Tick. Tick. Tick.

My OT and I reviewed each strategy, discussed where difficulties had plagued me, and reviewed every factor that had affected my reading. We created a list to help me decide what to read.

I walked home that day, list in purse, confused and despairing. I typed the list up on my computer in giant letters, printed it out, and pinned it to my corkboard where it remains to this day.

And then I picked myself up. I had homework to do. The strategies would help. The concentration exercises my psychologist had given me would help, if only I could remember to do them. I wasn't used to learning being hard. The harder the concept, the quicker and easier I had grasped it. Boredom was fatal. All my life, my father had instructed that I was not driven enough to achieve success though I found learning as easy and quick as breathing. Not reading again was not an option.

Tick. Tick. Tick.

Snow fell deep on the ground on December 12, 2000, and my husband pushed a way through the uncleared sidewalks to get to the hospital on time for my second insurance examination there, a medical DAC (Designated Assessment Centre). The previous had been for disability. I wasn't going to let them re-injure me as had happened during a similar functional assessment after my 1991 crash. The people at the functional assessment in the early 1990s had forced me to use injured muscles at the edge of their strength and endurance and so had re-injured my neck. I'd developed daily migraines. I wasn't going through that again! I felt strengthened with him beside me. As I awaited my turn to be tested on the old equipment, I watched a man with a cane and a bad knee be forced to bend and straighten that knee, agony lancing lines across his face. *He dared not protest for fear of being labelled as having a bad attitude, automatically disqualifying him from treatment,* I thought.

In a room with utilitarian stretcher-type beds and curtains separating them, the doctor asked me to lie down while my husband stood by. With my muscles not engaged, the so-called independent doctor was able to move my arms and neck to test the limits of my bones not my injured muscles. He declared me fine.

My husband erupted.

I stared at him.

My husband had only ever defended me once before. I watched as he used his height and his intelligence to flay the doctor for testing me in such a way to give the insurance company permission to turn the key against my treatment plans. The doctor wasn't about to be swayed. He'd objectively found my bones could move; ergo, my muscles were fine.

We returned home, my husband angry and I heading straight for the couch.

Tick. Tick. Tick.

My English aunt visited for Christmas 2000. She read the chapter for *Lifeliner* I'd written before my injury. She sat beside me at my computer and listened as I chatted about *Lifeliner*, a story I knew well because I had lived it and researched it all before my injury. She gave me a ten-pound note to tell me that she believed in me, that I would finish writing my first book.

Chapter 3

Journaling

My OT suggested journaling to help me sleep better, I wrote on the lines below my last entry from October 2000. My husband had walked out of our marriage but not our house that month, saying, "You oughta know why." *Crisis has a habit of disrupting things.* My hand, weak under the command of my brain, gripped my pen. It was mid-January 2001. I didn't notice that the next day was the first anniversary of the car crash. Instead the meeting the day before with the marriage counsellor, who was not counselling our marriage but the separation Mistral had demanded, filled my memory as I wrote: *My last entry became the last because after I wrote that...*I kept on writing, my aching fingers producing the words deep from within my subconscious while my mind read what I was thinking and feeling.

The day before, he had left our session, saying, "I'm going to the airport and will be back next week." He would not say where he was going.

I sobbed into the phone as I laid out the news to my pastor. The next day, I felt flat as I told my OT. It was like death had crept in. The day after, I smiled to my pastor and talked about my husband's walkout as if I was talking about a fantastic new play I had just seen.

"You're serene," my pastor noted. My eyebrows almost popped off. Me? Serene? But yes, my anger and irritation were almost gone. I felt fine. I could smile. I could laugh. My psychologist had taught me how to touch the peace deep within me. It was saving my sanity.

Or my brain injury was.

Tick. Tick. Tick.

I was making reading progress. I had begun with only five minutes per page of reading, and now I was reading articles in a journal! I picked up the journal and flipped to the article on tap. I laid out my notebook and pen and began to read. I wasn't sure how well I was retaining the information, but I was following my OT's suggestions. I was taking copious notes: read a point, write it down...except I couldn't remember the point. I read it again and wrote down another word about it. Oh, it's gone. Read it again. Ah, the point was there on the page, I was fired up to see as I watched my hand weakening from the effort of writing down the rest of the point. I moved on to the next sentence. This was working. I was following my OT's instructions, and I was reading! With relief, I heard my timer ding.

Tick. Tick. Tick.

I saw my husband again at the next separation counselling session where I sat inside my shell of outer detachment, my thoughts filling my mind, stuck within, unable to speak out, to bark that I knew where he flew to, as the counsellor listened and believed all that Mistral said.

"He doesn't love you," she repeated to me. "And you don't love him," she informed me. I said nothing. I couldn't. My eyes were dry as tears slipped down my husband's cheeks silently. Of course, I loved him. How could she say that?

We left together this time.

Tick. Tick. Tick.

My husband flew into TRI. Word of his arrival rang through to my SPT. She got me up and led me into the hall where my husband was striding to meet me. Glenda's newborn had died.

Grief shot up and crested like a tsunami through me. Gulps of sobs hiccupped my entire body. At the hospital, the sobs disappeared and took my thoughts with them. Where were my tears?

Saturday, January 27, 2001, time tricked me. It stretched before me, and suddenly I had to leave for a small meeting with a therapist and my closest kin. We were to discuss my behaviour. Lateness was the new me. Earliness no longer my way. I used to be organized, ready to spring into action when needed, part of a web of kin, kith, and community, I remembered.

Years earlier, Darius had cut his hand. I'd stared at the blood oozing in a slash across his palm then looked hurriedly away.

"What were you doing?" I exclaimed. I barely waited for an answer as I directed Mistral and Darius out the door after wrapping a rudimentary bandage around his palm. Mistral climbed into the driver's seat; only he could drive the temperamental beast of a car, which insisted on stalling at every red light then hiccupped its discontentment at being restarted. Of course, the very first light was red. Mistral kept one foot on the gas and held the brake down with the other foot, releasing it when the light at last turned green, letting the car surge forward, accelerating all the way to the next light, which was red.

I kept an eye on Darius's bandage. "Keep your hand up," I instructed. "It'll slow down the bleeding." At least he wasn't fainting like the guys in my physiology class had when it was time to take blood for whatever experiment our lab prof was having us conduct.

We rushed into the emergency room. While Mistral babysat the car, I kept Darius company, my eyes studiously averted, as the doctor attended to his hand. We drove home at a relaxed pace, all of us chatting in relief, Darius in much less pain and with a story to tell.

But that take-charge person wasn't me anymore. I drooped in my chair deep breathing while my closest kin spoke their thoughts in normal, rapid voices. I struggled to comprehend their words. The therapist had them stop so that I could summarize each point that they made, one at a time, understanding etching itself painfully slowly into my mind. My heart just watched.

"OK, we'll provide alternatives if we're going to critique your legal decisions," one of them said. "Your treatments are harming you! You're always negative!"

That's because I have to keep repeating what's happened to me.

"You're being made into a victim!"

The therapist had asked Mistral about that. It had puzzled him. By the end of the meeting, we agreed we'd speak directly to each other, Dad would speak to my psychologist, and Mum would help me more on Sundays. I was to filter all comments through goodwill lenses. And they agreed to visit me in my own home, small groups at a time except for Gertie who had her own difficulties.

We left together.

Tick. Tick. Tick.

Infection settled into my nose and crept into my sinuses and dripped into my lungs, turning me OCD-like with washing my hands over and over in my forgetfulness. I learned to fear colds. I hadn't had a puffer for asthma in years. I dug out my Flonase for my seasonal spring allergies. Later, my GP told me I had traumatic rhinitis.

Tick. Tick. Tick.

One day, Glenda had gently spoken to me about positive talk. She related that it was amazing how the corporate environment changed when people were banned from making negative statements. I listened, straining my brain to grasp what she was saying, to absorb her point that my talk was negative: the pain, the fatigue, my husband leaving, feeling unable to cope with taking on a tenant like he wanted me to, the insurance company denying another treatment plan, and the rehab homework and my hopes for it working. Her words echoed what others had said. My brain injury and seatbelt injuries had eaten up my life. There was no room for work. Energy drained out of my cheeks, and my body grew heavy as I struggled to shut my mouth against mentioning to her whatever sensation or thought or errant feeling popped into my consciousness to comply with what they all wanted to hear. It was a losing battle. I needed to talk out what I didn't understand. And I didn't understand this injury of the brain.

Tick. Tick. Tick.

Early in March 2001, my psychologist sat me down to tell me gently that my brain had plateaued. *This is my life.* He said acceptance wasn't giving up and that my brain would take its own time recovering from this bad injury. He suggested that it couldn't respond to treatment at the moment, and we should see how I do on my own for the month. The news ricocheted through me. The sound and light show he provided was the only thing that kept my brain working. I prayed before each appointment with him that I would receive life in my brain and hoped it would last more than a few hours or days. I'd arrive feeling so dead inside, like my brain was battened down. And then he'd put the giant sunglasses-like screen with its LED lights in it over my eyes, fit the headphones over my head, and adjust the light intensity and sound volume to low because the least amount of stimulation aggravated my brain. I'd lie back in his zero-gravity chair and gradually, gradually, as colours wove themselves into patterns in my view, thoughts appeared into the empty cave of my mind. Ideas and ability to converse popped up. At first, after the lights went off, I'd feel so tired. So, so tired. I'd nap within the cocoon of the crowd on the subway yet unable to sleep. And then I'd come alive like a mummy from out of a tomb.

After my appointment, I steered my feet away from Yonge Street into the deserted streets beyond it so that I could sob into my scarf unseen. Black despair surrounded me like death veils as

I walked with my drunken gait toward the road then lurched back to the middle of the sidewalk, unfeeling the increasing pain in my right leg, its muscles unable to relax and protesting against this unusually lengthy walk. I took so long to arrive home that my husband, the one who was leaving me, was waiting for me at the door, worried that something had happened to me. I cried into his chest the news, the last time I would be comforted with unconditional unhesitating arms.

Tick. Tick. Tick.

I forged on, committed to returning to *Lifeliner* in six weeks. The first week of March, my rehab team gently told me I was nuts and suggested I write a newsletter to everyone about my injury, where I was at, my goals, etc. It would force me to confront my reality and give people a clear picture of my situation. I agreed to do that and to take TRI's ten-week stress management course. My stress was high. I coped well. But I was at 80 percent risk of sickness. I blinked at that tiny piece of information.

Tick. Tick. Tick.

Mistral left. I slumped in the quiet house, staring into the dark. *I am alone.* My old dog licked my hand methodically. In his eyes, I could do no wrong. I could not cry.

Yet it was a relief to be alone because being alone with no one else around was truth. Being alone with a husband who wanted to leave was lonelier. But he kept returning to fix a wall, the garden, a dripping tap. I wanted him with me. His sadness flowed into me, and I wanted to reach out to comfort him. He asked for my hand as we walked one day. Our dog trotted ahead through the neighbourhood, and I said yes. But I grew weary of the back and forth. My social worker pointed out that the textbook answer to "how is she who has fibro, ABI, and been left, doing?" is depression. That's probably why people thought I should be depressed though I wasn't. Instead:

I sat behind the glass walling me from humanity.
Or in front of it.
I could not tell.
It was between me and the world.
Clear, transparent, thick, impenetrable.

The glorious sun shone paths of hope on your side, its warmth unfelt by me, its power seen but unfelt by me. The sunbeams wider, wide all over you and your doings. All over you and your words. All over you and your life.

I sat behind the glass and watched your arms bend and your agile fingers tap a rhythm out on your conversation, your deeds, your hopes, your dreams, your practical actions that bled you into the society beyond. On the other side of the glass.

I sat and watched.

And heard.

Your words pushed waves through the panes and panes that separated me from you. I sat and attended so that I could listen and understand, for I heard but could not grasp the meanings of these words. Their leading letters strained through the panes of glass and smacked into the waves, thrown up and down, until they hit. They entered my skin and entered my brain and entered my consciousness. But their following letters could not enter. They bounced off as if my skin was made of rubber that no longer belonged in this world.

Because it was injured by you and your kind.

The ones who were normal and cared not for their effects.

On me.

I was alive, yet I was dead. Isolated in this room where the sun did not penetrate. Isolated in this room, sitting immovable in my chair, sitting in the shadow thrown by you through the glass, the sun on the other side of you, its beams lighting you up, powering your dreams, your life, the works of your hands, and throwing your shadow across me so that I could not breathe anymore.

Because I was dead.

And you told me gently, the corpse me oh so kindly, to unpack the boxes of the new me.

The me I did not want because she was not me.

I heard your words. I comprehended your empathy, your compassion. And I sat on the other side of the glass, inside my cavern that I had begun to disappear into as my mind turned to blankness, the Indian man with his grizzled hair and southern-hemisphere skin silently sweeping the floor of my cave that I sat in at the very back looking forward toward the far-off craggy opening that revealed trees and flowers and houses and people I no longer belonged to.

And you told me to celebrate these boxes of blank mind, of isolation, of emotions gone. I was supposed to rip off the pretty paper and tape and yank open the sides and tops of these boxes in eager anticipation of what my life was never supposed to be about. And celebrate their gifts of broken thoughts and memories sunken into black holes of nothingness and kith disappearing and kin blaming me for sitting behind the glass that they refused to puncture a hole into to reach through to seize me and say to me:

"You are not alone."

I was not supposed to say, "Wait a minute! What has happened? Where am I? Why am I here in this chair, in this cave, behind the glass? How did I get here? And where are you going? Why are you leaving me behind this glass? Why are the ones who loved me nodding and agreeing and saying this is for the best and my healthcare team saying, 'you do not love, and so it is OK?'"

For me to be alone.

Sitting behind the glass.

Or in front of it.

With you on the other side, unreachable anymore.

Because I no longer belonged in the society of normals where people worked without ceasing and could play without flubbing up.

And I must sit here in my cave with the Indian man silently taking one slow step after another, from left to right across my silent isolation, sweeping, sweeping the dust away as I opened up the boxes of the new me and obeyed your instructions to grieve not the old me.

Who was dead.

In my alive body.

And whispered sobs from so far away at being ripped out of this world by the selfish actions of humanity that the tears tsunamied my emotions into obliteration.

And I must open up the boxes of the new me and rejoice in them.

But I did not know the new me. Who was she? Where did she belong? She belonged in this silent cave with the man sweeping for no one to enter and walk over its clean, grey floor of hard rock that pierced my soft feet.

I could not stand yet.

I sat and watched you talk and chatter and laugh and use your hands to carve out words in the air as you touched and were touched by kith and kin, neighbours, congregation as you and they walked away from me into the far-off maples, their red-burnt leaves jingling in the gentle breeze under the smiling sun on the other side of the glass.

I could not join you.

I would never join you again.

The memories of the old me rose in my broken brain, reminding me of my losses. I could not open the boxes of the new me while the memories of the old me clamoured reminders of how quick I used to be, how loved I used to be. I decided I had to paint black over those memories if I was to open up these boxes and be OK with the new me.

But the new me didn't live long.

As my brain healed, the new me changed. And changed again. Still behind the glass.

With no joyful relationship to guide and mould as we do for our children.

While everyone moved away from the other side of the glass into the certainties of their own lives, denying my existence so that my scars clotting from bright red to squiggling death didn't have to stain their happiness.

The contents of those boxes with their promises of lost talents, gone skills, fractured relationships, dependent life, I wanted no part of.

I pushed the creased flaps back down to roughly re-cover the boxes.

I kicked them out of my cave.

The old me was dead, but I wanted to live and thrive again. I couldn't with those boxes. And so I sat with my back to the craggy wall, my face to the distant rustling trees and flowers bursting orange, red, and purple under the sun, and pondered how I would return to that land, flow through the invisibly melting glass panes, and rejoin a humanity that wanted to know each other but not the new me.

Chapter 4

Staycation to Vacation

The sun dappled my skin as I sat in my garden chair, laboriously using all the reading strategies my OT had taught me: colouring the pages with lines of transparent yellow, scribbling notes, and wrestling with blank stark-white paper to cover off the text I wasn't reading. My staycation wasn't going as planned. I was failing at my writing goals, reading goals, and even my holiday with having to put my phone back on the hook and leave my haven of a home for yet another appointment with my physiatrist. But I was determined to follow my social worker's assignment to read the book on brain injury first, then lend it out second.

I'd lend it to kin first, for family is always with you no matter what. It was the mantra I grew up with, the one I adhered to, the one I knew. As I finished Dr. Claudia Osborn's book on June 18, 2001, the day after my holiday ended, I felt the thrill of achievement and thought about how her book spoke to me. Some of the changes in me that I'd revealed to no one because they'd seemed so wrong, she wrote honestly about. *She's brave.* I could not wait to lend it out, for loved ones to read all the aspects of brain injury that she disclosed so that they would know and understand without me having to speak about them. Speaking was a strange combination of what popped into my head popping out of my mouth, of dead silence as thoughts appeared then got stuck behind the cotton batting that surrounded my mind, and of shades of my old articulateness and rapid speech when I talked about things I knew prior to my brain injury. Fortunately, I had been a fairly voracious reader.

I looked at the pile of books I had intended to read during my two-week June staycation, most of them unread. My feeling of failure didn't last long. *I'll get my reading back. These strategies will work. The experts know what they're doing. And I'm not as tired as I was prior to my holiday. I don't ever want to become that fatigued again*, I vowed. *I must listen to my social worker and assert my boundaries!*

I returned to rehab. My team had told me I would have to be discharged early due to bureaucratic reasons, not clinical ones, but first, three therapists and I would meet with some of my kin, now that they had agreed.

I had prepped my social worker. My biggest question was, did kin believe the diagnosis. Did they at last believe I had a closed head injury? For months, they had insisted I was depressed, and just because I had been in a car crash did not mean I had a brain injury. To my immense confusion, they seemed to believe I didn't want to write *Lifeliner*. I couldn't understand that because I had never been so happy as when I'd gotten down to writing a couple of weeks before the crash. Why would I want to stop?

I didn't feel my team was ready to out-argue them. I tried to relay how my kin was intellectually rigorous, how they would expect evidence and learned explanations, and how they would ask skeptical questions. Dad was a Zoroastrian. Zoroastrians are raised to ask question after question, to drill down and find little inconsistencies. Generations of practicing in the law on my father's side flowed through our veins, and professional success was expected of every generation. Dad had reached the pinnacle of his profession of medicine as a clinical researcher whose work had worldwide recognition and impact. We were either lawyers or doctors; my mother was a trained registered nurse and a former midwife.

I was nervous. The rehab team sat on my left at the meeting, some of my kin before me and to my right. Dark fear weighted my limbs down. My body sat like a blob in the institutional chair. Fatigue threatened to shut down my brain. I had rested up as well as I could.

We asked the big question, and they answered, "Yes, we believe you have a head injury. But..."

"I am not depressed!" I shouted as the beast of brain injury anger shock-waved through my lips and into the air before me. I didn't know this beast was lurking and was going to let loose as some asserted that my real problem was depression, notwithstanding the opinion of a psychiatrist they had sent me to earlier in 2001.

Suddenly, I was flat emotionally again.

I cried, helpless to stop the tears.

And then I was flat again.

The meeting ended. We left in the time-honoured way of being socially happy as if no conflict had just happened, and Mum drove me home. I guess this way of coping with traumatic events, especially anything that affected our health, was learned during my parents' horrific childhood WWII experiences. Old, old memories threaded their way into my consciousness.

I didn't understand why Mum and the servants were hanging enormous black curtains over all the windows. I wasn't yet three years old. She explained that the government said we couldn't let even one sliver of light escape for aeroplanes flying by in the night to spot our flats. My young mind grasped that we were at war with somebody, and if they saw the light, they would know where to bomb us. Mum assured me the windows were fully blacked out, and we were safe. We were far away from the conflict. This was just in case. I carefully scanned the windows each night to ensure for myself the blackout curtains were fully closed. One day, Mum and the servants pulled them down. We were free to see the night through the shutters. At first, I was afraid. What if it was too soon? But then I forgot and enjoyed the freedom.

The rest of my life, I joined my Canadian generation in enjoying peace and the security of being an ocean away from conflict. My one and only brief war experience paled next to my parents, in which my father's family lost their home, their country, and their work. My grandmother told me that when they arrived in Canada that they felt at home for the first time since 1942 when Japan invaded Burma and they had fled, my grandfather overland in the great Burma trek, surviving by boiling all the water he drank from the rivers, which were full of cholera. They hiked up mountains and slogged through heavy jungle to rejoin the women and children in Simla in northern India and safety. For three months, no one knew if he lived or died. Meanwhile, my grandmother, seven-months pregnant with her third living child, a brother to my father, Dad, his grandmother, and a motley group of refugees boarded a Dakota. A Chinese pilot flew in a scary dance to evade Japanese fighter pilots chasing them until they reached the safety of Indian airspace. Much later, my father watched de Havilland Mosquito bombers land at night in Calcutta, their wooden wings tattered and aflame. He marvelled that they could still fly. Some catapulted on hitting the ground. When he related this story, I wondered at the traumatic impact on a youth.

Many, many miles north of where he watched men dying in flames, my mother found an unexploded ordinance and blew her eyebrows off. Mum had a habit of getting into scrapes: missing her bus stop as a six-year-old, breaking her collarbone, and arriving home bawling in pain. Her mother was strict and tough. When she was six-months pregnant with Mum, her husband came home and confessed that he'd made a mess of things. He needed a divorce immediately. He'd been having an affair with who he thought was an eighteen-year-old girl, but now she was pregnant too, demanding he marry her, and oops, it turned out she was sixteen, and if he didn't get a divorce and marry her, she'd have him charged with statutory rape. He'd go to jail! Wouldn't she be a darling and divorce him? My grandmother gifted his wish and went to work for her father in his grocery store, sometimes getting paid a pittance, sometimes nothing. The day years later her youngest came bawling into their drafty three-story brick house in the English market town they lived in, she was not impressed. She told her to be quiet. Luckily, her older sister noted Mum's fevered face and the tenderness of her abdomen and hauled her off to the hospital. She had acute appendicitis. Any further delay at operating upon her, she'd have died. Maybe that's why Jesus captured her heart, his sacrifice infused her heart to others, and she sees hope in all.

Back in India, Dad was more cosseted. When he'd been four years old, the centre of two wealthy parents, wealthy grandparents, and a household of servants, he had a younger sister. One day, they all woke up, and the two children were as active as ever. But then his eighteen-month-old sister developed a fever. The doctors were called. Not to worry. His socially busy grandparents went out that evening to a concert where my grandmother was playing the violin. Back at home, alone with the servants, Dad watched his sister die. My grandmother never played the violin again. As he grew older, doctors visited Dad constantly and overmedicated him for this thing and that. He had asthma, and at the end of WWII and beginning of India's War of Independence, he and his brother developed rapid pulses. The doctors became upset and recommended he stop exercising. Instead, he played cricket behind his mother's back. Of course, she'd find out and get upset with him. Eventually, their heart rates settled down to normal. Dad took care of his own health after that, no more henning over his pulse, breathing, and itchy skin. "Don't worry about it," became his mantra.

I became the first girl on my father's side to survive past five years old and not be associated with illness and death in three generations. And now here I was in 2001 quite injured. I found it beyond reasoning, yet it was true.

My kin, including those who weren't at TRI, stayed up all night discussing the incomprehensible and called me the next morning. I was told that these therapists didn't know what they were talking about otherwise they wouldn't have accepted the head injury diagnosis and asserted that based on the doctors' reports and their own experience, I wasn't depressed. "We love you. That's why we're challenging you about your diagnosis and treatment."

It was a very bad day.

Tick. Tick. Tick.

I turned to my reading goals and books. I couldn't afford to buy books regularly, yet the library had morphed from a haven to a horror house. Library fines kept accumulating. Over and over as I passed the library after one or another appointment, I'd remember that I'd forgotten the fewer and fewer books or audiotapes I'd borrowed at home. I didn't have the energy to retrace my steps back to the library to return the books. Surely, the librarian would understand if I returned them the next day and forgive the twenty-five-cent fine.

Uh, no.

Hostility oozed from her dour expression. "You're late. The computer can't be altered."

Furious at the tears that welled up, at the sobs that wanted to break my face into shattered glass, I fled. I tossed my library card and aimed my feet to my favourite large bookstore instead to buy *What's So Amazing About Grace* by Philip Yancey. I fluttered the pages and quailed. But I needed to feel better, to figure out why this was all happening, and how I could make it right.

Tick. Tick. Tick.

The heat of the summer settled in to my place and amplified the heat in me. So hot. I struggled to stick to my writing goals: two hours and three pages. I celebrated the day I made it to two hours. Three pages was a bit tougher. I kept my eye on September when I would get back to writing *Lifeliner*. It was hard work, but these strategies I was taught would get me there. I made an effort to write down goals I made. I adjusted the goals I typed up with my OT: dishes and cooking. I stuck them up on a bulletin board and referred to them every day. How was I doing? I remembered to high-five myself when I went from a -2 to -1 in achieving my goal. I began at -2 or two steps away from my goal. Each step up from -2 to -1 to goal to +1 above goal to +2 above was an achievement. My OT and I decided my goal for keeping my kitchen clean was at least *one sink clear, counters and table have no obvious sign of food, and pots stacked neatly*. I began at the -2 level of *some assistance required to manage in between housekeeper/homemaker and has run out of dishes and cutlery*, my usual way of being.

They were small achievements in the estimation of people in my life, yet it took two years to achieve -1 level: *manages independently in between times that housekeeper/homemaker come and does not run out of dishes and cutlery*. The +2 level of *sink is clean, counters are spotless, and kitchen immaculate* seemed out of reach. No way I could reach Mistral's level of making the kitchen literally shine. What my OT cheered me for, my kith and kin implied was not good enough and that I must speed up.

Tick. Tick. Tick.

Nausea and dizziness became my more frequent companions. I began to notice a pattern. First came those twin evils, then came an improvement. I felt the edge of alertness. I felt my observational ability re-emerge in part. Thoughts arrived more readily. Still, fatigue dogged me and blank mind time remained. I remembered a day back in the late 1980s when I visited a woman I had first met in my teens. She prayed for people, and I had gone to ask her to pray for a job for me. I was at the tail end of the baby boomer generation, and the older boomers had hogged all the jobs. I had graduated with a Bachelor of Science (B.Sc.) and couldn't find a job that paid well enough to live on my own. Lily had prayed, and the day she had done so was the day my next boss had begun to make inquiries that had led her to offer me a job.

Now in 2001, I called her son, and he relayed my message. I waited.

I wrote on August 3:

> They say I'm aware of the problems (imp't first step!) & smart & I can figure things out. 2 weeks to figure out how to change the porch light! So now I'm in the scary stage —being launched onto my own. But now I'm ready (I hope—no, not be negative, be affirming I AM!)

I was free of weekly rehab at TRI.

September arrived. And Lily called me! She came over to pray for me with her companion, bringing peace from God, messages from God that I was a blessing and needed practical help.

But life worsened. I was failing more and more. October 2001 trundled by, time stretching and contracting, confusing me as to the day and the hour. Distractions abounded, my phone calls were no longer being returned, and I remembered only once to do my concentration exercise and then couldn't reach the requisite three minutes before writing in my journal. I met my writing goal once that month.

Tick. Tick. Tick.

In the black aloneness of my bedroom, I prayed for release, for forgiveness. The next morning, Lily called. God had spoken to her, and she had to lay hands on me. Stunned, I agreed.

Her time-worn hands pulled her anointing oil out of her cavernous purse. She began by praying for forgiveness of our sins, for the Lord's mercy, for me to forgive. *Who had I not forgiven?* I wondered even hours later, searching my soul, as she prayed for mine.

She anointed my head as she continued to speak to God. She placed her roughened palms on the crown of my head then moved them down to my forehead, my temples, my back, and over again. In her French-Canadian accent, she relayed how God had commanded her to forget what she had previously told me a week earlier and instead to pray for, "my deranged mentality, the spirit of oppression and depression, and my eyes." *My eyes?* Maybe God meant my masked observational ability. But after she smoothed her hands over my head, she anointed my eyes and placed her hands right over them. The pressure on my eyeballs told me that God meant my physical eyeballs.

I didn't know what to make of that. My vision had been improving. My blind eye had begun to see beyond shapes and colours. I had begun to be able to identify objects with it. It was like looking through a black moth-eaten veil, but I could see them! Was God going to heal my blind eye? *Well, I hope He will instantly*, I thought.

(Uh, no, of course, He didn't.)

The power of Lily's voice crescendoed as she prayed. I became dizzy. I felt sick and hot. My good eye teared, and pressure built up in my temples. And then...

She prayed for happiness. Joy bubbled up into laughter like when Q blessed Data in *Star Trek: The Next Generation*. Genuine laughter like I hadn't felt since the hours before my injury filled me. Pure beautiful emotion.

Weight lifted from my heart. Good, positive, humorous, hopeful thoughts filled my brain. God had said I was a good person. He at least was with me. But I looked in the mirror after she left and jumped. I did not recognize the reflection staring out from deep within me through my eyes. It was inexplicable.

Tick. Tick. Tick.

"You need a vacation," my mother informed me. I frowned. I had work to do. "Your aunt is turning seventy, and she's having a birthday party with all her family." *Oh, right. England. See my aunt. I have work. I must get back to Lifeliner. I'm so tired. I have no money to pay for a plane ticket to England. Points.* Mistral, who was still popping into my life to fix a sink or go for a walk, got in on the act and told me he'd give me his points and babysit the dog.

We flew out on the morning flight to Gatwick in February 2002. Ever since I could remember, when my eyes spotted London through the thinning clouds, my spirit reached out and felt home. I'd been born there. Like a homing pigeon who nested elsewhere nevertheless knew this was the place where it began.

I looked out the window. The clouds parted, and I felt...

Nothing.

I blinked. I swallowed. I stared down at the rapidly growing brown brick houses, at the sinewy Thames, and felt nothing.

After the first party for my aunt, my mother and my aunt spent a sisterly week together while I hung out at two of the cousins' houses. The second one I stayed with was so excited because she didn't often make vegetarian meals and had spent some time deciding what to cook for me. I stared at her stunned, thoughts banging around inside my head. Back home, they instructed me that if I wanted to eat vegetarian at their barbecues or dinners, I'd have to make it myself and bring it over. *How?* I used to wonder.

My brain couldn't decide what to make, planning eluded me, burning or undercooking had become my norm, the energy demanded to stick with it, the muscle pain involved in repetitive chopping all made cooking my meal to take to a party impossible. Maybe one of my homemakers, when I managed to have one for a few weeks, could chop for me. But that help never lasted long. So I made do with foods like hot dog buns as my vegetarian meal at a party. And here I was, sitting in the warm kitchen at my cousin's square table, watching her eyes dance with delight at this new adventure.

I didn't know what to say except to apologize for being a burden. She informed me that it was easy to cook for me. *I was easy?* She explained that my vegetarianism didn't have any restrictions she found difficult to accommodate.

Early the next morning, my mother and her sister picked me up, and we drove west to my older cousin's place where we'd have another family party. On the way, we stopped at a lay-by. We went our separate ways, me to the bathroom, them for snacks and gas. When done, I returned to our meet-up place and hugged the wall in a brown-tiled corridor waiting for them as people hurried by chatting, their noise echoing around my head, shutting down my brain.

"You have a brain injury," my mother told me.

Huh? When did my mother decide I had a brain injury after all and wasn't depressed?

"We met a physiotherapist," she continued. At some point on their road trip, they'd stopped and like British people everywhere got chatting. The young physiotherapist worked with people with brain injury. They'd told him all about me. This didn't surprise me. Stories were my kin's métier, and stories about relations topped the list. He'd nodded at the familiarity of their description of me.

"She's typical," he had told them, echoing my TRI OT. *Oh. Why did she accept his word, the word of a man who'd never met me over the word of my entire rehab team who'd assessed me, treated me for months?* My brain began to understand. The physiotherapist was British. The mother country had the final word.

Since I couldn't feel laughter, I smiled to show my relief and understanding.

We walked into my cousin's house, greetings shouted around. I looked into my cousin's eyes. The cousin who had being held up to me as the model of brain injury healing. He'd been in a coma after an assault nine years earlier. Yet he had recovered fully in only two years, I had been informed. He had a job, a family, a house, all this after a brain injury worse than mine. They knew it was worse because he had skull damage, he'd been in an induced coma, he'd been hospitalized for a long time, and he'd lost his speech. I'd had none of those things. So what was my problem? Why didn't I want to improve?

I looked into my cousin's eyes and instantly recognized myself in them: the lack of concentration, the memory issues—he, like me, had also had a photographic memory—the inability to make a decision. He was definitely not back to normal. The external was not true to the internal. I felt safe with him, not judged, not vilified, not rejected for having a brain injury. He understood me.

While my mother stayed in his living room with the rest of the crowd, happy to get a break from taking me shopping, my cousin drove us to the supermarket to buy some grub. We began with thin French beans. The store had green beans and yellow beans. In Canada, beans lie in open bins. In England, they come prepackaged.

He asked me, "Yellow or green?"

I stared at the unfamiliar packaging of the beans. I shifted my eyes from the lovely yellow to the deep green and back again. I raised my eyes to his and shrugged.

"I don't know. What do you think?" He was older and the host and the one further along in his brain injury healing, I thought he'd know. He didn't.

Wow, he's just like me! He can't make a decision, either! This is so cool. I'm not alone. He won't care how long it takes me to decide, and there's no normal person waiting for us, forcing themselves to be patient or futilely hurrying us along. We stood before the two colours of beans, both of us stuck in our indecisive broken brains happily discussing whether green or yellow was better. For five minutes. We chose the green beans.

Days later, my cousin drove us to the train station as we began our journey home. He'd spent time explaining to me the ins and outs of brain injury. He'd made me feel less alone. I wished we could stay in touch, but my cousins were not ones to do that. In person, chatter filled the air. Distance silenced it.

I arrived back in Canada, unlocked my door, and my dog practically climbed into my arms, his entire body wagging relief and joy. Renewed determination filled me. I was going to get a new lawyer to represent me in my claim for accident benefits with my insurance company and in the tort claim against the drivers who'd injured me. The first lawyer had begged off when I'd received my brain injury diagnosis; the second lawyer was terrible. I needed one to go to the mat for me. And I was going to find a way to write *Lifeliner*.

The Honeymoon Learnings

Chapter A

The Details

The collision of brain against the inside surface of the skull happens because of Newton's Laws. Simply put: the energy pent up in a moving object keeps it moving until stopped suddenly; then it gets transferred into the object that stopped it. That energy will move anything that isn't planted or pinned down a.k.a. the brain. Unless someone comes up with a force field that both cushions and protects the brain from ping-ponging inside the skull like a ball of Jell-O, the brain will shred. Cell membranes rupture, axons stretch and shear, neurotransmitters release indiscriminately, the energy molecule Adenosine triphosphate (ATP) drops, and the normal balance of cell metabolism goes haywire. The cells need more energy to repair, but with reduced blood flow and ATP dropping, less energy is available, and fatigue results.

Imagine a hockey player zipping along the ice and hitting the maximum speed of 45 km/h.[2] Assume the average hockey player has a mass of 100 kg,[3] excluding equipment. When that player hits another one, the kinetic energy[4] transferred could be 7,812.5 joules. In comparison, one small apple dropping one metre to the ground will release one joule. Or a tiny 50 kg human moving at 0.2 m/s will release one joule of kinetic energy. In contrast, the muzzle energy of an elephant gun is about 7,000 joules while an

---

[2] https://www.quora.com/What-is-the-maximum-speed-ice-hockey-players-reach
[3] http://wiki.answers.com/Q/What_is_the_Average_weight_of_nhl_hockey_players
[4] http://www.csgnetwork.com/kineticenergycalc.html

alkaline AA battery contains about 9,000 joules of energy.

The player will absorb some of that violent 7,812.5 joules of kinetic energy through falling, but much will remain to push the brain until it hits the skull and bounces back in a coup-contrecoup motion. The injury occurs at the site of impact (coup) and the site opposite the impact (contrecoup). This action repeats for each impact. Think of a bouncing ball, how it bounces up and down on its own and more when it's hit again.

Car crashes are worse.

The average mass of a car[5] is 1,500 kg. Drifting at 10 km/h or 2.78 m/s would equal a kinetic energy of 5,796.3 joules, less than a hockey player going full tilt. But at 60 km/h, the kinetic energy would be about thirty-six times that of a hockey player or about thirty elephant guns at 208,416.7 joules. The force of about thirty elephant guns shot through me. Twice. From behind.

Although improvements in safety technology have made it so the victim's car, instead of the humans, absorb the kinetic energy, the neck and the head remain vulnerable to being whipped by the force of that energy. Also, double-jointed necks stretch farther forward and back until hitting the headrest, overextending the muscles, and inflicting a coup-contrecoup injury, one for each impact.

Car crashes are traumatic, probably with the highest kinetic forces of all causes. But then because of how our legal system works and our insurers operate, it's a trauma that keeps on giving for years. We don't know how much of a negative effect emotional trauma from insurance claims has on a brain already injured, whether it makes the injury worse, permanent, or simply harder to deal with.

Several blows to the head will always be worse than a single impact. And the closer together in time those impacts are, the

---

[5] http://hypertextbook.com/facts/2000/YanaZorina.shtml

worse the effect on the brain. I don't know if you can fully recover from a concussion, such that your brain returns completely to its pre-injured state. It doesn't seem logical to me. After all, broken bones, no matter how well set, never look like unbroken bones. Weather will make them twinge, even decades later. And so why would brains have a restore-to-pre-injured ability? Thus, for doctors to say, "Rest, show normal on tests, and you're the same," seems to be optimism at its most Pollyannaish.

Diagnosis

Examining damage at the cellular level is tricky. These are the available scanning technologies to detect brain injury. Note: standard CT and MRI scans do not.

qEEG. Quantitative electroencephalography reads the brain's electrical activity or brainwaves through electrodes pasted on to the scalp, using the ears as the ground. Wires from the electrodes feed the electrical information they pick up into a computer. Computer software shows the brainwaves, compares them to a normative database, interprets the information, provides a detailed analysis of the brainwaves, including 3D modelling and MRI-like pictures. It's inexpensive and not used enough.

DTI. Diffusion tensor imaging[6] maps white matter tractography. It's used to study and treat neurological disorders. It apparently reveals the extent of injury to brain networks, which helps to understand one's difficulties and how to treat them.

SPECT. Single photon emission computed tomography requires the injection of a radioactive gamma-producing isotope that the brain takes up proportionally to blood flow. The scanner reads the location of the radiation, thus showing how much blood is flowing through the brain, a measure of how well the brain is

---

[6] https://en.m.wikipedia.org/wiki/Diffusion_MRI#Diffusion_tensor_imaging

working. The pictures can be either 2D slices or 3D images.

Observation

The art of medicine includes learning to recognize observable patterns of brain injury. Some non-professionals too can observe. I met a woman who had a grade ten education in my Bible study group. She asked me with great hesitation if something had happened to me.
"Closed head injury," I said.
"I thought something had happened to you," she said. She explained how she knew intelligent people, like me, but they spoke rapidly. I did not. That created a question in her mind. A friend noticed I couldn't hold a conversation. Yet another close friend insisted there was nothing wrong. The need to deny bad news can drown one's ability to observe. In that case, objective evidence becomes critical.

My Brain Injury

In a diffuse injury, the entire brain is injured. A diffuse injury is worse than a focal injury, where just one area of the brain is damaged. After the initial injury, a cascade can sweep through the brain, worsening it (see below).

My brain damage included, in no particular order,

- slow processing;
- inability to pay attention (think ADD);
- inability to focus on one person talking to me in a crowd or group;

- inability to refocus after being interrupted;
- inability to multitask;
- loss of mental flexibility;
- problems with reading and writing (It was years before I fully grasped the extent of these problems.);
- problems with memory;
- problems with communication (e.g., hunting for words, circling around what I wanted to say);
- problems understanding others (The more attention required, the worse I got, and I often wanted to scream "I'm not going deaf!" when I couldn't "hear" them.);
- bad vision in one eye that began to heal, leading eventually to new vision in 2016;
- loss of self ("who I am");
- olfactory hallucinations (e.g., toast);
- fatigue;
- initiation deficit;
- pain (and sometimes feelings of coldness) behind my forehead whenever I concentrate during learning;
- changes in sleep (taking a long time to fall asleep, waking up several times, waking as tired or, worse, more tired than when I went to bed);

- irritability and anger issues (Brain injury anger is not the same as normal anger.);
- vanished emotions (I wasn't numb. My emotions were gone except when every now and then they'd fire on violently and take me on a roller coaster ride for about two weeks then disappear again.);
- impatience;
- increased stress levels;
- apathy;
- problems with time (reading and perceiving time);
- denial (a combination of perception difficulties and a normal coping mechanism after trauma);
- loss of curiosity;
- loss of humour (This began to return gradually after one year, but it wasn't the same.);
- loss of empathy and compassion;
- loss of listening skills;
- altered perceptions;
- dizziness, nausea (Lying down made it worse or brought it on.);
- loss of decision-making skills; and
- loss of problem-solving abilities (I only discovered this five and a half years after the crash.)

Dr. James Kelly on YouTube describes the parts of the brain likely to be affected by a concussion: http://youtu.be/9izH26JzmIo

Diffuse Axonal Injury

Diffuse axonal injury (DAI) occurs when neurons tear, stretch, or shear, blood vessels shear, and small tears occur between the junction of grey and white matter because grey and white matter have different densities. Axonal separation and death occurs not just in response to the physical injury but also the biochemical cascade that occurs hours or days after. The brain goes into shock or diaschisis. Glial activation results in inflammation. Extensive, densely packed, reactive microglia persist for up to eighteen years.[7] Microglia are the brain's immune defence and brain maintenance system. Fever or sub-febrile temperatures of 37.5-38°C from nervous tissue regrowing is nine times more likely to occur in those with DAI after a trauma. Fever is associated with more severe symptoms; people don't sweat when they have fever. Thalamic inflammation leads to a damaged corticothalamic loop, creating electrical blockages that interrupt the normal synchronization pulse that creates alpha brainwaves. Carla Shatz in 1992 said, "Neurons that fire together, wire together, and neurons that fire out of sync, lose their link."[8] With no synchronization pulse, neurons become isolated and randomly fire at 1 to 2 Hz, the sub-delta frequency. They lose their link to each other and to other areas of the brain that would normally send or receive information from them. In addition, EEG shows choppy beta brainwaves. The result is that the traumatically

---

[7] Dr. Lynda Thompson. Slide at Healing the Brain Conference. 10 May 2017, Toronto, Canada.
[8] Dave Siever. *Audio-Visual Entrainment and Diffuse Axonal Injuries/Interruptions*. 11 June 2016. http://mindalive.com/default/assets/File/AVE%20and%20diffuse%20axonal%20injuries%20for%20publication2.pdf

injured brain with DAI no longer has a ratio of 3:1 alpha to beta, but 1:1. Agitation and anxiety result. Meanwhile, the brain consumes vastly increased energy as it attempts to repair itself.

Every injury, though widespread, can lead to different neurons being torn, thus creating different symptoms with similar brainwave patterns.

One person may exhibit slowed cognition, another explosive emotions, a third discontinuous speech. Since there is no bleeding from the scalp or broken skull, probably no paralysis and no massive speech problems, and most of all because we can walk and talk, we're deemed to have "mild" brain trauma. However, a brain injured at the cellular level will result in multiple functionality issues and cannot be scanned, poked, or prodded with traditional methods. Experienced observational and critical thinking skills and going-outside-the-establishment use of several technologies creates the complete picture. In short, the art and science of medicine.

For references and further reading, go to http://wp.me/Pf8xE-169.

Chapter B

Anger and Perception

Are adults likely to exhibit dramatic behavioural changes simply because they feel like it? Would you suddenly choose to go from being a friendly, hard worker to wooden and humourless with angry, scary outbursts?

I learned in February 2010, no training manual, no cohesive approach, no general knowledge exists on what brain injury anger is and how to deal with it. This is why most of us with brain injury are not taught how to effectively manage brain-injury anger, despite the fact it destroys relationships and costs jobs. And, no, regular anger-management training doesn't work.

Brain-injury anger is like a wild animal that leaps into your brain screaming and gnashing its teeth, hurtling you into a freakishly strong fight response that shocks you as much as it does others. It can manifest from simple bellowing all the way up to yelling while hurling an offending object. Ignorance of how this anger is different can inadvertently escalate it.

There are several issues with brain-injury anger:

1. Understanding that it's a physiological process impervious to behavioural therapies

2. Understanding its locus in the brain

3. Understanding that the affected neurons and neural networks need treatment

4. Understanding that everyone, from family to psychiatrists, not just the behavioural therapist, must learn how to de-escalate it.

Acupuncture, brain biofeedback, and audiovisual entrainment (AVE), treatments that I underwent for other reasons, had this rather nice effect of reducing my irritability from sensory overload and thus calming my anger.

Ultimately, I discovered that a combination of avoiding my severest triggers, my hypothalamus fix (Chapter Q), and gamma brainwave enhancement (Chapter R) led to my brain-injury anger becoming rare.

However, being misunderstood, disrespected, put down, acted thoughtlessly toward, being overwhelmed, being refused to be accommodated, inaccessible public transit and city systems, abandoned, and betrayed creates moral anger. A psychiatrist or psychologist familiar with brain injury, willing to keep up with the latest understandings of brain injury and how to treat it, helps with extensive talk and psychodynamic therapy. That is difficult to find.

A second hidden anger issue is response to others' anger.

A neurotypical person would at least step back from in-your-face, sudden, top-volume yelling. After my brain injury, I don't. Although I startle when a squirrel bounces by, I don't even flinch when a stranger yells in my face. My brain blanks. My body freezes. In response, people either leave or begin to speak to me slowly and carefully like I'm extremely stupid. But none have analyzed why this happens or treated the involved damaged areas so that I can be safe.

In Arizona, a man shot a number of people, killing six, wounding fourteen, including Congresswoman Gabrielle Giffords. The killer's skewed way of perceiving the world had urged him on. His colleagues and friends identified him as "obviously disturbed," possibly due to brain damage from alcohol poisoning that had apparently interfered with the man's ability to perceive. We had dead people and intensive use of police and healthcare resources because it had not been treated.

Not everyone who is mentally ill or has brain injury has damaged perception. But if the ability to perceive oneself is diminished, then understanding other people's body language, verbal communication, and written language may become difficult. For example, when someone obeys police slowly or stares blankly, it's clear the ability to understand may still be there but in slow-mo. We must give them patience. It's the human thing to do.

People who know little about brain injury mistake the fatigue, initiation deficit, lack of motivation, cognitive deficits, anger and irritability, and/or lack of affect as behavioural or psychiatric and ascribe personality defects instead of understanding brain injury is physiological. Such a distortion results in the injured person not receiving support and having to fight for the treatment they need. In that case, privacy laws protect them.

Perception includes perceiving one's own body. You may lie down straight but feel crooked. One side may dominate your perception, yet it feels normal. How do you correct?

As my perceptual abilities improved, each month I'd look back and go, *where was my head last month?* But in that month, I'd think, OK, I'm healed now. Then the next month realize nope. Still, I often had no problems assessing situations for what they were, and that would be confirmed by the professionals.

So how do you know what is skewed and what is not? Look for cues from other people or take the time to assess before making a judgement based on your own perception. For example, read and reread an email, and reread it one last time before sending a reply. Language centres probably only work well when internal knowledge long held from before the injury is being expressed in ways said many times before. Impaired sensory inputs create confusion over what facial expressions mean, miss subtle tones in the voice, and cloud body language. Brain injury anger can manifest when the brain is overwhelmed and unable to process and respond to normal levels of information in real time. Fatigue robs whatever ability is left of its fuel to work. Transmission to external expression can take hours or days, which is unlikely to be spoken once an event or conversation is ended.

Basically, problematic social interaction is physiological not behavioural, worsened by stress, fatigue, medications, and alcohol.

Even if perception is off, self-awareness may remain intact. Although I don't think you have to have brain injury to be missing self-awareness, lack of self-awareness means you can't recognize how you've changed and how extensive your difficulties are after your brain injury. Thus, why would you seek help or understand why you need treatment? How can you see it's helping you? How can others help you perceive that?

When you mishear and misperceive actions and words and others refuse to accommodate by clarifying what they're saying, you can't have rational conversations, you can't sustain meaningful relationships, and you can't hold down a job. Yet that's when you most need to rely on the people around you to get you back to health. The appropriate response for them is not to worry about TBI snafus but support treatments that repair the damaged areas because your friend, daughter, brother, or parent is worth it. In that case, privacy laws and reluctance of people "to involve themselves" may hold back healing.

For updates, go to http://wp.me/Pf8xE-182.

Chapter C

Traditional Strategies and Therapies

Compensating strategies are, to me, minimally effective ways of coping with physiological damage. But they help one begin the process of regaining a sense of control and competence, even though strategies seem to work 50 percent of the time when all are used and used well.

Pacing

According to a Scientific American article,[9] "two thirds of the brain's energy budget is used to help neurons or nerve cells 'fire' or send signals...remaining third [used for] cell-health maintenance." The study's author stated that housekeeping power keeps the brain tissue alive, and energy demands jumped when the subject was visually stimulated. This study seems to suggest that the injured brain's increased demands for the housekeeping portion for self-repair, the greater difficulty of damaged neurons firing, and stimulation all combine to increase energy demands. Pacing in time and steps conserves energy. For example, work ten minutes, break for three. Repeat. Break a task into specific, measurable steps. Write each step down either in a smartphone checklist or on Post-its stuck in chronological order on cabinets while cooking, for example. Sit or lie down between each step and deep breathe.

---

[9] https://www.scientificamerican.com/article/why-does-the-brain-need-s/

Deep Breathing

Deep breathing calms and provides energy. Deep breathing continuously during stressful events helps one cope. Learning meditation may also help.

SMART Goals

Specific: Specify the goal, e.g., pay bills.

Measurable: Measure it, e.g., bills are paid.

Attainable: Establish a realistic goal, e.g., pay bills on a day you have good energy and break it down into steps.

Relevant: Ensure it's relevant to your daily life, functionality, or immediate projects, e.g., everyone has to pay their bills.

Timely: Goal achievable in realistic time, e.g., can you pay your bills before they're due?

Reading Strategies

Highlight sentences you want to remember. Write margin notes about key ideas. Cover off the text you're not reading to reduce visual distraction. Summarize what you've read in a notebook. Handwriting encodes differently than typing and seems to force the brain to pay more attention to what you're focusing on. Maybe do both.

Decision-Making Strategies

Begin by talking it over with people you trust. If you feel driven to talk it over with everyone, don't worry about it. It's how you are.

Write down what you need to decide on. Set an alarm for a month later to look at it then. If you still cannot decide, reset the alarm for two weeks hence.

Recurring decisions can be decided once then done the same every time, e.g., always buy four apples of the same kind when grocery shopping.

Use a decision-making method, e.g., the decision tree.

Decision Tree

At the top of the page write the two halves of the decision, e.g., "Visit England." "Don't Visit England." Draw a vertical line down the page between them. Underneath each, write "Pros" and "Cons." Draw vertical lines separating each. Then write in each column without thinking. When done, you'll notice what stands out. Discuss with your OT or trusted person.

Therapies help you relearn how to think and to process what is happening to you. Because the brain is poorly understood, its injury even less understood, and accelerated healing not often encountered, these therapies require a therapist who listens carefully, respects your understandings of what is going on in your head, and understands that emotions are physiologically mediated and thus need physiological and psychological healing done in tandem with healthcare professionals working as a team.

Cognitive-Behavioural Therapy

Cognitive-Behavioural Therapy[10] (CBT) is a way to perceive current problems and to learn how to deal with them in a manageable way. A therapist structures appointments and homework with accountability with the understanding that brain injury increases learning and mastering time and that you may not have emotions to guide you or that chaotic emotions will interfere with CBT.

Talk Therapy

The Canadian Psychology Association found that for anxiety, talk or psychotherapy is superior to medication.[11] Social isolation, confusion, anxiety arising from brainwave changes all lead to the need to talk things out with a calm, empathetic, empowering individual who will understand gender differences, cultural effects, and what is physiological and what is personal. Medication cannot substitute for the healing presence of another.
For references and further reading, go to http://wp.me/Pf8xE-16b.

---

[10] https://en.wikipedia.org/wiki/Cognitive_behavioral_therapy
[11] John Hunsley, Katherine Elliott, Zoé Therrien. *The Efficacy and Effectiveness of Psychological Treatments.* 10 September 2013. University of Ottawa.
http://www.cpa.ca/docs/File/Practice/TheEfficacyAndEffectivenessOfPsychologicalTreatments_web.pdf

Chapter D

Technology Assistants

Post-it Notes, notebooks, paper, and pencil are the traditional way to compensate for memory and attention loss, but they are not searchable, have no audio, and require you to remember to look at them. You may remember to check for days at a time, but then for some mysterious reason, you'll totally forget and keep on forgetting until suddenly you realize much later you're supposed to be reviewing your schedule first thing. With brain injury, habits have a habit of vanishing. Poof.

Technological assistants work better.

Artificial intelligence is the holy grail of technology assistants.

But right now, smartphones or tablets can make themselves heard and visible independent of your memory. It doesn't matter if you misread times. They audibly alarm you. Colours and icons make important events stand out visually. "You can't function independently if you don't know what you're going to do next," wrote Judy Steed quoting Brian Richards, a psychologist at Baycrest, a research and educational hospital specializing in geriatrics, in "Surrogate Memory," in the November 8, 2008 *Toronto Star*. Steed wrote, "What time is my dentist appointment? Your dentist appointment is 1 p.m. tomorrow." Technological assistants reliably answer those kinds of questions and can be with you at all times and places. They also let you fit in with everyone else who has smartphones glued to their persons.

How you use them determines your success. Setting only a few SMART goals per day or week is wise, otherwise, the alarms will overwhelm and irritate you, leading you to ignore them. Note: the feeling of competence they give you may lull you into believing you can do without them.

The problem with this solution is threefold.

1. People with brain injury find it difficult to learn new ways of doing things. They require patience from their technology teacher, external motivation, to be reminded why the technology assistant is a good thing, and must be taught over and over how to use them.

2. Insurers and lawyers may agree to buy the first one but don't seem to build in the continuing costs of devices breaking, becoming obsolete, and being needed for life. A useful service would be donations of old but still useful smartphones and tablet computers.

3. Too many Canadian healthcare professionals know little about smartphones, tablets, and computers beyond typing. Some choose not to get them or their employers won't provide them. Thus, they can't convince their clients to get them nor teach them how to use them well, securely, and privately. This incompetence inhibits a person with a brain injury to gain independent functionality and competence.

Every member of the healthcare team needs to understand how to use technology assistants to reinforce learnings and enable communication and functionality, whether by phone, email, text, or video calling. Physicians, psychologists, and therapists can reinforce assigned homework by using the device as a planning tool and by watching their client input the homework. They can enable their client to communicate emotions more readily by being open to alternative modalities using secure technology like Signal. They can empower their client's return to health by showing them health/medical/sleep apps and discussing regularly what the apps reveal. They can assist with return to work by finding and reinforcing use of appropriate apps.

For further discussion and updates, go to http://wp.me/Pf8xE-17h.

Abandonment

"I have a fucking brain injury!"
I yelled.
To no one.
Because no one wanted to hear.

Chapter 5

My Fortieth Year

"They said I can't write," I cried, referring to the vocational testing my diagnosing psychiatrist had sent me to. "Maybe in five to ten years. I can't wait that long!"

"What are you going to do about it?" my psychiatrist challenged me that June 19, 2002.

I was going to take an online writing course with a freelance writer I knew from before my injury. That was what I was going to do about it.

People around me in a classroom were a cornucopia of distractions, and fatigue stalked me like a hungry wolf. It wasn't a sure thing that I'd be awake at the time the class met. But at home, on my computer, I could use my strategies to absorb the words and understand the instructions at my own steady and glacially slow pace. I could work on my assignments in the moments I was most alert, in the morning and in the early evening. I couldn't understand why my psychiatrist was worried about me, about the insurance fight, the Mistral fight, and what I would do for income. Maybe I should have been worried? But I had continued my stress management on my own; I could do what it took to get better! Six months earlier, I'd bought Dr. Phil's *Life Strategies* and *The Life Strategies Workbook*. He'd talked about it on the *Oprah* show. Maybe his books would help me get better. *It was just a matter of changing my thoughts*, I thought. I'd scheduled fifteen- to thirty-minute weekly sessions to do the assignments. I'd used my reading strategies and worked my way through to the end of Life Law #7. But now I had to put my energies into relearning how to write, and I was beginning to doubt strategies were the way to treat my injured brain or fix my life. I forgot all about my psychiatrist's worry as I signed up for the course.

I began on July 22, 2002 and learned to write in a new way. No more handwriting. Toss out the mind maps. Use free association. Put fingers to keyboard and see what appears on the screen. Write short pieces. No more long ones. Only eight hundred words. Let my subconscious flow through my fingers and not worry that my conscious mind hadn't a clue what I wanted to write.

Tick. Tick. Tick.

My fortieth birthday was flying toward me. Big number birthdays were a cause for extended celebrating. One of my favourite ones I'd partly organized was for my mother's sixtieth.

The package in my living room had stood almost as tall as Mum. A gold bow dangled down from its gift-wrapped top strut. I confined my excitement to my grin and instructions for her to wait. I had to get in the right spot with my Minolta. And then I clicked rapidly as Mum ripped down the flowery wrapping paper while her sister and Mistral watched in contained glee. I can still remember her open-mouthed "oohhh" that I captured to my immense satisfaction on film when she saw what was inside: her older sister-in-law. Mistral and I had organized her flight from England in secret to attend Mum's sixtieth birthday party. A two-peat! I'd similarly surprised Mum about six years earlier when I'd worked with her sister to bring her over to Canada for her first visit ever.

After that surprise, Mistral and I hosted a pre-birthday bash barbecue. Summers meant gathering together at one birthday party after another under the warmth of the Canadian sun, usually in Mum's backyard with me baking the birthday cake, and Mum and Vashti cooking the meals, with Dad attending the barbecue and Arta helping to clear up. But that day when the sun chased the clouds, we hosted. Inside and out, Azriel told his stories; Gracious hid from my roving camera; and Imeda giggled. Mum usually wandered through birthday crowds with her video camera, but she was too stunned and too full of laughter from the continuing festivities, one after the other that several of us had organized for her, for her to remember. Vashti was there chatting with my aunts; Kurush talked a mile to a dozen with Imeda while Arta smiled on and Glenda interrupted with her two cents. Freny shyly watched everyone, and Ebenezer quietly joined in here and there. Laughter punctuated the air as the crowd feasted on my chicken wings, sliced potatoes barbecued in milk, and Mistral's famous creamy green bean salad. Mum shouted over the din for everyone to pose for the obligatory group shot. Loud, that's what I remember most about our gatherings. Loud laughter, louder talk, and dogs weaving in and out.

But my injured brain couldn't handle such hubbub anymore, I was struggling to admit. Still, I wanted to hold on tight to my former life, to the idea of having fun on my fortieth.

"What would you like?" Mum asked. I knew what I wanted, a traditional strawberry tea. Strawberries in November might be a bit bland, but Earl Grey tea, fresh scones, lickable whipped cream, and delicate cucumber sandwiches promised sweet interruption in my descending life. Her expression made me add vegetarian Pilau as an alternative. I loved my grandmother's Pilau recipe, a thick rich sauce on the bottom, comforting rice on top. I didn't eat chicken anymore, but I'd figured out how to make it with Portobello mushrooms. Heady, fragrant, bestrewn with sautéed cashews and sultanas, saffron threading through the pea-dotted rice that blanketed the korma, Pilau would do. For once, I'd have a meal I loved where I didn't have to check out which dish was meat or bring my own. Mum would even buy organic ingredients so that the food didn't interrupt my sleep. And the flavour would dance on the tongue.

As November approached, Mum told me that the extended circle of kin had decided that since I'd had a party for my thirty-ninth with gifts, it was a bit much to invite people over again for my fortieth, and so it would just be a small circle. Thoughts disappeared. I had no response. My heart flipped into memory of how years earlier I'd begun to plan my husband's fortieth, how I'd wondered how he'd top my thirtieth, a surprise of kith and cookies all waiting in our home, yelling "happy birthday" as I walked in the front door after a long day out interviewing for *Lifeliner*. I'd laughed, flabbergasted that he'd kept this surprise from me so well. I hugged him thank you.

In 2002, I walked in the front door of my parents' home. Mum had relinquished the dinner to another. The smells of Southwest cuisine greeted my nose. It was my least favourite food after an unfortunate stomach upset in California twenty years earlier. And was that meat? Yes. I had to check each dish for meat since I wasn't sure I remembered which was vegetarian after they'd been pointed out to me, as well as checking which I could tolerate for politeness sake, for she had cooked for me all day.

As I lay in bed that night, I felt outraged for myself, for where God had brought me, for another dream flung into the abyss. Maybe a trivial dream, but one everyone had. I was the first of our generation to turn forty, but I doubted any of them would have a party like the one I just had. I decided I would not attend any of their fortieth birthdays. I'd buy them gifts. But never would I grace their festivities. My revenge. Unknown to them. I huffed and rolled my eyes at myself and didn't change my mind.

Tick. Tick. Tick.

After another abysmal Christmas, I stared at my instructor's kind email of January 4, 2003. "What you need is focus. Maybe in your case you need to focus on personal essays as opposed to fiction." It squeezed my heart. My precious stories. Gone. My mind that had seen a person talking on the street or a memory fragment that rose up like a perfumed muse and turned it into a short story, couldn't do it anymore. My brain's networks, the neurons of creativity, were blackened and unfed.

I felt dead.

And then I told myself I still had *Lifeliner* to finish. *I can still write nonfiction*, I assured myself. The need to write overpowered my senses.

Before my injury, I wanted to write. I enjoyed my two hours every morning of nothing but the sound of my pen on paper under the requisite beat of the music for the story's emotions.

Post-injury I had to write.

My fiction was gone.

My breath sighed through me. I let go.

I began to read the instructions for the next module.

Tick. Tick. Tick.

Meanwhile, ever since February 2002, for a couple of hours many Sunday afternoons, Freny and I sat close, her high voice chatting, asking me smart questions for a child while we played on my computer or piano. She liked watching me play the concentration game my psychologist had first shown me back in mid-June 2002. As the cheap battery of my energy drained quickly, my heart filled up with her presence. After my brain injury, I suddenly preferred being around children than adults. Children accepted me unquestioningly as a person they liked and wanted to be around. I could be silly and stupid. The best part about time with them was baking for them. Brownies, cookies, doughnuts, pancakes. I was still burning or under-baking things; they giggled over that. I read about a chef who used Post-it Notes. I copied his style, and the bottom of my cabinets sprouted yellow stickies whenever I cooked and baked.

I began to let go of my old standards and accepted my new level because it was still good. And the best part was: I still had people in my life who wanted to eat my goodies.

Chapter 6

Year of Hell

My faithful dog died two days after the third anniversary of the crash. I killed him. He had aged beyond his lifespan. His heart beat strongly, but age had claimed his sight, his hearing, and his bowels fell silent on January 17. I called my mother. She told me to call the vet, and the vet came. I laid my dog's head on my lap as we sprawled on the floor of my kitchen, my homemaker silently cleaning up. The vet injected him. And he died.

Love photons burst into me, flooding me. I sobbed with guilt, the flow of love and forgiveness that came from outside me, from my dog's spirit, devastating me.

I collapsed.

My mutt had stuck with me while the cats in my life, my kith and kin, had jumped one after the other from my sinking ship, their tails spinning like whip tides to get themselves away from me. He was my comfort, my companion. He forced me out the door to walk and kept me anchored to who I used to be until he felt I'd be OK on my own. I had looked after myself and him. I hand-fed him and struggled to remember not to let his water bowl run dry. Day after day, week after week, months stretching into each other, I will-powered through fatigue. But he was gone, and fatigue won the battle. A month-long cold wormed itself into my lungs.

Tick. Tick. Tick.

My hand cramped, my fingers ached, my neck threw striations of pain down my shoulder swelling with deep ache while my hidden pressure cooker of thoughts and boiling cauldron of emotions spoke to me through my writing. Talking enticed them out, but it took time as I meandered through spoken words. Few had the patience to listen.

My journal didn't care how long it took.

Tick. Tick. Tick.

My husband reduced my monthly spousal support as the dog was dead.

Meanwhile, Freny was sick, that's why we couldn't have our alone time together, I was told. I accepted that unquestioningly. The next week, she had a birthday party to go to. And another the following week. I frowned when I was informed. I began to feel like she was being kept away from me.

Mum assured me that this was normal for girls her age, to be invited to many birthday parties. Maybe. I hoped, Freny could come to my home for my traditional Good Friday hot cross buns. Nope. Her mother had other plans, I confirmed. I began planning. Should I make two batches or one for this year's small group of nephews and parents? I settled on eight buns as doable. I mixed the dough one day, formed the buns another, and froze them to bake on Good Friday itself. My TRI team would be proud of my pacing.

Friday morning I was late taking the buns out of the freezer. Some remained half frozen! *Would they rise OK?* I worried. I popped them in the oven and prayed that I would not, as usual, take them out before they were fully baked. I knew how to bake—I'd been baking bread for decades—yet since my brain injury, the hollow sound I thought I could hear as I tapped the bottom of the buns would often prove false. As I closed the oven door, the doorbell rang. Freny stood there!

My brain refused to compute.

I blurted, "I don't have enough buns."

She replied, "That's OK. I don't want any." And then her parents appeared behind her. I invited them in automatically.

They entered my narrow hallway as I returned to my buns in the oven, trying desperately to hold two things in my head at once: the baking buns and the unexpected people at the door. The boys were elsewhere playing with Lego, my parents at my kitchen table. I wanted to go back to the front door. *No, stay by the stove!* I'd realized years earlier that if I let my thoughts wander me out the kitchen, things burned. I had to stay by the stove where the timer would penetrate the cotton wool wrapping my senses and thoughts.

They shouted down my long hallway, "We haven't had lunch. We're going to get Swiss Chalet and bring it back here."

My broken neurons fired chaotically. *I'm a vegetarian. I can't stand the smell of meat in my home. I'm OK with it elsewhere but not in my home. I have buns to bake. Are they baked yet? No, people are at the door. I have to feed them with only eight buns. But they're bringing Swiss Chalet in. I can't have chicken in my house.* The smell memory wrinkled my nose.

Brain-injury anger blasted out my mouth. "No!"

"We haven't had lunch," they bellowed back. "What's wrong with bringing Swiss Chalet in?" They continued that they didn't expect buns. They turned up to visit me.

I didn't do well with no warning. I began to spin around. *Do I have food other than buns to feed them?*

Good Friday is about buns.

I'd invited them over for buns.

They'd said no.

Why are they here? All of a sudden? And not wanting buns?

I can't feed them.

"You have to be flexible!" came the shout down my unlit hallway.

I yelled back from the oven, "You didn't tell me!" My brain injury anger was throttling me. *I can't burn the buns. I can't underbake the buns. I don't know what to do.*

The door banged.

They'd left.

Half hour later, I found their cell number and apologized for yelling. They told me I'd traumatized Freny. My stomach hollowed. My chest burned. My brow furrowed: *No! I didn't want to do that to her! How could I have?* But they said I had. I hung up, no reciprocal apology made, their words whirring in my head until my reason returned. I wrote an email. I feared confrontation. Hated it.

But I made myself sit down at the computer. I wrote. I edited. I stared. I edited. I sent to all.

Hi all,

I'm sorry about the kerfuffle today. But it's made me realise that perhaps I need to clarify a few changes that my brain injury has caused in me and what that means to all of us.

I have come a long way in the last 3 years, but, among other problems that remain, my processing is still slow. You may not think so, but it IS the reason why I have trouble making decisions, why I need time to respond to a question or request or invitation, why I seem sometimes to not respond in a discussion or am slow in starting one (silence in conversation does not mean I agree or don't care, just that I'm processing what you've said and trying to respond; if I'm talking on a topic I've been familiar with for years then it's like my old self) AND why I do not do well with surprises.

Surprises like today do not give me enough time to process what's happening. When I don't understand and am not given time to process what's happening or given the opportunity/time to work through it, it is for me like being in a panic situation. It's not a panic attack, rather a sense of being discombobulated and wanting to get out of the situation cause my brain's shut down. It's not something I can control. It just is.

On a related note, I still have problems with my attention. The injury created problems in all 5 types of attention and, of course, it takes far more effort for me to focus than previous to the accident. Added stress and illness always makes me worse. I've improved more in some types than others. For example, groups still intimidate me, and I cope by talking to one person, which I can do when the noise from the rest of the group is such that it sounds like white noise. If I'm aware of different conversations, then it's much more difficult to participate in one.

So I'd really appreciate it that, to ensure a good time had by all, you call me at least a day ahead about any plans (more is preferable or, for example, give me a heads up a few days ahead and confirmation the day before, not night before) to give me time to process and to decide what I can do. I do want to spend time with you and love to talk with you on the phone or in person, and I ask for patience and understanding so that we can all enjoy each other's company and grow in our relationships.

Cheers,
Shireen

I searched my inbox. I checked my email program was receiving. "Good message," Mum replied. No other replies. It didn't used to be like this.

On Sunday, Freny grabbed my hand, grinned up at me, and skipped with me up the church steps and into the cacophony of people joyfully greeting Easter.

For a moment, I was wanted, like that summer I went away to Europe when I was in my early twenties. I was fêted goodbye by all my extended gang of kith and kin. Lunch out, dinners in, phone calls, gifts of key tags and notepads, and Gertie tagging along as I organized suitcases, clothing, and knitting for two months of travelling the day before I was to fly. She talked about what was on her mind as our school year closed, and the summer opened up to lead into the next school year. I was used to working summers, not seeing much of people I usually saw during the falls and winters of studies, and so I'd thought nothing of going away from the last day of my part-time job until the first week of another year of university. But as Gertie watched me, confiding her troubles, talking as if already pining to see me again, I absorbed with growing wonder that I would be missed.

Not much missing going on now, I thought near the end of July 2003 as my brain descended into chaos. I had to flee my life, to a weekend with the family patriarch and his wife. I'd miss Gertie's daughter's birthday. But I hardly saw her anyway. I could make it up to her when I returned with ice cream out. The little one loved it as much as I did. I phoned and explained. Darius seemed cool with it.

An email arrived to say if I really cared I should've called her on her actual birthday.

> *Also, we have concern about your current situation especially having to leave to escape. Once you have a more stable outlook upon life we will be happy to reconsider.*

Glenda tsked, livid on my account, and shared how Freny's mother was considering limiting or stopping my contact with Freny, too. Glenda had said to her, "That will kill Shireen."

Tick. Tick. Tick.

August and September migraines clawed into my skull, and fatigue shoved me down. August 12, 2003, I began to see a spiritual mentor. She became a rock I swam to every month. I asked to meet with Gertie, maybe Freny's mother, and any others, with a therapist. I needed desperately to find out why this was all happening.

I met with my family lawyer, who told me I qualified under the Supreme Court of Canada ruling that a spouse disabled during a long marriage was entitled to spousal support, but Mistral's strategy of reducing his offer every month by the amount of temporary support nonplussed him. He pointed out, "You have three legal actions, and you cannot keep this up." My case would probably have to go all the way to the top court, and then what? Given his attitude, I would probably still be out spousal support plus the cost of the legal action plus the stress of trying to cope with three lawsuits. I nodded. I felt nothing as I saw poverty grasp my future. Meanwhile, the insurance company kept me locked into battle with it. I had thirty dollars left. *Should I cash out more of my RRSPs (Registered Retirement Savings Plans)? How long would this injury last? It had already been two years longer than I had ever imagined. Could it last much longer?*

Suddenly, the insurance company agreed to back pay for lost income, as well as the recommended devices and treatments. Relieved, I deposited the first cheque. But the second one didn't arrive.

Tick. Tick. Tick.

In seven days, I could have that meeting with Gertie and others, I was told. What? When? How? So soon? I was told it may be late November before they could all find time to do this again, and they're meeting with me to resolve my problem. I had to rest up.

My spiritual mentor doubted the wisdom of the meeting.

I said, "I have to know why I'm no longer allowed to see the children, why people are leaving me." I had no choice.

Tick. Tick. Tick.

We had arrived a small group, my parents, my brother, and me in Canada decades earlier; slowly my parents had drawn into our small circle their parents, siblings, friends, my kith, in-laws, and sundries. In early October 2003, some of that extended circle filled my parents' living room after church. The therapist took me up to Dad's study to discuss the agenda and my expectations. She did the same with everyone. I dropped into the IKEA chair, its back supporting my head. My parents sat on the couch to my left, the therapist to their left, the rest across from me and to my right. Light flung itself against the windows. The therapist explained the meeting format and how we had to use "I" statements. How we had to listen and not interrupt each other. How I would begin. And then each would have their turn. How we were not to insult each other. After she'd confirmed everyone knew the agenda, she turned to me. I began.

From deep inside the cave of my mind, my words exited monotone, clipped. They were making decisions about me without speaking to me. I didn't understand these decisions. I didn't know why they weren't discussing them with me. Did they want a relationship with me? Why didn't they want their daughters to have relationships with me? I was hurt. I was confused.

Imeda spoke. Sentences battered me.

"Your requests for relationships are me-focused."

"All you think about is yourself."

"You're using your brain injury to make excuses."

"You have something wrong, but it's not a brain injury."

"You need to change."

A car sped past outside the window. I watched its rear lights glow red as it braked at the stop sign beyond my sight. I had to focus.

Imeda asserted that they were here because they loved me. He said that they stand together through crises and the fact they gave up their pursuits and time to be here is evidence of their concern and love for me. The others nodded.

I thought, *Friends are your family, and blood is thicker than water. Which is it for me?*

Trees waved hello to me through the tall windows.

What was that? They're holding an intervention? For a brain injury? Who does that? The therapist is OK with this? My mouth wouldn't open.

Imeda blurted, "Why don't you treat us the way you treat the kids?"

Breathe and focus. He was saying that I was good with the kids. I remembered how I used to be with kids, so awkward and unsure before my brain injury. Everyone knew to give the baby to my husband because I just looked like a deer in the headlights. Give me older teens and adults any day.

"You have to change. You can't have good relationships with the kids unless there are good relationships with the mothers."

Vashti took up the thread. Her sentences slingshotted my head:

"I have to trust you."

"It's easier to be uninvolved with you because it's so difficult to talk to you due to fear of outbursts."

"I need to see you actually care about us and you're not so self-focused."

A couple walked by the window walking their dog, drawing my eyes outside.

I have to focus, I berated myself. *All my energy must be to listen. I'll remain confused if I don't listen,* I lectured myself.

"Good Friday." The words seemed out of nowhere.

My body tensed, I commanded myself to continue deep breathing. *I'm coping,* I told myself. *I'm finding out the answers to my questions.*

Freny's mother was saying, "My own reaction was to flee, then to protect. My daughter was affected by your outburst! She was more fearful and unsure of you!"

Would she have taken my hand on Easter Sunday if she was fearful? Do traumatized children do that? I have to explain my injury to Freny, explain she can ask me anything. Knowledge and education quell fear.

"You didn't apologize," she added.

I stared.

My parents' mantle clock struck the hour, each intonement of the chimes reminding me I was supposed to be listening, supposed to stay focused.

Peace from outside my being filled me.

My eyes moved from one to the other as they took up each other's threads. "You have to acknowledge you've done things that've hurt and offended everyone. You can't always be making excuses, using your brain injury as a reason."

Gertie asserted that all she did in our phone calls was listen to me. *How could I remember the details of her last day in our last phone call so many months ago if I was the only one talking? How could I recall those details when I'd forget important events like the day of a birthday?* I dragged in breath and tuned back in. "I heard little empathy from you for me. You cannot just listen. You always give forceful responses, and you get offended if we don't take it."

How was she any different? I grumbled to myself inside the cavern of my mind. Since when was anyone I knew anything but forceful?

Darius took up the thread, questioning my diagnosis.

Mum leaned forward to interrupt, "Shireen does have a brain injury."

The voices came at me.

"There are older pre-accident emotional problems."

"You've always blown up."

What? Yelling and arguments filled my childhood, but I remembered being amused at how mellow I'd become in my late twenties and thirties, not even alpha male doctors with their down-their-nose talk bothered me. And what about all the times we spent at each other's houses? Them pitching in with our renovations? Us helping out with their kids? The lavish meals I cooked for them? What about the ice cream party I'd hosted the summer before my brain injury or the multi-course Christmas Eve dinner? What about the times I'd listened to tales of childhood pain? Or trotted over with my camera to take photos of Imeda's children on a warm summer day?

Imeda said, "You have to change."

Change? I change all the time. Every day I don't know what will have changed in my head. I can't keep up.

The voices took courage.

"You've tended to isolate and feel persecuted within your family. I wish you'd get help to address this emotional issue as it is long-standing and not related to the accident or brain injury."

"You have to get help."

What the fuck did they think I was doing? I was exhausted working this health job!

"We can't talk to you because of how you'll react."

I'm not taking responsibility for your choices!

The words never exited my mouth.

Words exited theirs. Childhood battles leapt into the recent past. Chronology became topsy-turvy. My pre-injury photographic memory pieced together their vague assertions and slamming emotions and re-sorted them into a time long past.

They believe I won't get better.

I'm a writer. Writers write what they know. They don't believe I will ever write again.

The horror froze my mind.

Vashti said, "Each of us has a family. I wish you'd kiss my ass if you want to see my daughter. You should give me credit for cooking you dinner." I remembered the tiring drives to eat those occasional dinners, the din of her full house, the ping-pong of trying to decide if the fatigue was worth it, wondering why they didn't bring it over when even the act of eating required rest time. The way she did it fed her need, not my practical one.

And then they answered my question. I sat silenced in my chair as I became a being unrecognizable, a being who should not exist. Eyes black with death, hands curled into hammers, heart carbonized into molecules that vanished into the maw of space. A mind filled with anti-positive. A brain shooting electrons that pierce bodies and fling them dead to the ground. Mum objected, and they changed tact. I was now a being with lips stretched wide, eyes gleaming with bright amusement as blood spilled on sidewalks.

Dad said, "Shireen needs more love than the rest of us. Nothing is truly curable but is in fact managed and endured. I worry," he expressed, "that Shireen has a tendency toward isolating herself. I wonder if she has a deep-seated fear of failing. It's affecting her life and outlook."

The meeting wrapped up. Laughter and small talk about work rang over my head as I knew without a doubt that God had made a mistake. I was not the kind of person who should live.

Mum drove me home, the older children returning from their babysitter insisting they join us.

I climbed into bed in the wee hours and wrestled with my sheet and duvet as I perseverated: this was unsolvable. My frozen feet demanded more coverage. My neck itched from burning heat, and my chest was scorching, yet my shoulders craved warmth. I turned on to my right side, adjusting my arm until the pressure of my body dulled the deep ache in my shoulder. I hugged my pillow in the dead quiet of my home.

I ate yogourt for dinner Monday night, fatigue bloating my cheeks, weighting down my muscles so that the yogourt lid resisted my weak hands as hunger gnawed at my stomach. I couldn't wait until Wednesday when Mum would take me out for lunch. I still couldn't figure out why I ate so much more than I ever did. I never used to clean my plate except for dessert. Mum used to complain how I wouldn't finish my dinner. And worse, I needed an alarm to remind me to cook before ravenousness drove me to grab the quickest thing.

Emails flowed through invisible lines between me and the therapist. She suggested that my apology could have been more helpful.

I thought, *I have apologized so much for my brain injury. Yet I don't recall apologies to me.* Maybe they have, and I don't recall. But they didn't in that meeting. And every time I have a TBI snafu, I apologize. Do people go around apologizing for their cancer? For the chemo throwing their hair out of their scalp, a bad situation but a normal state of affairs for a person with cancer? For staying in bed all day after their latest treatment or when tumours displace neurons and cause them to space out? *No!* I screamed, my pain ricocheting through my split axons, my inflamed neurons, and my blackened blood vessels. I was done apologizing for an injury I did not give myself. An injury others inflicted thoughtlessly on me.

The therapist sent a summary of the meeting to all of us. I thanked her.

Thursday, I woke up and realized I hadn't asked and asked and asked myself, *Why don't they call? Why aren't they emailing? Why won't they come over to chat? Why don't they talk to me? What happened to our relationships?* I yearned for a voice that cared. But I no longer cared to stop my kin and kith floating away from me. I turned toward the future.

Tick. Tick. Tick.

I read my diagnosing psychiatrist's report to my lawyer to support my tort claim:

The published literature indicates that the persistence of SPECT scan abnormalities for a year or more is associated with social and vocational failure...Ms. Jeejeebhoy was an unusually capable, imaginative and intelligent woman before the accident with a multitude of intellectual pursuits...I worry that fatigue and pain will undermine any efforts she makes to sustain herself financially. Ms. Jeejeebhoy is a young person and she has a long way to go. Not only has she lost important skills which would have sustained her and, I suspect, have made her very successful over time, she has lost a husband who found that he couldn't live with her after the accident. As I described earlier, there was a change in her personality. She was either very irritable, explosive and angry at him for reasons that he could never quite figure out or was she exhausted and had no desire to engage in any of the pastimes they had once enjoyed together. Shireen Jeejeebhoy had been replaced by a stranger. Her husband felt that he had to get away from her but even months after the separation he wrote respectfully about the talented person he had married and the damage that had been done to her in the accident. Ms. Jeejeebhoy has been abandoned by friends and even members of her own family appear to want to stay away from her. She is much more lonely and day to day life is far more difficult. She is working hard to recover but I do not see that happening.

He's exaggerating, I thought. *I will relearn to write!* On December 10, I finished my writing course. My instructor wrote, "Focus on the book."

Tick. Tick. Tick.

Hope flowed into me in 2004. It was strange being alone. The adult chatter, the banging of chairs against table, the stomping up and downstairs of little feet gave way to quiet lunches with my mother alone. I still had her to bake for, or at least cook for, in my home. My OHIP-paid psychiatrist continued to monitor my progress while only my psychologist agreed to see me unpaid until the insurance company met their obligations. I begged my old acupuncturist to see me; her grandmotherly presence eased my pain as much as her needles. The insurance company and my lawyer settled the accident benefits claim.

Chapter 7

Shattered

My spiritual mentor leant me *Don't Forgive Too Soon*. I yearned for guidance after all the cats in my life had dived off my sinking ship. The book had sketches to illustrate points, white space to ease reading, and except for what "turn the other cheek" really meant, the rest of the concepts I had known from my Bible studies. The book put these stories of forgiveness in a new, practical way.

I scheduled my reading for Saturdays and Mondays beginning January 10, 2004. I followed my OT's instructions. I set a timer to pace myself for fifteen minutes of reading; pen and notebook to take notes; and blank paper to block off the text and facing page I wasn't reading. I couldn't use a highlighter because it wasn't my book. I was secretly relieved. One less chore to do to sap my energy. I began with my concentration exercise when I could remember that extra step.

For a year, I filled pages with notes and summaries. Each reading day, I turned a page in the book. It was slow. I felt guilty about borrowing a book for so long, but my spiritual mentor was cool with it. I came to accept the time it was taking. But what did "turn the other cheek" really mean? I frowned. I couldn't recall. I deep breathed. I flipped back to it. I remembered. I just had to stick to my OT's strategies. I didn't let it bother me. But my memory of that concept remained blank as the months wore on no matter how many times I reread that passage and my notes.

I began to doubt the strategies.

Yet I still attended social functions, feeling like I must cling to my old life, hoping strategies would work. I laboriously dressed myself in my outdated cocktail wear on Sunday, December 12, 2004. The night glimmered cold. The front door to the party opened, and I entered the warm babel. People held glasses that sloshed wine as they laughed, their lips moving and widening as they chattered. I squeezed through the spaces between perfumed bodies, my brain demanding flight, my mind trying to drag in my old social skills of small talk. I was introduced to a pleasant man, his face inquiring as to who I was. I knew of him, my father's colleague of the last couple of years. He couldn't hear me, and I said my name again, pulling on my meagre puff power so as to be heard above the happy throng. His face registered shock. He hadn't heard of me. I registered how far I'd dropped out of life.

He didn't know what to say. I felt bad for him. I felt nothing myself. No surprise, no anger. Just this crawling all over my skin as vocal cord ululations all around me pinged my ears and the elegant black dresses and dark suits sucked on my eyeballs. I slithered and contorted my way to the basement. I sat winded in the dim, low-ceilinged room and let the quiet soothe me. Why did I still try to attend parties? My TRI team had advised against it and had suggested quiet small get-togethers. But this was the only way people would socialize with me in the long-standing party tradition. They didn't want to see me; they wanted me to attend their functions.

Tick. Tick. Tick.

I dragged myself to acupuncture two days later, whining to my acupuncturist that I had a cold. She examined my tongue and my pulses. She didn't think I had a cold. I had a slight fever. *I always seemed to have a slight fever*, I thought. She treated me minimally with needles in case I had allergies then with a lighter heated up the inside of glass suction balls and popped them down my back on both sides of my spine in case I had a cold. They pulled painfully on my flesh. My lungs opened in relief. She told me to sit in the waiting room while she prevailed on one of her other patients to drive me to the subway. I sagged in my seat. I felt mothered, like I could get home.

Tick. Tick. Tick.

Twelve months after I began, I flipped open *Don't Forgive Too Soon* with dread. I read and reread and reread the first sentence of the last page. Suddenly my brain caught and absorbed the words. I understood. I read the next sentence, its words pinging off my forehead until finally my reading engine roared to life again. I came to the end of the paragraph and began to summarize it in my notebook.

I couldn't recall the first sentence. My timer declared break time!

I deep breathed for three minutes, letting my stomach rise and fall rhythmically, calming my fear and panic that after four years, I was having the same trouble reading as when first diagnosed. What did "turn the other cheek" mean again?

I resisted the urge to check and attempted the next paragraph. My forehead grew cold behind my skull as the familiar concentration headache crystallized. I'd forgotten to do my concentration exercise first. Again.

But did it really help? Was my reading worse? I had to admit that it made little difference. I still couldn't recall what "turn the other cheek" meant to people two thousand years ago.

I forged to the end.

I stared at the back cover of *Don't Forgive Too Soon*.

I cannot read. I don't remember one single new concept and not even some old ones. My utter failure sank my mind into paralyzing anxiety.

I turned my back on reading.

I kept writing, practicing, practicing, for I had to get back to *Lifeliner*. I had made a commitment to so many people. How could I let them down? Besides, I couldn't let go of my dream!

Tick. Tick. Tick.

Angst grew within me.

The dark cloud that obscured my perspective of the world, keeping me from being in the world, seemed to be a permanent part of me now. Trying to write a chapter of *Lifeliner* eluded me. But I needed to write. Pressure cooked and carbonized deep within me. I wanted to join the online community. Maybe I could write a blog to practice my writing and get this angst out of me.

But my lawyer warned that the defence would use it against me. "Every word you utter, every sentence you write can be turned around and made to sound different from what you intended." He wasn't too happy about my request.

"I can make it anonymous," I said.

He thought about it. He assented but with conditions. I wasn't to write about health, the law, insurance companies, or myself.

OK, I could do that. I had set up a website for *Lifeliner* back in the 1990s. I didn't know how to use it or design it anymore, but I had seen the Blogger platform. I wrote my first post on it. The obsidian block of angst vanished. Weightlessness lifted my soul in my dense fatigue. In the vast bad news of my life, I had a success!

I rose stiffly while I danced in my head. I couldn't wait to tell Mum, to spread the joyous news! I had set up a blog. I had written a post. This was an achievement everyone could celebrate with me.

I posted every time that black angst began rebuilding itself. Some times I could read what I wrote to edit it, to make it better, to fix it to say what I really wanted to say. It was difficult. It took more energy to take in information (to read) than to express what was already in my head through my writing. Some times I couldn't, and I'd tell myself, write and post, if you try to read it, it'll take so long, you'll never post it. Just write. But was anyone reading it? I learnt of a service that gathered blog stats, and I added it. Suddenly, there they were, my readers, identified by country and ISPs. I had ten!

I didn't know any of them, but I had readers. And even better, people began to comment on my posts. They thought I was male, and I didn't disabuse them. It wasn't new for people to confuse my gender, and anyway, it would make it harder for the defence to find my blog. I tried to reciprocate by reading their blogs, pacing myself as my OT had taught me, to let their words process in my head until I understood, until a response effortfully emerged into my consciousness so that I could comment on their blogs.

On Canada's birthday, Mum checked out my blog and liked my collage of old photographs.

Tick. Tick. Tick.

June 2005. Anger and irritation. Out of the cut off emotional centres of my brain, only those two bled through into my consciousness as frontal neurons refused to moderate the neurons deep in my brain. Since my injury, anger and irritation had chained me. The beast of brain injury anger joined forces with moral outrage at the broken bricks of injustice being tossed at my heart. Anger told me of my desperation, desperation my despair's voice.

From inside my mind's grey cavern, I looked out to the fresh green of the gardens that all others lived in, their trees sturdy, my father's soon to turn seventy. Flocks of memories flew past me, cawing stories of how I used to plan birthday surprises. I stood to grasp an errant bird that had strayed too close above the heaped-up bricks. He eluded my clutching hand, but I remembered. I struggled on tottering feet toward that garden, to plan, organize, create a gift so stupendous, it would shock and last, it would bring joy and satisfaction at a life loved, lived, lauded.

Lauded.

What gift could laud a man who had re-landscaped nutrition, drove patients to move to Toronto to receive his care of hope, generated invites from all over the world to speak, to teach, to show them a better way to care for patients?

An award.

An award at my alma mater and the department that brought him and us here to Canada.

My legs bent; my butt landed on the basalt floor of my cavern. Trees in those gardens burst forth pollen in the springtime air, and I stretched my hand out for a touch of that golden productivity. My hand couldn't exit the craggy walls of my vacuumed mind.

The gardens receded as the walls imprisoned me, scattering my thoughts into disconnected shards. Women outside peered in, babying me, watching their words bounce off my besieged brain. Try, try again.

I. Can. Not. Plan.

I. Can. Not. Organize.

I. Can. Not. Problem. Solve.

I phoned my mum, my siblings, friends of my parents. I phoned the University of Toronto, Faculty of Medicine. I scribbled furiously in my phone notebook what to say, what was said to me, clutching at these words, to remember and plan how to set up an award in Dad's name. His birthday present. For his seventieth. In August. I had only two months, time for pre-injury Shireen to wrap up an idea she'd have been cogitating on since January. For me, an unknowable entity, an eternity of spinning thought out of baffled uncertainty in between days of rest.

I met with three women. Fund-raisers. Businesswomen. To plan and organize the award in my father's name. Mum the fourth as my brace and connection to them. Pure happiness as frond tips from the gardens caressed me, guided me to answers, but they slowly left me behind. Mouths moved; talk chattered in my ears; fingers typed at speed on Crackberry-Blackberry; and my hands lay still in my lap, my Palm forgotten, as my eyes flitted from one face to another to the Shih Tzu trotting happily past the restaurant windows to the tiny Blackberry screen, envying, lost, confused.

Head home. Head on kitchen table. Alone. Memories of the fundraising plan our five-woman committee had organized burrowed themselves into my disconnected neurons, taunting me to apprehend them. My Palm, my second brain, offered no help, its blank notes adjuring me for not filling them while we'd conversed and I with horror realized I could not figure out how to find a paper clip in an office.

Five years, five months, and thirteen days after my injury, comprehension like a cresting wave splashed into my empty cavern, filled my lungs, drowned my emotions, and flung me like flotsam against the craggy back wall of my detached mind.

Oh. My. God. I. Cannot. Return. To. Work.

How much can one person cry?

Abandonment Learnings

Chapter E

Evidence-Based Medicine Fails

Scientifically objective evidence is considered superior to the art of medicine. Yet evidence-based medicine prescribes coping to treat brain injury—coping with deficits, worsening social situations, deteriorating brain function, and death while physically alive. In no other area of medicine would this be considered treatment.

Treatment isn't feeling better about the deficits; it's actually feeling better. Treatment restores lost cognition and automaticity, restores emotional centres to normal functioning, regenerates damaged physiology, and heals the autonomic nervous system, internal organs, muscles, hormones, and skin.

Pacing, compensating strategies, acceptance, meditation do not lead to recovery but put people into a repetitive pattern of being unable to sustain work and relationships, with worsening health.

Evidence-based medicine doesn't respect the brain's regenerating and electrical properties as central to repair. The brain being the final frontier, by necessity, requires treatments that are mostly in the research phase, requires physicians to work within a healthcare team, requires respecting the internal experience of the person with brain injury as believable and pointing the way to treatment, and requires understanding the deficit is physiological not psychiatric and then using logic and reason to think through how to use the brain's sensory inputs and plasticity to change itself. By ignoring serious cardiac ramifications, evidence-based medicine is essentially medical malpractice that consigns a person to an early death and low quality of life, especially if given fatiguing medications to inadequately prop up their heart.

Chapter F

Medical Team, Social Support

Through *Lifeliner* I learnt that the road to thriving has four legs: something within yourself, faith, medical team support, and social support.

Medical Team Support

Healthcare professionals work in silos. It confounded me that people with intact brains, responsible for my brain injury treatment, expected me to remember and coordinate my care, ensure lab results were delivered, carry letters from specialists to my GP, and communicate accurately and fully what one professional was doing to all the other healthcare professionals in my "team." The medical side didn't "speak" to the psychological side. Mediating care between professionals ate up the energy I needed for brain repair, homework, exercising, cooking healthy, etc. It increased my stress and gave me a profound sense of insecurity.

Stress is bad for the brain.

Every healthcare professional from neuropsychiatrists to psychologists to massage therapists are part of a person's team and as such need to communicate regularly without depending on the person with the brain injury. If the GP can't coordinate the care, then one of the specialists must. Technology can enhance regular communication with less effort. And medicare should pay since effective, timely communication and coordination of treatment results in better, quicker recovery.

Without the team approach, you get trauma and much less recovery.

Social Support

Equally important is social support. A talk at the Irish BIM Innovation Awards 2016[12] acknowledged a person's social life after brain injury:
"Nobody wants to know you."
"I don't mind being alone, but I would like someone to share things with."
"They're just not willing to listen to me or get to know me."

Social support confers a sense of worth and security, encourages one to stick to difficult treatment, and gives the certainty that it's worth it. It's difficult when a person you love changes fundamentally. But when you leave that person, you're saying that they are not worth saving. With their confidence in themselves already crushed, they're likely to take that message on and be unable to stick to the unrelenting work of recovery. They will accept the lie that this is all they can achieve and carry the burden of grief deep underneath the mask of a diminished life is OK.

But how to provide support when the tragedy of the injury hurts like a flame licking its way up your skin until it chars your heart?

Learn: brain injury is different from other disabilities.[13]

Share the load.

One person—perhaps the mother, perhaps the spouse, perhaps the closest friend—becomes the expert companion on a life-long

---

[12] https://twitter.com/NicholasBehn/status/705778964825030656/photo/1
[13] https://cbirt.org/sites/cbirt.org/files/resources/How%20Brain%20Injury%20is%20Different%20from%20Other%20Disabilities_tips.pdf

journey.[14] They disseminate information on brain injury and how to accommodate it to others in the person's life. They help the person share their internal experience so that their social network understands. They organize a schedule of social support the injured person needs from coffee dates in quiet places to tasks around the house to drives to appointments to advocacy to phone calls or texting time. People with brain injury function better on predictable routines. A schedule settles their minds and allows their damaged social skills to work optimally. Schedules give the social network a sense of control, help them manage dates around their work and families, and allow them to see that their exposure to the tragedy is pretty limited.

When you withdraw support from a loved one—or a patient when you as the physician make yourself unavailable or usher your patient out the door because you don't want to think outside the box—you condemn the suffering person to carry a burden they can never lift off of themselves while being further weighted down by the label of "negative." When everyone pitches in, it lightens the load, gives the person with the injury the sense that they are not alone and are still valued. It gives the person the best chance possible to recover and thrive. Isn't she worth saving?

---

[14] https://twitter.com/VickiGilman/status/705775811744419840/photo/1

Chapter G

Remarkable Recovery

In the *Reader's Digest*, Canadian edition, April 2011 issue, the article "True Grit—Why an Axe to the Head Couldn't Stop Capt. Trevor Greene" outlined the effects of committed treatment and social support.

Captain Greene recovered because he received the two keys to healing: (1) full-time rehabilitation for the years he needed, not for some predetermined, too-short time period and (2) the unwavering, committed, and involved support of a family member.

No miracle. Just what happens when someone gets proper support.

His rehab understood that the damaged part of his brain had to "grow up" again, to do everything that happened in the first twenty years of life all over again with damaged or dead neurons in an environment of bleeding and inflammation that may have had cascading effects on intact areas. Brain cells dedicated to reconnecting neurons work extremely slowly so that spontaneous healing happens over decades. It is a strange feeling when that last connection is made, like suddenly a part of you is plugged in and no longer short circuiting or off.

Healing from brain injury is like going through childhood again. But you don't have a child sitting around, watching TV, expecting the child to learn how to walk, bathe, eat, read, write, and think all by themselves. You teach the child. Every single day. The whole day. For years. Even play is teaching. So why would you expect a person with a brain injury to be able to relearn with only one or two hours per week of rehab over the span of six months to two years? And why would you ignore that a person with a brain injury has to relearn what a child learns in twenty years in a lot less time and with much less support and guidance? Why would you throw away a life? Giving it back requires effort and thought, sure, but that's part of a doctor's job. Isn't it?

Greene had his miracle because his fiancée Debbie Lepore did for him what we do for our children: support, encourage, and teach daily. Lepore was really the miracle. What she did for him was like a rare, beautiful bird creating a nest for a wingless one. What makes her especially rare is that it sounds like she did it mostly on her own with no other family members to spot her.

But most of us don't receive that nor have families who are willing to make that years-long sacrifice of full-time, hands-on rehab and caring. Some of us even have families who tell us to get over it or that we are thinking ourselves into a brain injury, as if we can reach into our skulls and smash neurons.

Worse, no medical establishment is willing to provide that kind of intensive, years-long rehab, especially not true cognitive rehab, treating us as fit only for day programs, not as having the potential to become members of society once again. Lack of funding doesn't cause this attitude; it enables it. I fought for my life, but few have my kind of background with persistent stubbornness against the establishment to do that for themselves. I don't know if I will ever stop being angry about this injustice.

Greene is no miracle. He is what everyone with a brain injury should be. When a person has committed social support and a medical team, remarkable recovery is the norm. Perhaps one day it will happen for everyone.

To read the original post in full, go to http://wp.me/Pf8xE-16d.

Chapter H

Insurance Principles

Ask yourself how much you earn annually, multiply by forty years, and record the total. Is it more or less than $250,000? Would $250,000 cover your living expenses for four decades or the rest of your life? Now figure in $10,000 to $20,000 per year for health-and-assistance-related expenses. Would living off $250,000 plus $11,000 annual government disability cover all that?

That's what the insurance industry, legal system, and most uninjured people seem to believe.

Is $250,000 a generous insurance settlement? Many seem to believe insurance claims pay for frivolous healthcare and goodies like giant TVs. Most people probably haven't needed to think about the difficulty of cleaning a home or cooking when your shoulders spasm, you have zero energy, or can't remember. Or you believe medicare pays for treatments. But medicare doesn't pay for brain injury therapies and compensating gadgets. That's what insurance is for, to cover medical expenses, housekeeping, and lost income.

But in my experience insurers only pay out after consistent, persistent badgering over years.

When you're injured in a car crash, assume you have a day to make a claim. Call your insurance company or broker immediately or have another do so. Some insurers may try to fob you off until you're past the cut-off date so that you can't make a claim, saving the insurer money but costing you a lot. Don't stall.

Hire a lawyer. It may seem silly, but the insurance system is impossible to navigate on your own. Don't put up with any lawyer you feel isn't representing you as the full ramifications of your injuries unfold.

Make your health your number one priority. Ensure treatment plans are complete and include supporting details, always be kind and civil to treatment providers, and don't wait for your insurer to give its blessing. Your body and brain will deteriorate while you wait, making recovery harder or even impossible, ensuring chronic pain becomes lifelong. Your insurance company may give you heck and ascribe bad motives to you for not waiting for their approval of your treatment plans. It's psychological warfare. They want you to quit so that you and the taxpayer will assume the financial burden of your healthcare. Resist it. You paid your premiums. Fight for your claim. Keep up your treatments.

Some insurers seem more willing to pay for IMEs and DACs than for what will return you to work. They can because people underestimate how much medical care costs and how much they actually earn when multiplied over decades; people give in under the onslaught, thinking an inadequate offer will be enough. Do a hard financial costing of lost income, new homecare, and new medical treatments medicare doesn't pay for. Then ask yourself if you can afford it all on your own. If no, dig in for years-long fight. Take the approach of not thinking about it for months at a time until your lawyer calls. Then focus on it until that part of the legal action is done. Then forget about it again. Be mindful of how your public utterances will be twisted against you; think through anything you write before clicking that Send button.

Resistance is worth it.

For insurance-related links, go to http://wp.me/Pf8xE-16g.

Salvation

Treating my neurons
Saving my life
Giving me
The possibility of hope.

Chapter 8

Brainwave

I launched Firefox and stared at the Google search box. Maybe instead of typing "brain injury treatment," I should search for ADD, a condition I'd studied and researched back in university. I didn't have ADD back then, but it sure felt like I had it now. Maybe I had googled ADD treatments before. I couldn't remember. I would try again. I found my answer! The ADD Centre.
But it was too far away.
I'd call anyway.
First thing the morning of Thursday, July 14, 2005, I phoned Lily to pray for courage. I hung up. Prepared to ask if they knew anyone in Toronto, I dialled the number from memory, fearful I'd gotten it wrong like I usually do. To my utter shock, the medical doctor, the husband of the Clinic Director, answered, not voice mail. I learnt later that him answering was rare.
He told me that their primary clients were those with ADD and they had not treated many with closed head injuries. But they could assess me in Mississauga and treat me in Toronto. *I could do that.* He was very interested in seeing what they could do for me. It took all my effort to focus on his neuroscience talk. He told me they had a cancellation; I could be assessed in only three weeks. *God heard me! Would this be my salvation? Maybe I could problem solve again. Read again. God had finally made an opening for me to get help. About damn time too.*
Tick. Tick. Tick.
A yellow Lab wandered past me in the coolness of the ADD Centre on Thursday, August 4, 2005, and I smiled inwardly, amazed I had found my way despite being confused over the streets.

"Hello!" a high, chirpy voice greeted me. "I'm Dr. Lynda Thompson," said a slim woman with shiny black hair in a classic bob.

This was the clinic's Executive Director, I remembered. I stood up, spoke my name, and followed her into her office. My senses reeled. So much to see from her large dark wood desk to prints to carpets to books to prints to the windows to papers to her to books.

Two wooden chairs with country-style pillows on them waited for me. Choices, choices. I focused effortfully, finally choosing.

She was speaking.

This was my chance, my last chance to get help. I had searched for so long, and this was it. What if they found I was normal? The neuropsychological tests I'd taken had always shown me as normal. I shook my head internally. *Focus on the now.* In her neutral, quiet tones, she was asking me the same questions the IMEs and nice doctors had. When were you born? What happened in the crash? How long ago was it?

I handed over the sheaf of information I'd brought with me. I was well versed in seeing new practitioners who wanted to help me, and I knew to bring test results and reports.

She got up and walked around her desk to another one behind me. I struggled upright and followed her. An IBM computer!

Something familiar.

I'd started my work life using computers like this one. I hadn't seen one in years! I sat down in another wooden chair in front of the computer as she instructed me. She said that I was to do a boring test. I nodded, trying to keep up. She handed me earphones, their small, foamy pieces rough against my ears. The computer would instruct me. She pointed the mouse out to me. I was to use it.

I felt comfortable with mouse and computer. I felt connected to a time when I was competent. I felt I understood the simple instructions: click the mouse if I hear or see the number one; do not click if I hear or see the number two.

As the program began, I became unsure of what I was supposed to do. But I had faith in computers. Computers were my friend. The male voice precisely spoke the instructions to me through the old earphones and led me through a practice. I felt I knew it.

Left alone to do the test, door shut, I stared at the screen. A number one flashed on in the old 1980s' green pixels. I clicked the mouse. I heard intoned in my ear: one. I clicked the mouse. A two flashed. *No,* I told myself. *Don't click. Don't click.* I thought I heard one but wasn't sure. And now there was a one on the screen. Click. It felt easy. Click. Don't click. *This isn't hard.*

The minutes ticked by.

They slowed into hours.

I had to talk to myself more and more to keep going. Boredom dragged my neurons. When would it stop? Wait, did I miss one? No, I didn't think so. I was acing this. I was sure of it. Suddenly, it was over.

I sat back, exhausted. I slowly removed the earphones. Again, I was going to be told: nothing wrong here. Try harder. Be grateful. Get on with your life.

I wondered what I was supposed to do now.

Lynda came back in and asked me how I found it.

"Boring," I confirmed. I didn't speak my worries out loud.

We exited her office and entered a room with a modern computer. She said they would do a single-electrode EEG on me. As she used a flexible tape measure to measure my head, I felt familiarity creep in. My psychologist had done a similar test on me when I first saw him in 2000. Her capable fingers scrubbed my ears and top centre of my head firmly with granular gel to clean them so that the electrodes would pick up my brainwaves. The granulation dug into my skin like extra-hard pumice. I kept my face neutral, I hoped. It had to be done, so there was no point complaining.

She clipped my ears with round pieces of metal and pressed another tiny round piece of metal on the top centre of my head. Fine coloured wires snaked from them to a little plug she clipped to my top. More wires snaked to a small rectangular box on the desk.

I watched the black screen light up. She checked the connections; soon I was seeing my brainwaves. She told me to deep breathe. I settled right into the rhythmic motion of inhale slowly, exhale long. She said to focus on one thing and not move my eyes. I tried.

It was difficult.

My eyes were demanding to move. My mind instructed them to stay put.

"OK," she said.

It was over. The program showed the results. I was fascinated deep inside me, yet I couldn't absorb it. I understood what she was explaining, yet the information skipped right on out of me except for one piece: I had low power. I knew that because that was what my psychologist had found and had explained to me several times.

I was led into another room divided by glass display cases where their Chief Operating Officer would conduct and read my EEG. Sailing ships seemed to be everywhere.

"Hello," a man seated on the far side of the room greeted me, his cheerful voice dragging my eyes away from the massive painting on the wall ahead of me and giving me a direction to walk toward. This was Michael, the one I had spoken to on the phone. I knew him! He explained that Lynda would not be present during this test. He did his test, she did hers, and they didn't speak to each other until the assessment was over. That way they didn't taint each other's testing or results. It was the most objective way to conduct the assessment. My scholar mind liked that.

As we waited for the one who would put the nineteen-point electrode cap on me, Michael introduced me to a student who was there to learn from him. Time flitted, and I had a cloth cap with two ear clips and nineteen grommets in it fitted snugly over my head, electrogel squirted and swirled with painful intensity on my sensitive scalp into each grommet so that the grommet electrodes would pick up my brainwaves. I was glad to have no mirror to accidentally catch my reflection in.

Michael instructed, "Now sit back." I leaned back in the black, high-backed leather office chair. "That's it." He concentrated on his screen for a moment. "Now I want you to relax your jaw, and I'm going to record your brainwaves."

I suppressed my automatic nodding and tried to relax my jaw.

"Relax, just relax," he said, pulling long on the words in low, somnolent-inducing tones. "Let your jaw fall. And I want you to focus on this," he said pointing to a box. "Let your eyes relax. Don't close them though. Now, your left jaw is tensing up. I want you to relax it, let it drop."

I felt like an idiot with a snug cap on my head, my jaw hanging slack, my eyes half closing.

"That's it," he said absent-mindedly. "That's it." He said a little louder. "Now, don't move your eyes. Keep them on this."

I was never going to relax, never going to stop moving my eyes. Every muscle was jerking to move, to tense, to flinch. I stared at the box and struggled to keep still.

Satisfied with my attempt at relaxing, he began recording. Lines flowed in jagged waves across the screen. Nineteen lines of brainwaves. He watched them, and I watched what I could through my lowered eyelids, taking it in, wishing I understood, wishing I could nap, thinking how the old psychology student in me would have been enthralled. She would've asked so many questions: what each line meant, why the waves were different heights, why some looked sort of like heartbeats while others looked like squeezed-together sine waves. I tried not to worry why they were so short in height.

"Good, good," he said soothingly. And then the recording was over. But the test was not.

He asked me to close my eyes and again instructed me to relax my jaw. "Let it go slack. That's it," he said. Satisfied, he began another recording. He had me read a book clipped to the desk with a paragraph on squirrels. Squirrels haunted my neighbourhood, startling me with their twisting, jumping antics. And they dogged me here, too.

He had me do math in my head. The moment he began talking numbers, every muscle relaxed. I got this. When I was done, he smiled and told me that I had done better than most accountants! I felt puzzled but pleased.

Exhaustion stalled every neuron. At the end of each recording, as he saved the information, he explained what was going on to the student and to me. At the end of the assessment, he pulled up other programs. I saw my brain mapped out like an MRI. He reminded me of my father, enthusiastic about his subject, explaining what it meant as he brought up images of section after section of my brain, showing how the back of my brain produced a lot of delta. A lot, he emphasized. The back, I wondered, dying to go to sleep, confused because the SPECT scan hadn't shown any anomalies in the back, wanting to remember what he was saying, wanting to want to know. But my curiosity was dead. And exhaustion was shutting me down.

He produced a report and showed me my various results as the cap was removed, my scalp cleaned up. I was relieved it wasn't like the concrete paste used in sleep studies. Still, my hair stuck out in all directions.

His voice recalled me to my results. "See here. Your alpha is 2-3 Hz lower than it should be. Because you're intelligent, your alpha should be here. But it's down here. And you have an acquired learning disability." *What? I have no learning disability.* Acquired, settled in to my brain. Acquired. The brain injury gave me a learning disability. I told him I wanted to read again. He explained that he wasn't sure they could help me with my reading, but they would try. They could help me with my concentration.

I was back in Lynda's office.

She smiled at me as I plunked down. I feared what she would say. Go home. Nothing to see here.

Lynda picked up some white sheets, turned them around, and showed me the results of the boring test. She explained that the bars representing auditory and visual response times were scattered like a wide city of low-rise and mid-rise buildings. I was at the extreme end of hyperactivity. I looked at the line with the square on it representing me. You couldn't get more hyperactive. And I was slow, real slow. I couldn't understand the rest of the results, other than...

I was not normal.

She told me I was articulate.

My heart dropped. *Did that mean I was fine? That really despite all these tests I was OK?* Imeda's long-ago words yelled into my head. "How can anything be wrong with you when there's nothing wrong with the way you speak?"

Lynda spelled out the problems uncovered by the objective tests, the ones that peeked inside my brain. Not like the neuropsychological tests I could ace because of the ceiling effect or endless questionnaires that didn't actually see what my physiology was doing.

She was telling me my injury was real.
She wasn't telling me to get over it.
She wasn't saying, "Get on with your life."
She wasn't saying, "You're depressed."
She was itemizing my physiological problems.
And she was telling me they could repair my attention.

Was this for real? Was this true? Was hope being stretched toward me, healing what mattered? I kept my eyes on her face, trying to absorb words I had longed for. They could fix the damage to my concentration.

The rest they didn't know. The research was new with closed head injuries. I hardly cared. Restoring my concentration alone seemed like a miracle, a miracle so commonplace in this Victorian-like office and absent in the modern hallways of hospitals. The reading would come, too. I believed it had to.

Salvation sprouted from a concrete plan and evidence!

Somehow, I was on the subway train. Through the exhausted folds of my cortex began to seep the ADD Centre saying that my problems were not psychiatric malingering or illness or simple depression. Injured neurons had caused these problems.

Why didn't any of the people I'd seen, all kind, nice people, ever order these kinds of objective tests?

Why had they and their tests been all about my subjective answers, coping, and being at peace?

Peace!
Peace with a person not myself!
Peace with no more talents!
Peace with skills that had vanished like smoke and defied resurrection!
Peace with no affect alternating with rocketing emotions!

Peace with a beast of brain injury anger that defied management!

Peace with feeling like nails on chalkboard scratching around me almost all the time, driving me into irritability!

Peace with being abandoned!

How could anyone have peace with all that? And why didn't they give me real peace, the peace of regeneration? The peace from healing the damage, not inflicting more damage on me?

Why had no one considered me worth saving before? Only my psychologist had given me direct treatment. No wonder I thirsted for his light and sound show. It was the only regenerating energy my neurons had received for five years.

Five years lost.

I wept in bed that night.

Heaving sobs of loss and grief and abandonment.

I could never get those five-and-a-half years back.

I shed tears that maybe at last salvation had come.

Chapter 9

Brain on Training Wheels

Monday, August 8, 2005. Another hot day. My skin burned from Toronto heat and my own heat. At last, I had figured out how to have a cold shower, to run the water until it splashed off my skin cool instead of scorching, without having to strip fully or get my long hair soaking. It was too tiring showering daily or twice daily, but my skin and mood demanded cooling down. Glenda said I had to arrange and keep the threesome ice cream date she had to beg out of. Trying to think how made me cranky. I remembered being able to plan so easily, even a wedding.

That long-ago day, I had had barely any time to finish icing the three-layered chocolate wedding cake I had settled on making for Glenda after poring over my collection of cookbooks before the guests arrived. The day before, Mistral had helped me grate from my ever-present five-kilogram bar of chocolate, the large amount needed for each layer. His sinewy arms were still tired. I wanted the cake and our home to look perfect for Glenda and Ebenezer's wedding reception. I wore my dark green dress, which set off the corsage of pink roses Glenda had ordered. Mistral wore his striped grey suit with his grey silk tie with black dots. I took a moment to admire him and grin. I directed Mistral and whoever else I could find to twist and affix pink and white ribbons to our living room ceiling, clocks, and chandelier and place the crystal jug filled with pink roses and white baby's breath on the table.

Glenda arrived, radiating contentment and discreet perfume in her sea-green filmy long jacket over her shimmering grey gown, her new husband Ebenezer a happy backdrop in his dark suit and elegant tie she'd picked out for him. She bustled in to the kitchen to ensure all was in order. I shooed her back into the living room where the crowd of parents, in-laws, Imeda, Vashti, Arta, and more were gathering to congratulate them. I followed her shortly, placing the cake in front of the jug of roses, an icing sugar heart standing out against the chocolate. Glenda and Ebenezer sliced it together as we toasted them with champagne. None of us could stop smiling.

I couldn't smile now.

Tick. Tick. Tick.

August 25 via FedEx the black box Lynda had told me to get arrived. Mind Alive, an Edmonton company that designs and manufactures devices to improve brain performance and treat mental health issues, called what it did "audiovisual entrainment" (AVE). My psychologist, the one I had recently decided to leave, had called it "neurofeedback." The ADD Centre called what they did "neurofeedback." It was all too confusing. The black box was AVE. The ADD Centre appointments I had yet to start I'd call "brain biofeedback." Satisfied with my sorting out of same-word-different-meanings, I fished the manual out of the black carry bag the unit came in and stared at it hard through my usual mental cotton wool to spot anything familiar. SMR. I thought that Lynda had mentioned that. My psychologist too had said "SMR" a long time ago. I read and reread the description. "Sensory Motor Rhythm (SMR) with HRV," whatever that was, "Use to achieve relaxed attention." Attention. Yes, I needed to focus.

That sounded good.

I sat down.

I slipped the large shades called the Tru-Vu Omniscreen on and fought with the headphones not to slide off my hair. I pressed the on button.

Lights flashed into my eyes. Too bright! Pulses thrummed into my ears. Too loud! I fumbled with the brightness and volume levels. Ah. Better. For twenty-four minutes, I lay there, thinking how my psychologist had been using shades with red not white LEDs in them for quite some time now. *Would it be OK to go back to white? I wasn't sure. Did I make the right decision?* The thought faded as sleep began to overtake me.

The lights and sound powered off.

I struggled out of the chair and stumbled to my bedroom. I fell across my bed and slept.

For one-and-a-half hours I slept the sleep of a person who hadn't slept in five-and-a-half years.

I woke up not feeling like a zombie.

I blinked. I looked around. Yes, I could see clearer, just like after my appointments with my psychologist. I effortlessly raised myself. I was thirsty as heck. I craved water. My mind felt...like some cotton wool had been cleared out. By 2:00 p.m., I was fully awake. Really awake.

I had to do this again! I must remember to drink water after each session. But I couldn't wait until the next day to try another session.

After breakfast, I grabbed my new Mind Alive device and its manual and hunted for another session to try. *What to try? What to try?* Oh, this one looked good. "Low Beta Perker with HRV" at 16 Hz, 2 Hz more than yesterday's. I turned it on. *Water!* Sheesh. I went back and forth so many times from room to room, forgetting this, forgetting that, remembering, then immediately forgetting why I turned back. I didn't need to go to a gym! Impatient to lift my brain out of its wool prison, impatient with myself for forgetting, I poured myself some water and returned. Time seemed to tick along slower than I felt. I felt like I'd been quick, only a minute, yet many minutes had inexplicably passed. It reminded me of how once a friend had said, "I can see you thinking." That still made no sense to me. I shrugged off this confounding time differential between my inner clock and outer reality. I placed my water carefully on the table beside my chair and picked up the device before I sat on it. I turned it on again and succumbed to the light and sound show. Slight stimulation and no nap required.

I was in heaven.

Chapter 10

Biofeedback Begins and *Lifeliner* Ends

Tuesday, September 6, 2005. The trainer's nail-bitten fingers scrubbed my ears clean with the gritty cleanser that rubbed sharp little pains into my lobes and the top middle of my scalp. I cringed inwardly. I wasn't going to complain, though. I didn't have the patience to endure cleaning a second time. My mental clock ticked down the minutes as she checked the impedance. Every second counted to me.

She explained the first screen of the brain biofeedback software on the ancient, fat monitor, its greyness a hulk on the heavy desk. I threw all my effort into following her words. She said that the first thirty seconds were assessment. Just sit, and the computer would read my brainwaves. The seconds clunked by, like drops of liquid lead hanging off the tip of a dropper unable to fall. She clicked the stop recording button, and I sagged into the back of the chair.

My trainer—in my head, I called her my "brain trainer"— explained we would now enhance SMR at CZ using a neurofeedback screen. The acronyms sounded strange. CZ? She explained CZ was where the electrode was on the top of my head. I resisted raising my hand to touch it, fearing I would disrupt the connection and it wouldn't read my brainwaves anymore and she wouldn't know it and all the work would be for naught. I swallowed nervously as she asked me if I was ready. Yes. She clicked Record, and indicators went up and down. I stared at the screen. *How was I supposed to do this? How could my brain control those indicators? And what was I supposed to do with them again?*

She told me to relax my muscles. I followed her orders and forgot to think. That worked!

Suddenly, she clicked Stop, and it was over.

"Good!" she said. She wrote down the numbers from the screen as I wondered what I was doing.

I crawled home late: 6:00 p.m. I ate a salad and collapsed in front of *Canadian Idol* with a bowl of popcorn. Yet email sang out to me, and I had to check it. No matter how dog-tired I was, I needed to see if anyone knew I was still alive and wanted to talk to me or say hi. An email from Dad awaited me. He had written a letter about his children for the award I was spearheading in his name, his seventieth birthday gift, and had described me as a writer. He desired my feedback. The word "writer," his laudatory words emblazoned themselves on my heart.

The phone rang. Glenda said, "You need to call yourself a writer."

"How can I? I don't get paid. I can't work as one."

"Because you are."

Oh.

"You have value," Glenda told me. I nodded emptily at the wall.

The next day, I went to massage before my brain biofeedback appointment. My massage therapist kneaded and pushed my pain-filled muscles into some semblance of relaxation. The difference showed up on the computer when my brain trainer connected the electrodes to my ears and head and began recording thirty seconds of assessment. My scores were amazingly different! I felt chuffed. She told me that I was an excellent deep breather. Who knew? Until I arrived at the ADD Centre, I hadn't seen the slow, sine curve beauty of my breathing on a computer screen. I was doing one thing right!

I finished my first neurofeedback screen and spouted off about how I don't find stories where people have support structure inspiring, and I don't like being compared to them. Show me a story of a person with a brain injury who doesn't have anyone helping them out, finding them treatment, or participating in it with them. Show me that person, and I'll be inspired.

"I find you inspiring," she said.

My brain stopped working. *How could she?*

In between the next neurofeedback screens, she played Connect 4 with me. She monitored my brainwaves as we played. I looked at the holes in the vertical board, picked up a yellow round chip, and had no idea what to do with it as my hand slipped the chip into a gap at the top of one of the columns. Swiftly my subconscious mind beat my brain trainer. She said it was similar to the phenomenon of people blinded by brain injury who can navigate with ease as if they can see (because their eyeballs still work).

She also began reading with me after a neurofeedback screen. I read one page of an article, and she asked me questions. She gave me big hints as to the answers as I stared at her, thinking I understood her questions until her umpteen emphasis on a word made me realize I'd forgotten what I'd read seconds earlier.

Well, I had told them I wanted my reading back, and this was the way to do it.

I fought sleep after the final neurofeedback screen even though it had a good ratio of SMR to muscle tension. As she removed my electrodes and cleaned me up, she couldn't answer how I could be focused and almost sleeping at the same time. So I finally said I'd go home and think on it. Later I recalled my psychologist explaining it takes much more effort to do what was once effortless. Maybe that was it. When I didn't focus, I felt better, more awake. When I did, I felt heavy-eyed. I was supposed to pay attention to how I felt when I did well during a neurofeedback screen so that I could replicate it at home when doing tasks. But I didn't want to feel like that every time I worked!

The second week of brain biofeedback, understanding seeped in. The indicators were not random lines jumping up and down. They meant something. I fixed on one of them. I was to raise it above a threshold. My forehead grew cold behind my skull, and the batteries powering my neurons died. I struggled to hang on, to keep going. Fatigue smacked my focus.

The person in charge of the Toronto office said hello as I was leaving. I asked her, "Why can't I read? Why can't I learn?"

She explained patiently, "Your theta is too high. That's why you can't learn. We're bringing it down." She said something about meta, but I didn't understand.

I'm never going to read like I had, I realized with pain that sliced through me like a butcher knife. All I wanted to do was curl up in a chair with a cup of chocolate and get lost for a couple of hours in a book, not have to cover off, highlight, and ask myself recall questions after each bloody paragraph. But I had to. So I might as well suck it up and get with the program as Dr. Phil said on Oprah. *Does it suck? Yeah. But it's the only way God will let me read now. Bloody hell. Oh well. Crap.*

I looked around the room, wondering which door to exit. She led me out. Dazed, exhausted, worried about where I was going, I went to the elevator. I hated elevators, but I didn't know where the stairs were. I pressed the button and swayed.

"Pop!" my mind demanded. Pop? I hadn't drunk pop in years and years. "Ginger ale!" my brain screamed. The doors of the tiny box opened, and I stepped in. Down one floor, I peered out. This looked like the hallway I'd entered when I'd found the building earlier. I followed it to two glass doors and hesitantly reached out to try which one opened. Always a conundrum figuring out which door to open. The door resisted the pull of my weak arms.

Finally, I was outside in the late-afternoon September air. I somehow made it home though my eyelids kept resting on my lower lashes. I fell through my front door and leaned against my wall, relieved I'd arrived.

My brain screamed for food. My stomach ate me up. But fatigue dragged my cheeks, my shoulders, my arms down. Worse, something had pissed off my neck and jaw in the last couple of days. How was I to make anything for myself? I pulled on the fridge door with all my might and staggered back hanging on to its handle as it popped open. I leaned in and stared sightlessly at its contents. Was there anything I could eat as is? My brain refused to compute its contents. I shut the door and leaned my forehead on it.

Chocolate.

I'd have to buy frozen meals. And ginger ale. I wondered if organic ginger ale existed. I staggered up to watch TV from first a chair then my bed and ate chocolate. Counting and recording the calories of every meal, every snack, which I had done to lose 5 kg in early 2005 was beyond my energy.

The next day, a new brain trainer took over. Perhaps she could answer my question, "Why when my SMR scores are so good am I falling asleep? Why am I so tired?"

She suggested I try the ADD session on my AVE device at home. It was the one they used with all the kids.

Blood beat in my right ear, like the drumbeat of doubt from my tribe, bothering me as I tried to sleep. I counted the sessions I had done so far: four down, thirty-six to go. I tried the ADD AVE session in the morning. But week after week, deathly fatigue nailed me in my chair for the rest of the day after biofeedback.

Tick. Tick. Tick.

My family's patriarch, an enormous man with a powerful voice that brooked no dissension from anyone, phoned me from Ottawa on September 20.

"I talked to your parents last night," he informed me. My heart quailed, wondering what was to come. "I informed them that you had had a coup-contrecoup injury and explained to your father how rotational forces can shear off neurons, resulting in your flat affect and wooden speech." I blinked. "You have no prosody, Shireen." *Prosody?* He talked about my lack of gestures. I wondered, *do I gesture in my speech anymore?* I looked down at my still hand lying on my lap, pain flooding down from my neck into my fingers, weakness travelling down for the ride.

"But you know, Shireen, I think I hear less flatness in your voice. What are you doing?" I explained. "Good," he replied. He was the only one to say so.

I trudged to my fifth brain biofeedback, fighting back the doubts. I had seen no change, and all I was doing was fighting sleep by the end of each expensive session. Surely, I was supposed to be alert by the end of my appointment? Was I wrong? No, I shook my head. My psychologist had said my logic and my reasoning were intact. Slow but intact. This treatment made logical sense to me. Changing brainwaves in order to stimulate regrowth made sense to me. If you could change chemicals to effect change in the brain, why not electrical? They had said forty sessions. Besides, I was committed and nothing else worked. The price was worth it.

I wondered if Lily could pray for me. I phoned her and phoned her. She answered and began to pray, her voice growing powerful then disappearing as she prayed and praised the Lord.

Suddenly, she boldly stated, "You are in my care. Fear not." My face froze, my heart leapt. I wanted to cry. Someone was caring for me. She added, "Write that down and put it where you can see it. And write down the date, too."

I obeyed. I pinned it to my office bulletin board next to a picture of a clay sculpture—a hand cradling a girl child—my spiritual mentor had given me. Safety, love, caring. Words and photo together to remind me every day.

Tick. Tick. Tick.

AVE became a regular companion to me to wake me up, to calm me down, to keep me going to my rehab job of acupuncture, massage therapy, monitoring psychiatrist, and brain biofeedback. I stacked appointments one after the other so that when I shoved and cajoled and pushed myself out my front door, I didn't go out for just one thing but for many treatments. I was efficient, and my body began to pay the price while my words ranged all over the place like Waldo rambling through a tortuous maze.

But my spiritual mentor was used to it during our monthly meetings. Near the end of October, she instructed me to write on a sticky note and put on my computer, "I will not be diminished." I nodded, dragged myself home, and obeyed. I always obeyed, yet somehow, I managed to rebel against those who told me I was simply depressed, must stop this treatment, and get on with my life.

I shivered with cold, yet my skin pocked lava bubbles of heat that moved and grew and disappeared under a strong stream of cold, cold water and a slathering of melaleuca cream. My inner core cried out for a hot shower; my skin demanded cold as it swelled from water flowing into my flesh and not flowing out. Fat expanded, and the weight scale numbers began to climb again.

Four days after Halloween, a miracle. My stomach shut up.

Every day since the crash, my appetite had relentlessly signalled imminent starvation no matter how uncomfortably full my stomach was. But on November 4, after once again getting lost in the grocery store as Mum followed my wanderings through the aisles, I didn't order dessert at lunch. My brain had registered being stuffed and shut off my appetite!

On Sunday, November 6, 2005, emotions rocketed out of me like fireworks set ablaze by an arsonist. Every emotion from every event since my injury blasted into my mind. Happiness, humiliation, feeling stupid, blind, taken advantage of, laughter like gunshots, losing things and not knowing how, losing my tribe, forgetting possessions and parts of my life, they hit me all at once. Grief pined to vomit out! My hands startled me. Wild hands gesticulating, catching my eyes, after years of lying in my lap or silent by my side.

I broke through my barricade of not questioning the experts and phoned Michael on Monday about the emotion tsunami and how I really wanted to stop falling asleep during SMR. Michael explained that I'm one of the few who training SMR sends to sleep. He transferred me to Andrea, the Clinical Co-ordinator, to work out the details of switching to enhancing problem-solving beta brainwaves at 15-18 Hz at PZ. No more fighting sleep at the end of each appointment. And surely training the problem-solving brainwaves would give me back my problem solving. Not only that, we would change up the work on my reading. Tears pricked at the edges of my eyes as I hung up.

A fellow Canadian blogger, a man living in the Northwest Territories, inspired me to join Flickr. As usual, action took months to follow thought. I joined on the first day of my new brain biofeedback protocols: enhance beta 15-18 Hz at PZ and inhibit theta/alpha 6-9 Hz. After that, my trainer could move the electrode to F3, C3, or Wernicke's area, to aid reading. This part was going to be trial and error. I suggested F3 to my brain trainer because the next day's trainer was going to go for C3. I went home, marvelling at my boldness at directing people who knew far more about brain biofeedback than I did and glad that for once I didn't have to fight sleep.

Another day, another lawsuit-related phone call. My lawyer needed affidavits from people who'd known me prior to my brain injury. A former boss had been publishing audiotapes on voice disorder from the Mayo Clinic when I called him with my lawyer's request, and he recognized something in my voice. He heard spastic dysphonia, fading away but there. *What?* He explained it to me. It made sense. I wrote it down as "dystonia," my injured brain mishearing the phoneme as it did at times. And then promptly forgot the term and couldn't find my notes in my journal, but it didn't matter. My speech wasn't some nervous tic, I knew now. It was another manifestation of my brain injury.

The next day on Remembrance Day, I greeted my mother warily as she walked in the door. I needed her for shopping, but kin and kith were regularly using her as a messenger. What was today's? Ditch your pride. Relationships were more important. Her words lit the pain of humiliation my brain injury had brought down upon my head: the memory lapses, the confabulation of writing phantom cheques, my inability to decide on how many apples to buy week after week, the walking down the sidewalk like I was drunk for reasons I didn't understand, the stuttering as I struggled to produce a word, the weirdness of feeling nothing at funerals as people cried all around me, my alienation from laughter for year after year, my recognizing a joke only by others' laughter and prompting myself to smile so that I didn't look like a complete freak. How could I possibly have any pride left? When they could admit to me that I had a brain injury, then we could have a relationship based on truth. But without that, I was OK with things as they were. My mother said my brother now knew I had a traumatic brain injury.

"He has to tell me himself," I replied. Mum hugged me.

Two days later, I was showing off my Flickr page to Freny and told her that I'd received an invitation to join Gmail. She practically bounced in her chair.

"Join!" she insisted. "So you can send me an invitation to add to my email collection!"

"Well," I said, "When I hear it directly from your father's lips that it's OK, I will."

"Yeah, but you have to join now."

I wasn't sure. My injured brain toiled to think about it. A friend had been bugging me for two years to get a Gmail email. I had tried to sign up when he'd first asked me, but the fields I had to fill in flummoxed me. Now I looked again at those fields.

Oh, they're not difficult to fill, I realized to my puzzlement. *Why were they before?* My neurons were healing, and Freny's enthusiasm was pushing me to click on the invitation and to acquire a Gmail address.

Tick. Tick. Tick.

My emotions settled back into the abyss, and once again I felt nothing. I had dialled back on my AVE sessions. I had been in such a hurry to get better. *The more I could do to move my brain,* I thought, *the better.* But those emotions...that was awful. But now I knew that I had made the right decision.

On my birthday, another problem. Where was my massage therapist? It was 2:00 p.m., the time of my appointment. My watch said so. She walked into view on her way back to her office where I was waiting for her.

"It's three p.m.," she said. My face sagged in disbelief. Three? I looked at my watch, and this time my brain understood what my eyes saw. The hand was on the three, not the two. I shook my head. How did I misread the time? I had been doing so well.

My massage therapist was understanding. They'd been worried because it was so unlike me. She gave me a quick shoulder knead before her next client. I went home in pain, aching, stiff, weary, perplexed. I walked in my front door. I had to change my alarms on my Palm. They just weren't registering, and despite feeling like I was on the right path, I still misread numbers. And spoken English turned to gibberish while words morphed, like when strongman became sidethrough or string. I called those mysterious mistakes "verbos." Meanwhile people continued to confound me. Their voices said they wanted to see me, but their actions absented them from my life. My spiritual mentor told me to set boundaries. "You can't let people walk all over you," she said. I nodded.

The next day, as I was washing my edematous hands at the sink, I tugged at my wedding ring under the suds in the way I did every now and then. I'd begun to gain weight again and didn't expect to be able to pull my ring off when it hadn't come off after I'd lost several kilograms. My ring moved. I stared down at it. Could I pull it past the puffy fat and water? I tugged properly. It slid off. I felt nothing.

Tick. Tick. Tick.

The ADD Centre and I continued to hone in on what would help my reading.

Michael advised me, "It's important to ensure you're alert when reading." I wasn't sure how to do that. I wasn't a zombie anymore, yet alertness eluded me.

I thought, *I suppose alertness is relative. My psychologist had told me that when I don't practice, my brain reverts to its default state.* I had to keep reading and do it at my peak energy level.

I called Lily. She asked the Lord for a word. Diligence. I frowned.

"I'm bad at definitions," I told her, as my memory refused to cough up that word from my internal vocabulary. She looked it up. It meant industrious and careful. She said it applied to my life. Don't quit. I'll get to where I'd like to be through my hard work. Don't get discouraged with my blog or photos, how long it takes me to figure out Flickr, or how few kith and kin are interested in my writings or photos. I hung up. When I loaded my Flickr page, I was astonished and delighted to see the Northwest Territories' blogger had added me as a friend.

Tick. Tick. Tick.

December arose cold. Money continued to drain from my bank account, and I kept the thermostat low. I tired of being cold. My muscles enjoyed an entire hot shower whenever my skin allowed it. I began to stay in bed in the warmth under the sheets until I had no choice but to get up.

My traumatic rhinitis returned. Zombie mode returned. I became cranky. I despaired. I didn't have many sessions left. I had to get better before the forty were up to prove the rightness of my decision. Instead, my body was breaking down. Fat cells swelled and multiplied like cockroaches. More water gathered in the spaces between my cells. Except for that one moment when my brain had shut down my appetite, I remained perpetually hungry and my stomach expanded, demanding food all day long. And on November 1, I'd gotten the horrifying news.

A former psychiatrist had called me. She'd received a request to copy every single page of her notes to send to the lawyers. *What?* Provincial accident benefit regulations stated that the insurance company couldn't view mental health records older than one year prior to the accident. Mine were much, much older. What possible relevance could they have?

December 4, like magma rising, my anger exploded. *Why would anyone see a shrink when the expectation of privacy is a mirage?* I raged to the uncaring walls around me. *They're invading my own personal, painful words that I said in confidence. They're alleging my old shrink is a liar, that somehow she could predict years into the future my car crash, that her summary for them wasn't good enough. Why is a fishing expedition allowed? God is nowhere. Why believe? You're still strung out to dry like the wretch in the old marketplace scaffolds. Not a shred of dignity left. I'm not a criminal. I didn't harm anyone, the only justification for unsealing private emotions. The two drivers who hit my car, the defendants, un-fined and un-convicted, were the ones who harmed me.*

A couple of days later, after doing an AVE alpha session, I happily travelled to my twice-weekly brain biofeedback.

"Your busy brain is up," my brain trainer said as he frowned at my scores. "Why is that?"

I couldn't think of what was worrying me. Puzzlement wreathed my brow till I was on my way home. Oh yeah: lawsuit. Meanwhile, my second brain trainer listened as I cried that the reading wasn't going well. No matter what I did, I couldn't see the big picture of what I was reading. I was stuck in the moment of the page I was on with no past remembered, no future to predict. She described a new strategy to help me. I didn't understand her. She drew it out, and my brow cleared. I'd try this gridding method where on one page along the top row of a chart I'd list the article topics and in the left column the five Ws so in each cell I'd write something I'd learnt.

The next day, I reread a section of my current book for the third time. It took me five to eight minutes to read a page using the grid method and writing notes in the margins. But I remembered what I read! It worked!

Daytime TV kept me company during the monotonous hours of recovering from my appointments. Oprah talked about how she surrendered to Jesus and then immediately got the call about *The Color Purple* role.

I tried it. In my inside world, I saw Jesus hold out his hands, giant hands, waiting patiently as I put each of my cares in them. When I was done, he continued to stand there patiently holding out his hands. What had I forgotten? Was I hallucinating, making it all up?

The book!

I placed that and all the things I could no longer write, my dreams, in his hands. With his hands full, he turned ninety degrees and walked away to the right.

Peace relaxed my whole body as he walked away carrying my cares, worries, lost dreams, and people in his hands.

But peace didn't last long. The legal invasion into my past encircled me. I huffed to myself that so many had documented my case that there's no way anyone can claim I'm faking.

"It's like the courts reward bad behaviour by those who don't want to pay out!" I vented to my lawyer.

He explained that the Master of the Court had ordered it, and we had no choice. Besides, he soothed me, "They're so old. They're irrelevant."

I filled in the mental health release forms. I scribbled angry words in my journal. And my brain trainer asked me later that day if I knew the something or other that reduced busy brain? His words turned to gibberish in my perception, so I replied, "No." He explained this stopping ruminations thing. My mind cleared. It's what I did in my journals!

The next day on December 14, 2005, my other brain trainer explained the smurf thing is pretty close to my journal writing. *Smurf? Did I hear the word right?* I didn't ask her to repeat it. I was concentrating hard, trying to remember this busy brain-reducer thing, feeling good I was doing something right. She added that I was looking less anxious and more focused when reading.

Yeah! I thought. *My mind isn't bopping like some sort of superball out of control. This biofeedback thing is working!*

After my second neurofeedback screen, she excitedly told me, "I've found you a new game. It's taken us a long time to figure you out, what's needed to get to your problem areas," she admitted, "but I think this one will challenge your visual-spatial skills."

Oh? A memory bounced out of its vault, of how the vocational assessment a few years ago had said my visual-spatial skills were ranked high, at the top. I knew they'd been wrong, like they had been about my writing.

Pay attention, I snapped at myself.

My trainer was unboxing the game. She explained it to me. We'd learn it together by playing level 1. She placed little toy cars and trucks in different colours inside a black box with short walls and one exit. I had to get the yellow car out the exit. To do that, I had to move the other cars and trucks out of the way, one at a time without bumping into or running over each other.

My subconscious couldn't play it.

It was all up to me to do the conscious work, and I couldn't. She had to help me figure out how to figure out the beginner level. The game became part of the repertoire. Meanwhile, she questioned me on my reading grids, fine tuned my method, and said she'd question me weekly to see if my reading was sticking.

Tick. Tick. Tick.

I need daydreams to fill my head and crowd out the circling.

I thought about how an old friend who sporadically stayed in touch had stood me up, got angry at my complaint, and then thinking about it, had come over in early December and had apologized in a way she hadn't before.

"It didn't matter what my intent was. It mattered that I really hurt you. I'm really sorry. Can you forgive me?" she'd said. The rare apology had hit me hard. Tears had flung themselves out of my dry eyes as I heard words of remorse and admission of how she'd affected me, words I'd longed to hear from so many but hadn't. The hurt dissolved. I forgave her. My thoughts circled round and round to that apology.

Tick. Tick. Tick.

I awoke on Boxing Day hung over with exhaustion from Christmas. My Flonase and puffer were my friends. My couch was my spouse. Over the next four days, energy began to flow through my neurons. And I began to think again. Time for the next step in my recovery.

Give up *Lifeliner*.

I could write. I could write lots in my journal, wandering thoughts, feelings peeping out, but I still couldn't write fiction.

I reminded myself, *You can write poetry*.

Yes, there was that. But the book eluded me. I couldn't write enough words, organize, problem solve, or make even the smallest of decisions. I needed a human resource, and I had no volunteers, no money to pay anyone, and no ability to find one if I did and no person willing to look for me. I had to face facts. Time to say good-bye to my past and to that commitment. Finishing no longer mattered. I was getting used to my brain injury causing me to cancel my commitments as I struggled to relearn what I could and could not do.

I chucked out all the publishers catalogues. I boxed up my stories and archived them. I set aside what I'd written for *Lifeliner* before my injury and, with a reluctant hand, wrote Christmas cards to Judy's family with the news. I had to give up writing *Lifeliner*. I was so sorry. I handed the cards to my mother to mail for me else I might confabulate mailing them.

That night, I walked into my office for a final check of my Flickr page. I had so many views. I was accumulating likes and comments from people I'd never met in real life. Gladness suffused me. I shut off my computer. I noticed my office denuded of all signs of the published life, all signs of *Lifeliner*.

I switched off the light and left the room.

I felt nothing.

Chapter 11

Becoming Me

Clouds chased drizzle in the light winds of early January 2006 as I made my way to acupuncture then brain biofeedback. During reading recall in my first biofeedback session of 2006, I'd remembered names! First time I had!

My male brain trainer said a couple of weeks later, "That's what I like about you."

Huh?

"You're a positive person."

News to me. I hear so often that I'm negative.

"You always look at the good numbers."

I do?

But I had more yet to accomplish, like remembering names without any help. I worried about my forty-session reassessment coming up on February 2, 2006.

The trip to the Mississauga clinic through haze and a stiff wind was different than in August, and it wasn't because of the weather. I was different. Chattier, livelier. I did much better than before on the boring test. That meant I really did have damage! Not malingering! The right treatment worked! The staff cheered my improvement in concentration and my normalized ADD scores, yet I had far to go. My response time had risen from less than first to seventh percentile for women my age. I'd gone from sub-sloth to sloth speed. I needed more sessions but only weekly. How to pay? I prayed. A way opened.

"You have a brain injury."

My brain froze.

My mouth said, "I know." Had Dad really said those words? My heart skipped into my throat. I couldn't have heard right. I kept talking to him on the phone. He kept talking to me as if it was now clear I really had had a brain injury, not easier-to-accept depression, because I had improved. Significantly.

Meanwhile, Miriam, Judy's youngest daughter, had asked me about *Lifeliner*. "Know anyone?" I'd tacked on to the end of my mid-January 2006 email reply to her after explaining I needed a human resource to finish it. She replied that she had a writer friend, Glen, who might be interested.

Was this hope? Was I to write *Lifeliner* after all?

A month later, the three of us sat around my kitchen table. Glen had one stipulation. My heart thudded.

"I must do your horoscope first."

Uh, sure. I gave him my requisite information, information that went beyond simply my birth date.

I waited.

Each day felt like a mountain. I tried to put it out of my mind, like I did with the lawsuits. Hurry up and wait. And while you wait, forget about it. Live life as if it wasn't happening, my draining bank account notwithstanding.

On February 20, Glen said that he wanted to help.

I could hardly believe it. I had a human resource! I had help! I wasn't alone in this humongous endeavour anymore.

He came over in early March, and we sat down in my living room on another cold winter day. He explained to me that 13 percent of the population is inner directed. They make decisions from principles and things inside them. The rest look to others. He said he could be truthful because Scorpios deal with reality, and I could take it. People lean on inner directed, and we are fated to carry others in how to lead one's life.

What?

Panic assailed me. I could hardly get myself breakfast. I couldn't even write a book on my own. *How could I lead anyone?*

He insisted. My horoscope told him this. Perhaps not now. But it was my destiny, that I'm meant to write, that I've been given the gift of aloneness, and one needs to be alone to write. And *Lifeliner* is not the main event. It's a necessary step to get me to my next project, a book about me, the story behind the story.

Um, OK.

I shoved it out of my mind. I had to focus on reality now. The best part was he was leading me. *Lifeliner* was no longer an impossible behemoth that would take me the rest of my life. I could finish it!

We reviewed the outline I had put together so carefully over the months before my brain injury. Since 2001, I'd slowly faced the fact it didn't work for me. The chapters were too large. I couldn't write five thousand words, never mind sixteen thousand as I had before my injury. I couldn't read the mind maps that I had effortlessly created before my injury.

We pared it down to what I could do. He introduced me to the screenplay concept of treatments and set me a word count goal. I couldn't meet five hundred words, but I wrote diligently every Friday and Saturday.

He told me to call my editor.

I nodded and swallowed at that scary task. Shame at my failure to write engulfed me each time I had called him to say that once again, I had to put off *Lifeliner*. I had failed to meet my goals, failed to return to writing my book. I had lost opportunities for agents. But this man said we could do it together. It had been years and years since I'd spoken to my editor. Would he even want to still work with me?

Yes.

"Come in to the office," Henry said.

I told him I would not be alone. He was cool with that.

Henry looked the same as ever with his long hair, quiet smile, and Birkenstocks. The days were lengthening into spring as we all sat down in his sunny boardroom on the first day of May, Henry at the head of the long rectangular light-wood table, me with my back to the door, Glen opposite me, and Henry's staff on my left.

I showed Henry what we had come up with. He noted it was disjointed. Because I was so visual, he agreed with Glen that the way writers outline screenplays would work well for me. I wrote the titles and names of the authors he suggested I learn from down in my notepad in the brown leather folder I had brought with me, the one I'd used to use before my brain injury when I'd visited potential clients in my computer programming and desktop publishing days. Glen and I left together. By then my neurons had hunkered down, covering their little dendrites from any communication with thought. Glen explained the meeting in three easy steps. Step one: buy the books on screenwriting.

I trundled to Theatre Books, a tiny store in an old mansion on a little street of pollen-hurling trees near Bay and Bloor. Warm and thirsty, with my two new screenwriting books in hand, I retraced my steps back to the familiar, wide intersection busy with cars fighting hordes to turn corners. I froze as my field of view widened. I blinked. Though I travelled through this intersection fairly often, it was like I had been away for six years and had just returned home. I could perceive the whole of it. I yearned for that same astonishing feeling with reading. Maybe with brain biofeedback reminding me weekly of how to read and to practice, improvement would stick. Glen kept me going with my book so that I began writing a two-minute treatment and step outline as per the screenwriting books. I read only the parts I needed to learn from, using all my strategies. I showed my outlines to Glen and Henry at our next meeting on May 25.

Henry liked my step outline the best and gave me a task: condense each chapter's description to one sentence. I nodded. As Glen and I left, I fought panic at the enormity of the task and lost.

Glen said, "We'll do it together." We went into a nearby restaurant for lunch, and he pushed two tables together so that he could condense my step outline. Although I knew the story inside out, he could see the big picture and I could not. He could see how to organize the book. I could not.

Focus.

Focus on what made Judy special.

Focus on the pioneering part of her story.

Let go of the injustices, the extraneous details.

I got so excited that when we left I followed him across the street instead of going in my direction. One-quarter way across, he asked where I needed to be. I swivelled and almost got run down by a rushing right-turning car.

He said, "I can't have an author getting hit," and steered me safely back to the sidewalk and in the right direction.

Tick. Tick. Tick.

Tired of my decades-old clothes that pre-injury Shireen wore, tired of the same cartoon-festooned T-shirts and flamboyant skirts, I walked into a clothing store. For once, I had enough energy to buy and didn't care too much about my tight budget. I wanted to wear a pretty skirt, and I didn't want to wear the clothes of another person one more day. I told myself: don't think, just try on what you feel drawn to.

I wandered through the airy, small store, letting my eyes roam along the rack of dresses. No, they wouldn't do. I scanned the skirts. My hand reached out to a pigeon-grey one that flared out like an upside-down lily. A thought bubbled up: *Shireen doesn't—*

don't think! I liked that grey. I liked the subtle flare and the white ribbon outlining its waist. I tried it on. I felt pretty. I felt calm. Oh so calm. I looked in the mirror and saw—me.

I didn't know who this me was, but I liked her choice in clothes. I wore it to visit my spiritual mentor. She noticed. And even before we sat down in her yellow-painted office in the glowing filtered sunlight of mid-June next to the table with its small candle flame swaying in the breath of the spirit, she was cheering with me over finally writing chapters for *Lifeliner*. I yearned to cheer with kith.

But their calls kept dwindling. I hadn't seen them in ages. She had been praying for new friends for me for almost three years now. But she assured me I'd done well because I'd focused on myself, that my life was full of confirmations that writing was my path.

She advised me, "Don't explain yourself. If they're angry, let it go." She spread her hands out, miming bad words falling away from me. She said, "Your Net contacts are so good for you. You're not responsible for them." My mind leapt to the previous day's miracle. I shifted in the enfolding armchair and told her how someone had commented on one of my photos on Flickr. My spirit lifted as I remembered out loud.

I thanked her, this kind Torontonian.

She replied!

Her sense of humour tickled my smile into being. I typed back, my fingers flying over the keys so that she could see my words before she logged off.

She replied again!

I laughed. And typed.

The conversation lasted a little while; then it was time to say good-bye. But not for long. She Flickr mailed me. She introduced me to a puzzle group. A British man chatted with me on the weather, said, "Blimey" to my puzzle solve. She and he gave me Flickr tips, and I had two new friends!

Was that answered prayer? I didn't know. But happiness bounced me out of my computer chair and out the door to my mother's for her mid-June barbecue. I wasn't going as the person left alone in her miserable injury. I was going as a person whose conversation was enjoyed, not one reluctantly replied to. I was going as a normal human being.

Chapter 12

Open a Window

I cleared my desk in late spring 2006 as my OT had taught me, except for my computer and the chapter notes I had painstakingly compiled from all my interview transcriptions, medical records notes, research articles, and various sundry notes. For year after year while I couldn't write *Lifeliner*, women my mother knew had helped me organize my research. Glenda had helped me put the interviews into Goldmine, a database management program.

As I perched at my grey melamine desk, I prayed. I worried I wouldn't be able to write long enough, that fatigue would grab me, slide my hands off the keyboard in weak surrender to it. I knew I didn't have the stamina to write the old way, of two handwritten drafts, the second one mostly crossing out the first one, then typing it in. Then massively deleting and adding sections. And typing and retyping four more times at least, each time editing less and less.

I could barely fathom writing a chapter once. I couldn't fathom writing that many drafts.

I prayed, *Lord Jesus, please give me first-draft writing.*

Inhaling deeply, not knowing what I was going to write, the length of the interview summary document beside me challenging me yet buttressing my memory, the new doable outline strengthening me, and Glen sending me on my way with a workable writing schedule—write one day, go over it the next—I placed my fingers on the keyboard.

My fingers flew. They had been waiting so long for this moment of return. I couldn't stop to pace, else I'd forget my thoughts and my place in the story.

Forty-five minutes later, I sunk into myself, chapter written. I was lucky to reach eight hundred words in one forty-five-minute sitting. But that was all my brain could perceive as one coherent story. That was all I could write and read to edit before wandering off onto random paths of thought. I smiled at the screen flickering invisibly.

I stood up stiffly; I walked the few steps to the room where my ancient black TV hulked and flopped onto the couch. I put on a fourteen-minute AVE alpha session to thwart the migraine coming on. My body relaxed into the rough fabric of my couch.

I had written a chapter of my book *Lifeliner!*

Tick. Tick. Tick.

Glenda called on her cell on her way home from a trip on Friday, October 13, as leaves flew off the trees outside my window. "What's up?" she asked.

"I've finished writing *Lifeliner!*"

She managed a bit of enthusiasm as I talked on and on about it. Then I paused. She told me about this buttery skewered meat dinner she'd had with her co-workers. I got bored.

Glenda assured me. "I love you. We're still friends."

Tick. Tick. Tick.

A specialist frowned over my blood pressure and instructed me to see my cardiologist.

"I don't want you to have a stroke after all the work you've done to heal your brain." I nodded.

Tick. Tick. Tick.

Another exam for my lawsuit. Another peg test. Using my shaky right hand, I pushed pegs into a column of holes with great effort. Time was up. Repeat with left. My left hand slid the pegs in smoother, quicker. Annoyingly, the tester talked to me while I was trying to put the pegs in. I had to stop every time to understand her. The same when one of the men overseeing my assessment came in to talk about some paper or other.

I griped to Mum afterwards, "No wonder I was one percentile for left hand and less for right. My processing speed sucked, and I kept having to stop." She pointed out they were testing my veracity, with the pegs, as most people who lie about not being able to multitask wouldn't realize that when the assessor spoke that if they couldn't multitask, they would have to stop. They'd be too focused on getting the pegs in their holes to think, *I'd better stop to show I can't multitask*. I never saw that! And I think I'm so clever.

Tick. Tick. Tick.

1:06 a.m. My heart pounded me awake. Again. I was panting. Hot sweat prickled through my hair. I flashbacked to my grandmother sitting up in the hospital in 1981, declaring she couldn't breathe. Then dying. I turned on the radio to hear human voices, to tell me I was alive. I raised the head of my bed, pushed down the covers, slowly lay down on my left side, deep breathed.

"*Rest* and *relax*," thundered the Lord through Lily when she asked him the next morning on October 25, 2006 if there was anything He wanted to say to me.

Don't tell me to relax! Tell me how to publish Lifeliner.

Lily said, "2007."

Tick. Tick. Tick.

I'll take Christmas week off, I decided, fatigue a Jupiter-sized soggy blanket that pounced out of the seeming blue to throw me onto the couch to watch daytime, nighttime, and morning TV. I crawled into bed, after cooling my skin down with cold water and melaleuca cream and elevating the head of my bed to futilely stave off edema bloating my features and the itchy, painful burning patches that encircled my neck every morning. *When will*

I ever not be panting again? I thought about time, about my book, about people's inexplicable reaction to me and them disappearing, about the lawsuit, about time, about the treatments I was receiving and if they would be enough. Before my injury, I had always been able to tell myself stories to get myself to sleep. Now...a giant hamster wheel squeaked and squeaked perseverating thoughts. Busy brain.

Tick. Tick. Tick.

I had to accelerate this treatment so that I could return to my self-publishing plans, to the website I'd coded back in 1999, to have the energy to market, to have my cherished self-discipline back to make it happen. Otherwise with no human resource help, how could I do it? All this writing, and for what?

Tick. Tick. Tick.

Six days after my birthday, Glenda emailed to wish me a belated and to say she'd call me when back in Toronto. My massage therapist was appalled. I was confused and sad. I ignored Glenda's calls.

Let her be as frustrated reaching me as I usually am with her, I thought pettily, the pettiness exposing I needed a break. I feared hearing my lips speak truth if I spoke to her.

Tick. Tick. Tick.

I poured out the deadly silence of my home, the loneliness, the hurt, the not knowing what to do to my spiritual mentor. How could Glenda say she loved me yet not want to talk to me? My life was one unending litany of medical appointments and difficulties with no sense of connection to the people who loved me when they called less than weekly, but I had achievements to share! My mentor noted that interactions with her diminished me, and it was discouraging to see. She suggested that in the spirit of St. Paul who counselled married couples to separate for a time to strengthen their bond, we separate for three to six months. Six months seemed a long time, yet...I'd had enough.

Glenda exclaimed, "Not six months!"

I struggled to express why six, to speak the words I'd planned and not get derailed by her interruptions, to stick to my decision.

I acceded, "Three months. And you call me." If she called, then she did want to keep the relationship. We hung up. All I felt was happy to get back to my friends on Flickr. It was Friday, December 1, 2006. I began the countdown to February.

Tick. Tick. Tick.

Wrapping paper ripped, kids scrambled, shrieks, and a cheque in a card for me. My Christmas gift. Camera body. But which one? I went with my parents to see, to see through, the viewfinders of each DSLR that the Henry's store employee suggested to me to replace my sturdy Coolpix I'd bought cheap. My faithful Maxxum. Time to say goodbye. My brain, my brain. It knows f-stops and shutter speeds again. Camera lingo. But which, but which Nikon lens? My hands shook, and my brain fluttered stress as Mum declared, "Our gift gave you distress." Their cheque the body bought. My cash the chosen lens. Mum slipped me some bucks. Boxes ripped open. Nikon D80 scrambled together. I shoot. I shriek. I share.

My Flickr friends swarmed in:

"awesome gift!"

"Just beautiful."

"he, he, shouldn't it be called a **Nikon** moment, LOL!"

"Points, that's lovely...Yay!!!!" (Points was the anonymous name my Flickr friends knew me by. My lawyer's instructions adhered to.)

"Welcome to the Nikon club Points!"

"I knew you would be thrilled with the D80."

"Congrats on the new toy PN :)"

My first D80 photo.[15] I showed my pleased parents, too.
Tick. Tick. Tick.
Bong!

---

[15] https://www.flickr.com/photos/pario/336798470

Salvation Learnings

Chapter I

Neurons and Brainwaves

Neurons are the brain's cells. They talk to each other through spaces called synapses via chemicals called neurotransmitters. They conduct electricity down their long arms called axons in response to neurotransmitters from other neurons. An EEG reads neurons' electrical oscillations or brainwaves. These are measured in Hz (hertz) and divided into named bands with each band corresponding to different brainwaves as described in the following sections.[16] Keep in mind neuroscience remains relatively unexplored and continues to evolve each year or decade.

Delta Brainwaves

Delta brainwaves are the largest waves at a frequency of 0.5-3 Hz. Sub-delta for AVE is 0.5-1 Hz. Delta waves appear during deep sleep, i.e., Stage 4 sleep, when it's posited that the brain cleans house and regenerates. Delta waves while awake are associated with daytime sleepiness and fatigue. In brain injury, they appear in damaged areas, as if those areas are snoozing. Also, if electrical blockages interrupt the corticothalamic tract that loops between the outer and deeper areas of the brain, neurons stop producing alpha brainwaves in sync with each other and instead produce delta waves at 1-2 Hz, resulting in chaotic brainwave activity.

---

[16] L. Thompson. *The Neurofeedback Book: An Introduction to Basic Concepts in Applied Psychophysiology.* Wheat Ridge, CO: Association for Applied Psychophysiology, 2003.

Theta

Theta brainwaves range from 3-7 Hz (or 5-8 or 4-8). Low theta is 3-5 Hz, high 6-7, and 7.5-8.5 is associated with visualization. As if in twilight, theta waves appear in the moments before falling asleep. They are also associated with daydreaming or tuning out. After brain injury, if neurons produce theta, instead of alpha or beta, you feel unengaged from the world and tend to lose attention.

Alpha

Alpha brainwaves are between 8-13 Hz (or 7.5 to 12.5 or 8-11). Low alpha is 8-10 (or 11). High alpha 12 (11-13).

Alpha waves are associated with creativity, thought, understanding, and a relaxed mind that is aware of its surroundings. High alpha with the big picture when reading and alert broad awareness. Meditation enhances alpha to produce peacefulness, warmth in the hands and feet, thoughts or ideas (e.g., turning on imagination), and better immune function. People of high intelligence may have higher peak frequency. Also, brain injury can markedly drop the alpha frequency.

SMR

Sensorimotor rhythm or SMR brainwaves at 13-15 Hz are generated in the sensorimotor strip that crosses the centre of the head horizontally from ear to ear. They are associated with relaxed, focused attention.

Brain injury can reduce SMR and cause SMR enhancement to induce sleepiness during brain biofeedback. However, they are fundamental to restoring brain function and to being able to think calmly and reduce anxiety and impulsivity.

Beta

Beta brainwaves range from 15 to 30 Hz. Beta at 16-20 Hz are active when you're awake and alert, having a stimulating conversation, debating, problem solving, deciding, or thinking. You require more beta when learning.

Busy Brain

Busy brain is about 24-36 Hz in the beta category and associated with anxiety and rumination on steroids. These brainwaves are implicated in perseverating, the round and round thinking that people with brain injury get trapped in. Busy brain drives the person physiologically into worrying, indecisiveness, and perseveration. The only thing that has effectively and permanently reduced busy brain in me is inhibiting it during brain biofeedback. It's like peeling back an onion. You inhibit the widest range first, then with each successful reduction, shrink the range, for example, begin at reducing 21-35 Hz at CZ, narrow down over several years to 24-28 Hz.

Gamma

Gamma brainwaves, at about 40 Hz, are the least well known. From my own experience, they feel like the foundation on top of which all other brainwaves sit and are enhanced. They are the seat of feeling coherent, your brain as one harmonized unit. They open perception up so that you perceive more of the external world and can engage in it. They markedly reduce stress so that whereas before a gamma brainwave enhancement session a small problem will seem insurmountable, after enhancement the problem is suddenly solvable or at least no longer overwhelms and rockets you into an orbit of uncontrollable frustration, anger, or tears.

Some posit gamma is associated with the conscious mind. It correlates with the neurotransmitter GABA, which is also poorly understood. Research seems to show that people with brain injury do not produce gamma under circumstances that normally would induce them.

EMG

EMG is muscle contraction, inhibited in the 100-200 Hz range, but EEG is monitored from 2 to 62 Hz. Thus, 52-58 Hz is chosen to reflect EMG and avoid artifact contamination by countries' electrical systems of 50 and 60 Hz. Muscles produce higher voltage than normal EEG. EMG is like an ocean that lifts and lowers all the brainwave boats. EEG/EMG ratios cancel out the EMG effect and show whether you've enhanced or inhibited the trained brainwaves. According to Dr. Lynda Thompson, "One has to be very strict about reducing muscle artifact whenever one works with EEG."

For further reading and updates, go to http://wp.me/Pf8xE-16i.

Chapter J

Audiovisual Entrainment

Seeing, hearing, smelling, tasting, and touch are the brain's sensory inputs akin to a computer keyboard and mouse. Audiovisual entrainment (AVE) harnesses seeing and hearing to guide your brainwaves into a desired mental state via LEDs and synced tones. AVE also induces meditative dissociation, increases cerebral blood flow, and alters neurotransmitters. Consider AVE as the conduit for the medicine. The specific session as the medicine itself.

Sessions range from delta waves for sleep to alpha waves for a coffee-like break to SMR for an energy boost to 18 Hz beta waves for enhanced mental activity. Its effect varies from hours to days; regular use may effect some permanent change. Some people use the same session every morning; some use a variety throughout the day; some only a few times per week. One of my blog readers found the ADD session made her feel "like a heavy weight on my head, very foggy thinking," while I found it at first overwhelming for a few years and used the gentler Brain Brightener instead though I liked the 18 Hz one the best. In 2017, I switched to using SMR/Beta almost daily when research showed it helped with diffuse axonal injury. Following the principle of stimulating neurons while using the damaged neural network as a way to harness the brain's neuroplastic function, I've begun using AVE with the Viewhole Omniscreen while reading or writing on the computer.

By lowering blood pressure, AVE can result in temporary dizziness. This is the only side effect I've encountered. It vanished once my brain was used to AVE. It's a good idea to lie back or sit in a comfortable chair to rest for a few minutes after and to drink water. The personal profile questionnaire in Mind Alive's AVE User Guide may help decide which sessions to start with.

For further reading and updates, go to http://wp.me/Pf8xE-16k.

SMR 14 Hz

SMR is relaxed, focused attention. This twenty-four-minute session helps me cope with crowds, noisy events, and handling public transit. SMR for Reading is used with the see-through Tru-Vu Omniscreen Viewhole to focus during reading for twenty minutes. For a small subset of the population, stimulating SMR waves induces sleep. I find the forty-minute SMR for Sleep session effective at bedtime or in the middle of the night.

SMR/Beta L13.5/R18 Hz

In his small-subject study on AVE for diffuse axonal injury,[17] Dave Siever showed that sessions with SMR in the left visual field and beta in the right paradoxically create 10 Hz brainwaves, re-establishing the alpha rhythm in the corticothalamic loop and thus reducing the anxiety and agitation created by the alpha rhythm being disrupted. Beta at 18 Hz is also associated with reducing trauma. SMR/Beta energizes me, makes me feel like I'm ready to write. I have also used it with the Viewhole Omniscreen while writing on the computer or reading (with reading glasses on). By stimulating neurons while using the desired neural network (e.g., writing), this acts on the brain's function to change

---

[17] http://mindalive.com/default/assets/File/AVE%20and%20diffuse%20axonal%20injuries%20for%20publication2.pdf

in response to mental activity in a way that could strengthen and heal the injured network.

Alpha 10 Hz

I find the fourteen-minute alpha session a good introduction to AVE. It perks me up sans coffee and generates thoughts again after fatigue has bulldozed my mind. I like its brevity. I sometimes get frustrated with how much time I have to spend being what I call "duct taped" together with gizmos, so using this one gives me some benefit without taking time away from activities I enjoy. The thirty-two-minute alpha session stimulates creativity, in a relaxed, happy way, and stops pain from worsening, especially neck pain, which is the cause of my migraines. Thoughts begin to appear, imagination sparks, and ideas flow. Research by D. Anderson in 1989 suggests that it can help with migraines with the visual intensity as high as one can stand. For me, it is most effective when used right at the onset of pain. In people with high IQs, alpha waves generally cycle at 11 or 12 Hz instead of 10. The 10.6 Hz thirty-minute alpha session is designed to re-establish that. At first, I used it occasionally right before I was going to tackle a harder-than-usual mental task. I, then, began to use it weekly.

Brain Booster/ADD L14-10/R19-10 Hz

The ADD study was published in the *Journal of Neurotherapy*.[18] I graduated to the ADD session when Brain Booster lost its effects, but I stopped using it when I discovered SMR/Beta is better for

---

[18] Michael Joyce and Dave Siever. *Audio-Visual Entrainment Program as a Treatment for Behavior Disorders in a School Setting.* Journal of Neurotherapy 4, 2 (2000): 9-25. http://www.tandfonline.com/doi/abs/10.1300/J184v04n02_04

brain injury. When you have a brain injury, you want to set yourself up for success and have things be gentle on you in the beginning so you're more likely to use it again. These sessions stimulate the mind through rapid transitions between beta and alpha frequencies and improve mental function and memory.

0.5–1 Hz, Sub-Delta

I found this passive session with no entrainment most effective when used just before going to sleep to induce sleep and reduce my body temperature at night. If I use it in the afternoon, it makes me very thirsty. Part of my hypothalamus fix (see Chapter Q).

Chapter K

Attention

Attention! Brain injury damages attention and reduces the energy required to use it. Without attention, you can't perceive what's going on, can't remember what happened seconds or days ago, and can't follow instructions. That's why restoring attention is the first task of brain biofeedback.

According to TRI and the 1994 McKay Moore Sohlberg paper "Understanding Attention Impairments," there are five kinds of attention: selective, alternating, divided, focused, and sustained. Attention is mediated through each sense differently, depending on the person's strengths and weaknesses. For example, one can have little problem paying attention to things you hear but struggle with visual stimulation.

Selective. This attention skill allows you to ignore distractions and focus on what's important. For example, in a coffee shop, selective attention allows you to follow the conversation not be distracted by clinking cups or passing cars. Or it allows you to read at home surrounded by piles of clothes, an overfull bookcase, and a coffee table strewn with magazines.

"People with impairments in selective attention may become easily irritated and frustrated by such extraneous noise." (McKay Moore Sohlberg, 1994)

Alternating. This attention skill allows a person to switch their attention from task to task or person to person in a group or party. Without it, a person makes mistakes when switching from one task to another. Sometimes they may continue with the first task after switching to another. Or after being interrupted, one feels discombobulated, frustrated, and overwhelmed at needing to switch back to resume the task.

Divided. This attention skill allows a person to pay attention to two or more things at once. Without it, for example, one may find the radio on while being driven in a car overwhelming. The brain cannot process the sensory information from both a moving vehicle and the radio.

Focused. This attention skill allows people to notice objects or events and sensory stimuli outside of themselves. Without this skill, a person will notice internal states like pain but not external ones like a friend's facial expression. Complicating this may be the ability to notice but not respond. For example, you may notice a birthday is arriving but be unable to send a card till long after.

Sustained. This attention skill gives one the ability to stick with an activity over time, like reading to the end of a chapter or talking on the phone to the natural end of a conversation or paying all the bills. Following step-by-step instructions also requires this skill. Fatigue and conscious direction of automatic tasks interfere with sustained attention. Walking, for example, is an automatic skill. Brain injury may change it back to requiring conscious self-guiding to direct your feet, which consumes energy and slows down the process. Without sustained attention, flow—the state of being absorbed into a task—is not possible.

Diffuse axonal injury lowers attention, muffles spoken and emotional expression, slows cognitive processing and reasoning, and decreases impulse control. Low voltage beta brainwaves throughout the brain can also lead to poor attention.

A party demands several attention skills with every sound perceived as piercing, brightly dressed friends like flashing beacons screaming, "Watch me. Watch me," and every appetizer, perfume, and shampoo shoving themselves up the nose, all demanding attention. Add to that people naturally placing demands on impaired divided, alternating, and selective attention just by trying to converse. Expression becomes wooden. And the bathroom becomes a haven.

The compassionate, human response is to understand these issues and listen, listen to the person with the brain injury who says, "I'd rather see you over coffee, in a quiet place, one-on-one, where I can be myself, and when I won't have to spend days recovering just because I chose to socialize." This physiological issue is not a personality failing. Seeing it as such leads to frustration and building a stone barrier between yourself and the person with the brain injury. You cannot overcome physiological damage by having a "good attitude" or "trying harder." Nor with medications that only manage symptoms. You need brain-based treatments that target and regenerate physiologically the damaged areas, which the brain learns is the kind of change to make and continues to do so after treatment stops. But until impaired attention skills are restored fully, accommodation reduces the cognitive load and releases more energy toward using the attention skills left, thus creating a better experience for all.

To read the full original post on attention, go to http://wp.me/Pf8xE-16n.

Chapter L

Fatigue

"Fatigue" inadequately reflects the unutterable weariness that comes on to a person with brain injury just because one got up in the morning. As mentioned in Chapter A of Honeymoon Learnings, the injured brain requires more energy than normal and diffuse axonal injury creates energy-sucking inflammation, but there isn't enough blood flow to bring the brain's fuel, glucose, to cells nor enough ATP to effect repairs, never mind execute normal functions. As a result, this fatigue feels different than at the end of a long day. It's physiological, not laziness or normal exhaustion.

After brain injury, every task exhausts. Whether you're breathing, eating, digesting, microwaving oatmeal, brushing teeth, opening the door, dressing, walking, feeling the wind, sitting in a car, reading signs on public transit, talking on the phone, having your heart continue to beat, having coffee with a friend, or paying attention in a crowd, everything requires way more energy. When the brain has to execute an impaired or absent skill or function, including regulating your heart, the energy drain is felt in the moment as well as the next days or weeks as the brain recovers.

The usual ways of recovering energy do not work as well or at all after brain injury. I found pain from injuries can be tolerated up to a point, and willpower can push through pain, at least for a while. But willpower cannot overcome fatigue. Brain injury fatigue enforces immobility for hours or days until slowly energy returns. Energy depletion results in the brain being unable to run the body. It feels like you're flung into a furnace or pumped up with water until your skin stretches painfully or swollen, itchy patches erupt or heart rate increases or blood pressure yo-yos or nose and sinuses swell up and block. You must scale back to restore energy so that the brain can regulate internal functions better.

Begin with a diet that promotes lower blood pressure, helps regulate a good weight, provides energy, and allows for best cell health possible under the circumstances. However, it's not easy, so don't beat yourself up if you can't maintain it 24/7. Also, *after*, and only after, intense cognitive activity such as brain biofeedback or reading, you may find you desire sweet like organic ginger ale or a cookie. That's because your brain is demanding its fuel—glucose. Being mindful in how much you eat, eating something sweet right after is like filling up the gas tank. If you perk up and don't have an equal crash right away, then your brain used it up.

Pacing tasks, setting doable priorities, and tracking to learn how many tasks and events you can do in a day, a week, or a month help. Planned staycations during your predictable worst times of the year like seasonal changes or crash anniversaries stave off long-lasting extreme fatigue.

Routines with rest times before and after events manage limited energy.

Single task, e.g., listen to music or read emails but not both.

But none of these restore energy. They only manage limited reserves better. *The key to restoring energy is healing the injury.*

For further reading and updates, go to http://wp.me/Pf8xE-16p.

Fear

In the terror
of the night
Lies water waiting
to feverishly swell
up spaces
between our cells.

Brain injury is not for sissies.

Chapter 13

Terror and Erebus

Thursday morning January 4, 2007, I awoke, heat flaring through me, erupting into red lakes puffing up hot rage all over my arms, my torso, my face. I ran cold water over my swollen eye and lower lip until the water ran cool off my skin. I stuffed down my fear and tried not to look in the mirror. I had a day to get through. I would be OK. I took Reactine. Maybe another one. They drained the life out of me, but my face looked better. I lived another day, tried to sleep another night.

Inky early morning light weaved through my eyelids Friday morning. My senses sent me incomprehensible information. My tongue was confined. I lifted my hand. My left cheek was swollen. I ran my tongue along too-smooth flesh. I whipped off the sheet in brain-injured slow motion. My feet painfully met the floor. I hobbled to the bathroom, my hips and legs protesting, my back straightening slowly. I flipped on the switch. Edema distorted my left under-eye, my left cheek, my lips, my face into a horror movie monster of death. Where it had been swollen on the right the day before was now bruised. Red dots decorated my stretched face. I averted my eyes hurriedly and cranked open my protesting jaw fearfully. I stared and stared at the glottis at the back of my throat. Back in the twentieth century, an allergist had instructed me that if it's bigger, I'm having an allergic reaction. My glottis was OK.

The inside of my mouth was not.

The inside of my left cheek swelled and swelled.

The red lakes with lines of white rough skin here and there in the flatter patches flooded down my neck onto my chest. Long elliptical patches clung to my forearms. I pulled down the collar of my PJs to stop it irritating my neck and growing the red lakes. I shoved up my sleeves. But the cloth stubbornly returned to lie against my raging skin.

I grabbed the Reactine. I took one.

What to do? What to do? What if my cheek kept swelling? What if my other one started up? I stared inside my mouth. Edema, edema, everywhere. I couldn't see the back of my throat easily.

It's not an allergy, I told myself. *It can't be an allergy!* I ate and drank absolutely nothing I'm allergic to. I didn't even go near any place where cross contamination could sneak an errant protein into my system and shove me into anaphylaxis.

My heart thudded in my chest: no!

I stared into the bathroom mirror again. Was the Reactine taking effect? I'd call my acupuncturist. She'd tell me what to do. She said it was best treated by doctors. I hung up, struggling to think. Doctors. Does that mean the ER? Should I call my parents?

Fear throttled.

I left a message for my GP. He'd call me back. He'd know what to do. I waited.

The minutes ticked by as the inside of my mouth didn't abate its assault on me.

I called Lily. She explained if I had hives, I had go to the ER and treat it within seventy-two hours or they'd stay for months. I googled hives, the typing and reading consuming what energy resources my brain had left, growing the burn on my skin.

I suddenly understood that I had to go to the ER. Hives needed cortisone.

I swallowed another Reactine. My brain was in chaos. Neurons vibrated independently. Neural networks freaked out, filled the spaces between cells with water and stopped regulating my body temperature. My mitochondria pumped out messages of heat, boiling my blood to scorch my skin.

I picked up the phone and dialled Mum, fearing my GP would call me back while I was on the phone because that's how things worked with me, yet terror clawed up my chest, scrabbled along my neck, and dug itself into my brain. I had to call. I can't go to the ER on my own! I just cannot! I listened to the phone ringing on the other end for interminable seconds. "Hello?"

Relief threw out fear for a moment.

"I need to go to the ER." That was the only thought I had.

"I can't take you," my mother replied. She listed the things she was committed to, the people she was at the beck and call of.

"How do I get there?"

"Take a taxi."

No! Not alone! I had needed to be independent to separate myself from Mistral, to cope with the lack of help. But I couldn't sustain it after years of making myself do it, especially since the treatments healing my neurons depleted, drained, devoured me until I literally couldn't move. The physical exertion, the constant self-talk, the necessary self-soothing after every instance of bad news ran me ragged. I couldn't endure the exhaustion of doing the treatment, recovering from the treatment, recovering my brain by myself anymore. I wasn't going to sit and listen to more bad health news by myself anymore and then manage my fear, my grief, my pain on the long, jostling TTC ride home by myself anymore, only to collapse in front of the TV, my brain swathed in deadening wraps of cotton wool, my body a morass of sweat-free burning, water retention, pain, exhaustion that dragged my cheeks down and drew lines of fiery lead through my legs.

I was not going to sit in the ER alone.

"I need someone with me! I'm not going alone!" I shouted.

I can't tough it out anymore, I cried deep in my heart. *God has broken me. He has hit me in my weakest spot, like with Jacob.*

She said she'd ask her neighbour. She hung up. I went to the bathroom and opened my mouth as wide as my uncooperative jaw would let me. Still swollen. I inhaled deeply, checked that little appendage hanging down at the back of my throat. It still looked OK. And anyway, this wasn't an allergic reaction.

I knew an anaphylactic reaction.

This wasn't it.

This was the nightmare extension of what had been happening to me for months. For years, my acupuncturist had warned me how it was a good thing I pushed myself hard because it kept me going to get better, but I could crash and land myself in a very bad place. I'd been in a bad place and hadn't seen it. For a long time, I'd gotten so hot by 5:00 a.m. I had to shove my sheets down and let the cold air soothe my skin.

But never—

The phone rang. I snatched it up. Mum's neighbour was coming to pick me up and take me to the ER.

I dressed quickly and waited.

The neighbour tall, slim, blonde, and understanding took me to the ER. The nurse triaged us. And sent us to the waiting area. I tried not to panic. I tried not to scream, "I'm dying! My mouth is going to close my throat shut!"

It hadn't yet.

I should be OK.

I talked to the neighbour. I tried to watch the others in the ER and guess why they were there.

I'm not going to be able to breathe!

No, no, I'm OK.

I needed to check my throat. There was no mirror.

"Shireen?"

I looked up and searched for the caller of my name.

The nurse, neighbour, and I shoe-horned ourselves into a tiny room with a solid exam bed between light wood cupboards and cream-painted walls. A paper sheet covered the centre of the bed, leaving the sides unprotected. I perched on it.

I feared lying down. The heat would rise and the water would pool even more in my mouth and face.

The Reactines finally began to diminish the rash. And that was when the nurse took my vitals and asked me questions. My heart rate was 137, and my blood pressure 140/80. She took my temperature with an ear thermometer. It was the first time I'd seen one. Neat! 37.5°C.

Is that all? I thought. I felt like oil was boiling inside me. She took it again. 36.4.

I said I was bloated. She thought I meant my stomach. My vocabulary failed me, but eventually by looking inside my mouth she understood.

She left, and the neighbour and I faced each other in the enclosed space. I saw her controlled horror as she watched little red patches with erratic edges appear and disappear like lava bubbles around my right lips and cheek, and I knew: skin cells turned red, the red spread, the red swelled up into small patches. The red disappeared and reappeared in another set of skin cells, like some sort of roaming alien infection

I tried to joke about it. I wanted to allay her fear and maybe allay mine.

The nurse returned with the resident and a nurse practitioner.

They said, confused, that it looked like an allergy. No! On top of everything else, I could not, was not, going to have a new health problem. I couldn't cope with one more new health problem.

This was not an allergy!

I did not have a new allergy! I had enough shit to deal with!

No allergy!

The resident agreed. The symptoms were atypical.

The brain injury was killing me.

The myth of the individual was killing me. Erebus, chaos in my brain, had strangled me. Terror had engulfed me.

I was going to die.

The ER professionals didn't know what to do. My cheeks were going to keep swelling and swelling like an alien demon was pumping water and air into every cell and every space between my cells to cut off my air supply, while they scratched their heads.

I wasn't going to be alive by the end of the day.

I could die in front of them while they wandered the halls looking for clues, not understanding, not accepting that this was my injured brain giving up on regulating my body. Not hearing me that the worst time was always the early morning. By the time any doctor saw me, it was a time of day where the edema shrank, the rash gone. But they had to do something! Now!

They gave me 50 mg Prednisone. I was to take what the nurse gave me now then the prescription for a total of five days. I was to take maximum doses of Benadryl, too. This would calm down the edema and keep my airway clear.

I thought dryly, *Well, the Benadryl will put me to sleep.* But the Prednisone? I wasn't sure. I knew that my adrenals were pumping out cortisol. I called myself the "Michelin Man" for looking steroidal, and so I wasn't sure giving me steroids when my body had been producing them for years was a good idea.

But what else was I supposed to do?

I left. My mother's neighbour took me to Starbucks. The cold drink soothed my heat as we waited for my prescription to be filled. I noticed I had more room in my mouth. She dropped me off, and I entered my home alone shortly before 3:00 p.m., Prednisone and Benadryl inside me, giving me a life raft of hope that I would survive yet terrified of what the night would bring. I ate rice because I had a headache. I had no desire to eat. What if it lodged in my throat?

I checked my throat in the bathroom mirror. Could I see it clearly? I wasn't sure. I had to see a doctor. My GP! He'd tell me what to do. I rang his number. His answering service assured me they would leave a message with him. I tried to watch TV. I returned to the bathroom mirror and checked my throat. I stood in an ice-cold shower to calm my fiery skin, to run cold water until the water coming off my head no longer ran fevered but cold. I slept on the couch, talk radio keeping me company in the silent streetlamp-lit night, not knowing if I'd be alive or dead by the end of the week, not knowing how to soothe my body nor prop up my brain. I berated myself for pushing so hard.

Chapter 14

Humans Aren't Tigers but Elephants

Saturday, January 6, 2007, I awoke and ran my tongue around the inside of my mouth, inhaled deeply, and felt the air flowing through my throat, filling my lungs. I sagged, broken in relief. I was still alive.

I looked in the mirror. Water swelled the delicate tissue under my left eye. My flailing brain had punched me. I iced it. I spread melaleuca cream on it. My brain found another spot on the right side of my nose to scream its exhaustion. I ate breakfast and swallowed my Prednisone. My energy fled, weakening my legs and wasting me like I had been after my injury. Only recently had I been able to eat breakfast and not need a nap after.

Now back to post-crash endless zonked.

My GP called me back from a party. His answering service had failed to deliver my Friday message. He said that he would have given Prednisone differently. He would've given first a huge dose then taper off. But, he said that he wasn't going to interfere.

Great, I thought, as I hung up. *Now what? I'm having it given all wrong. Would it work? Make me worse?* I thought back to the doctor I'd seen years after that day in 1981 in the ER, who'd diagnosed why I'd collapsed on a rainy hot day only a month after my grandmother had died. Her complex testing revealed that not only did I not produce enough adrenaline and norepinephrine under normal circumstances, they didn't rise under stress. That's why when I was stressed, my blood pressure dropped like a stone in a still pool.

But that was before my brain injury.

My blood pressure had instantly risen at the crash site. It had taken me all these years to remember why normal numbers were wrong for me.

I wished that physician was still alive to advise me. My GP did too and suggested I see an endocrinologist. My choice, he said. He'd always respected my medical knowledge and my self-knowledge. He'd always supported me in my medical choices.

I latched on to adrenaline insufficiency. I latched on to endocrinologist.

I googled adrenaline insufficiency. My brain in revenge swelled up my left eye again. I hurriedly got off the computer and checked my throat in the mirror. I could still see it. Maybe it was safe to eat. I poured out a small bowl of soup and ate an early dinner.

Licorice!

My old physician had told me to eat licorice to prop up my adrenaline levels. I searched in my cupboard for licorice tea. I'd thrown out my licorice years earlier after my brain injury. I couldn't quite remember why. But the tea would help. I inhaled its steam and sipped its sweetness.

Tick. Tick. Tick. Now the clock in my head added to the counting up of years *Lifeliner* was on hold, the time lost to my regressing health. Its ticking dominated me, and I strained to rest against its urgency.

After church, Mum took me out for lunch. It was safe to eat with another watching me. I was hungry. And if my brain fagged from eating and stopped regulating my body temperature or started shooting out swellings in bad places, Mum would see.

She could stop me choking to death, I thought but did not say. If I said these words out loud, the fear would grow like a giant, people would laugh at me, and throw me back into my home alone. What would happen to me when the Prednisone ran out? I had to see an endocrinologist now. My mother suggested we leave it till the end of the week when she'd next see me.

"No," I snapped. "I have to see someone Monday or Tuesday."

She said she couldn't drive me. I'd have to take a taxi. I didn't know how I'd do that. I ate the lunch she bought me. My insides grew cold, my legs weak. I couldn't walk far; fatigue clutched my legs. No, I wasn't going to listen to one more piece of bad news by myself. I didn't convince her.

Back home, the silence raised its tentacles and petrified my heart. I called Lily. The rhythmic rise and fall of her prayers of absolute love for the Lord, the certainty of her prayers in Him, the energy of her voice, rocked my fear into calmness. She said she saw me writing on paper. I furrowed my brow. I hadn't written anything since Friday. I couldn't.

She said she'd pray with her daughter. She called me back with words from the Lord. "Joy of the Lord is her strength. My Grace is sufficient, as power made perfect in weakness." Her daughter saw me rejoicing.

His Grace is not sufficient, I raged silently, as I burned in my light T-shirt and skirt, my home's thermostat set to 18°C. *When would I ever rejoice again?* The shade of the last time I'd laughed freely, loudly, two days before the crash, flitted in to taunt me. *But if this leads to a cure for my problems —*

Lily interrupted my angry thoughts. "You'll be OK," she said, "because God's promises have not yet been fulfilled. Read Psalm 107:20." Her pragmatic words and the verse settled me for a few minutes.

I began to write again.

I asked Dad for help. Maybe he'd taper my Prednisone dosage since he used it on his own patients.

"No," he stated emphatically. He wasn't going to do it. I was family. I despaired. I knew Prednisone was supposed to be tapered. I knew it was not a good idea to stop it cold. But I didn't know how to taper it myself. The ER had screwed up. My GP wasn't going to interfere. Dad said no.

I persevered. Maybe if I saw a specialist at the clinic he worked at, that doctor would help me. So I told Dad about adrenaline insufficiency.

"You should go see an allergist," he suggested instead.

Endocrinologist, my mind hung on to that word. "Can you refer me to an endocrinologist?" I pleaded.

"No," he replied. "Go see an allergist," he advised and followed up with those familiar words I'd heard my whole life: stop worrying about it.

It was threatening my breath.

It was not being treated.

It was ruling my tissues.

My brain couldn't regulate my body.

I couldn't recognize the chaos in my thoughts, the round and round, what if it was this, but this was happening. But I knew I needed to see an endocrinologist. Anger vied with fear as they marched on my mission: see an endocrinologist.

Mum called the clinic for me.

She got me in to see an endocrinologist on Tuesday.

She wasn't going to drive me.

I yelled that she had to.

OK, but she wasn't going to stay. She had to get to work. I could get one of my kith to drive me home. I began to plot how to get her to accompany me into the endocrinologist's office. I worried about getting back home. The clinic was so far. I flagged. I fought myself stopping in my tracks, standing, swaying, collapsing. Once I sat, I couldn't move again. Keeping going was easier, though the fatigue consumed me, sharding fire lines into my muscles.

If I have to, I thought, *I guess it'll be a return to that nightmare of 2000 and 2001 of praying not to fall over on the TTC, of talking my legs into a one-two rhythm.* I phoned Arta, the one who was on time when only a half hour late and who seemed to disappear during daily life and pop up during terrifying emergencies. She cheerfully agreed to drive me home.

Mum, in her lifelong forgetful way, went to work in Brampton Tuesday morning. I panicked. She had to drive me to see the endocrinologist! She said she'd come right away. I stared out the window, waiting, waiting, worrying, feeling my sinuses worsening, doubling my traumatic rhinitis medication, hoping the Benadryls wouldn't wear off, fearing the long drive where other sober drivers competed in who can threaten my safety the most, tailgating, erratically changing lanes, running red lights, speeding. I remembered my psychologist's visualization technique. See myself like an enormous giant, striding over the highways and arriving home in one piece while deep breathing. My breath slipped in and out of my throat. It wasn't being cut off, I assured myself.

As Mum and I waited in the gulag waiting room for the endocrinologist, I hadn't gotten any further along in my plot to get her into the office with me. He strode toward us, hand extended, my former now-semi-retired endocrinologist, happy to see both me and my mother. He ushered Mum in, taking it for granted that she would come in with me. I almost smiled in relief. Mum wouldn't counter the doctor.

She stood at the far wall in the tiny office, so reminiscent of my ex-husband on that long-ago day when I got the diagnosis of brain injury. I strained to focus on the endocrinologist's words. I must remember. I'd long ago learnt I couldn't take notes and follow along at the same time. I fared better by focusing as hard as I could and remembering.

He said authoritatively, "I'll order more thyroid tests because it can flip." He didn't think it was stress, and I recalled how ER said it was a diagnosis of exclusion. He said categorically that I did not and do not have an allergic reaction. This is dermographia. He pointed out to Mum, "See here, these red patches." I stared down at my forearms. Mum nodded, as if she was paying attention. "In ninety-five percent of cases, the cause is unknown." He pointed out my eyes. I didn't understand what was wrong with my eyes, something to do with what the eyelids were doing. Mum nodded.

She could explain it to me, I thought.

He took my blood pressure, said my heart rate was always high, so he wasn't concerned about that. But my blood pressure was another thing.

"Atenolol," he said. I was to take it.

I hesitated. My high heart rate concerned me more. My blood pressure couldn't be high; my whole life it had been too low. "Take half a tablet of fifty milligrams atenolol immediately," he instructed firmly as he handed me the prescription. It would drop my heart rate, too.

"OK," I agreed, wondering how I'd fill it, wondering how I could arrange to take the first pill in front of someone in case anaphylaxis drained my body and terminated my breathing.

Mum waited with me because Arta had gotten lost, and I asked her about my eyelids. She had no clue what he'd said, her brain's old habit of zoning out having taken hold. Despair, anger, and confusion competed for supremacy in my heart. What was wrong with my eyelids? As soon as Arta arrived, Mum left. Arta drove me to the closest Tim Horton's for an apple fritter for me and a large, sweet milky tea for her. Her young sons kept us company in her utilitarian vehicle. She helped me pick up my prescription. Back home, I cut it in half and swallowed my first dose of atenolol, fearing allergy would strangle me. I noted the time: 2:30 p.m.

Twenty minutes later, stress released me from its hold. And Arta and her sons left.

I began to document my ordeal to email my endocrinologist.

Document. Document. Document. Feel like I have some control. Be a partner in my health. I checked my pulse. Ninety. Noted the time. 6:00 p.m. Made a sandwich; ate it slowly so that I wouldn't tax myself; couldn't avoid the cold and weak-feeling legs that came on every time I ate since Friday. Noted I stayed in my chair and watched TV the rest of Tuesday night. Still...

Old tachycardia choked me, and I grabbed my throat, checked my pulse, noted the time: 7:00 p.m. on Tuesday. Ninety beats per minute. By 7:30 p.m., internal cold and the skin burning diminished. I checked my face in the mirror; it looked more normal, less hot. I boiled the kettle and poured boiling water over a bag of licorice root tea. It was 9:15 p.m. Somehow the minutes leapt to 9:40 p.m., and my pulse was eighty-four. It's 10:00 p.m., and I was warm, my chest tight. I inhaled and my lungs barked their unhappiness. No wheezing, though.

At 11:00 p.m., my pulse was seventy-eight. Filling and drinking a glass of icy water pumped it up to ninety. I didn't sleep. Heat from my face reflected off my pillow and irritated my skin. I turned onto my side so that only the top of my head lay on my pillow while my neck levitated to keep cooler. I dozed. My left shoulder powered me out of sleep with deep ache at 7:50 a.m. My sinuses dripped soreness into my throat. Pulse seventy-two. Eczema had disappeared from my wrist and appeared on my elbow. I calmed a new rash on my leg with melaleuca cream. Pulse up to eighty-four after cooling off my head and face in the shower then warming myself back up. I forgot to note the time. Dizziness assailed me when I stood up, and the air closed in around me. Ninety at 9:55 a.m. Blood coloured my face burnt and emptied out from my hands and feet.

Mum drove me to see my cardiologist, whom I'd followed from one hospital to another and whom I'd booked back in October.

How serendipitous, I thought. Mum wasn't going in with me. He shut the door and listened to my racing heart in multiple places on my chest and back. He noticed the tremors in my hands and legs that had been with me since the crash. He felt the beta blocker, the atenolol, would stop the tremors and settle me down. *Maybe I could raise a fork to my mouth without having to focus hard on getting it into my mouth, not around my lips. Or stand without shaking.*

He said that whatever I said wouldn't leave this room, and I began to cry over losing my identity. "Losing my friends never fucking ends," I cried out. Tears dripped from my lashes as his brown eyes watched me with kindness. He noted I was isolated within my family and even before my brain injury had much to cope with. My fears poured out. Then the heat of my eyes dried my tears. Softly, he told me he wasn't too concerned about my blood pressure and that I'd always had a fast heart rate.

He asked me if I'd taken the atenolol that morning. I admitted I hadn't. Fear of allergy had overcome me that morning. He told me to take it when I got home and to take it every morning starting Thursday, tomorrow, and then return after two weeks for twenty-four-hour blood pressure monitoring. I'd have to pay for that test as OHIP didn't cover it even though it was ordered through the hospital. Sixty dollars.

Afterwards, Mum took me to a restaurant I felt safe in. But I badly wanted to lie down.

I said, "I'm going to cancel my appointments next week."

"Don't do that. I'll drive you on Wednesday. Call Aunt to have her drive you home on Tuesday," Mum replied.

I nodded. I had to keep going. Maybe I'd been heard after all.

Tick. Tick. Tick.

1:00 a.m.
2:00 a.m.
3:00 a.m.
I composed my own Ecclesiastes in my head.
4:00 a.m.
For the first fucking time, I could lay my whole face on the pillow with no fever or puffy.
5:00 a.m.
6:00 a.m.
This was godawful. God was beyond cruel. No dreams. No plans. Not even a fucking daily goal. People talking about their dreams was like spitting in my face. For years, I'd enjoyed others' successes, but not now, six years, eleven months, 362 days after my crash.
7:00 a.m.
8:00 a.m.
9:00 a.m.
I staggered up and stared out into the mild day. Nine degrees Celsius the weather guy said. I gingerly stepped into the shower. Needles of cold drummed onto my head, and hot water splashed onto my shoulders. I waited for the head-heated water to fade into warmth, fade into cool, fade into cold. I turned on the hot, my kinked muscles shouting for the relief warm water would bring. Red furied down my arms. I turned off the hot water tap and waited again for the cold to run cold off my head. I turned the hot tap back on again to raise the temperature from almost frozen to just above ice cold to warm myself up quickly. I had to begin to adjust to no warming up, to cold showers, to slathering myself head to toe with melaleuca cream, to ice cubes and more cream on my skin throughout the day. I dressed in layers to stay warm because that's how I dressed all my adult life. But I was wretchedly hot

yet too tired to strip off the layers. Why couldn't I learn how to dress for being hot? Seven years and I still hadn't!

What worth was it to strive to get better, only for my body to rise up and bite me in the britches and my brain to revolt and push me back down a hill it took me years to climb one sore foot at a time? What worth was it to live like an adolescent whose future lies before her waiting to be filled, but knowing that future will never come?

Potential lay behind and taunted in front.

I excelled at watching TV. If I was real lucky, I could even listen to the radio, assuming the music didn't stress me out by blasting memories into my consciousness of when I had myself, talents and skills, kith and husband, kin around me. I had to stop myself crying, for the tears swelled my eyes up worse. I hated this joyless existence. I should have just watched myself blow up Friday instead of letting my fear drive me to get help. I had to suck it up. God hated me.

Eleven days after the ER, I went to biofeedback, but I didn't want to talk about the ER. My heart rate jumped to 150, dropped to ninety, leapt to 170. Sweat beaded out unusually onto my arid skin. My breath flattened and resisted my deep breathing attempts. Sympathetic and parasympathetic activity rocketed up. Document. Document it all. And email to my cardiologist, I reminded myself as my aunt and uncle drove me home, to my intense relief. My cardiologist increased my dosage to 37.5 mg every morning, assuring me that I would not become tolerant to atenolol and the main side effect was fatigue. As I leaned on a knife to cut a tablet in half and half of a tablet in half again for three-quarters of a dose, I thought that my fatigue was so enormous, I wouldn't notice any additional.

I sat down at my kitchen table, mind blank, and two cardinals flew by my window. I stood up and walked over to watch them.

They hopped up to a higher branch, bopped back down to a lower one. They flitted further away, then hopped closer to face me fully. I waited for them to fly off as cardinals were wont to do. They didn't. A thought crept into my head: *photograph them.* Malaise kept me rooted, but the cardinals didn't leave. I frowned. So unusual of these red birds with their black masks. They stuck around for about an hour, long enough for me to move my feet at last, find my camera, and photograph their upended tails, their aggressive stares, and finally their beautiful profiles. Awe and hope filtered into my soul. The two angels in bird form launched into the blue sky then and disappeared.

God sent them.

I put my massage and brain biofeedback on hold.

That night, I stepped outside in my short-sleeved shirt, knee-length skirt, and sandals, arms outstretched and let the frozen air caress the burning patches, soothing them to flatten, to fade to pink. I didn't shiver. As I turned the thermostat down, I thought, *At least I'm saving on heating costs I can't afford.*

Chapter 15

I Need a Therapist

The atenolol was the only thing keeping me sane. The moment I took my morning dose, I watched the slow second hand tick the twenty minutes down to relief. My skin calmed as the day wore on. By noon, I could put on a light sweater or sweatshirt and cover up my arms and keep the collar and stray hairs off my neck. The skin there hated being touched or covered.

Early March, pain began popping up here and there like bubbles in a swamp. My acupuncturist said lack of energy was the reason for my disconnect between internal and external temperatures and I should return to only one thing at a time. She said to pick one, brain or pain. I picked brain biofeedback over massage therapy. She was concerned about me walking in the cold. I wasn't. In the vicious wind that burned skin, I wanted to tear off my hat and scarf, I was so hot. But her words gave me permission to continue to scale back. Days dropped out of my consciousness, hours leapt ahead to land me in the future. I no longer heard the ticking away of my age as *Lifeliner* continued to languish, waiting for someone to publish it. I was too hot, too bloated to care.

"One thing at a time," she'd said.

I missed my Bible study with the WWII vet and the younger seniors, the way they accepted me with all my TBI snafus, made me feel like I belonged. But I had energy only for one thing: brain biofeedback or Bible study. As the veteran said, it was important to go for my brain.

I began to recover my energy. I kept up my Flickr socialization as my anonymous self. It had its advantages of shoving down my experiences, letting me escape to its island of photography. But there really was no escape ever from brain injury.

I dithered about what to do with *Lifeliner*. I had no publisher and no agent. I had no stamina to self-publish. I used to edit, but finicky detailed work requiring concentration to discern one word from another didn't agree with my damaged brain. Every now and then, I'd google and read for a few minutes on self-publishing companies. And then I'd crawl onto the couch for an hour or two, ruminating. *Could I afford it?* I brooded, *The insurance company was sending me to their usual charlatans for whatever diagnosis they felt like trumping up, anything but admit the fucking obvious: brain injury.* This fight of expert-versus-expert was dragging on. Was it wise to spend my savings on self-publishing *Lifeliner*?

I wished I was healthy. But God had condemned me. Only through my writing, with the time to let my neurons process and crackle through the damaged areas, could I be the person I wanted to be, the person trapped behind the damaged language centres, the misfiring emotional centres, the dead areas. I hovered in a deathly limbo between glimpses of improvement and the summer smog that melded with my internal thermostat and ratcheted me into an inferno.

And then to my surprise, Dad asked me, "Why don't you self-publish? I'll fund it."

Surprise spurted hope into me. But helplessness took over. *Are my writing and photography any good? Am I kidding myself?* I felt like a yo-yo.

On Friday, March 23, 2007, I finished reading iUniverse's publishing guide. Suddenly, I phoned iUniverse. I signed up and gave over my credit card number. In twenty-nine minutes, *Lifeliner* was on its way to being published, and I was assigned a publishing associate to guide me through the process. Once more, I'd have other humans pushing my dead initiation button for me. I began bouncing out of my skin. I dialled Glen's number, and to my shock he answered. Not getting his voice mail told me God must be for this! I asked him about possible cover photos. He said that everyone sees IVs on TV every night; her mug on the cover would be sufficient. I was relieved. I called my iUniverse contact about acknowledgements. She told me not to rush, to enjoy the weekend, and to ensure I was happy with the final manuscript. I emailed Dad. The heat crawling up into my head couldn't shake off my excitement.

On Wednesday, April 4, 2007, I published my website under my own name. I was so bloody organized before the crash that all I had to do was follow my 1999 plans and copy and paste the articles I'd listed. Putting up a blog was beyond me though. I lost days again. I became too tired to get up, too awake to sleep. It was so depressing.

The ADD Centre began coherence training at C3-C4—roll the ball along the virtual gorilla's arm from my left to the right to reduce my very high coherence. That ball defied my attempts to move it, and my entire head hurt. But my brain trainer said that I did well for a first try, to get the two areas above my ears to work separately but connected instead of as one unit.

Mere days later, my asthma returned. I counted down the hours to take my asthma medication, my sinus medication, and my atenolol. I tried the 18 Hz beta AVE session and found my mood liked it. At the same time, Mum told me the family all looked at my website and photos. My aunt called to exclaim over them. My niece chatted with me on the computer and left me my first guestbook entry. I chuckled at her wit. My mood soared then returned to neutral as phone and inbox fell silent again.

As spring rolled toward summer, Michael became vociferous with my brain trainer that I was to relax and must not try. I must just let the coherence ball roll or not. And only she should see my heart biofeedback as me seeing my wonky heart rate tensed me up. He adjusted my training as well to include both single electrode at FZ and coherence at FZ-F7. Shortly after, on a muggy June day, Dad became intrigued enough by the brain biofeedback that he met with Michael to observe me during brain training. And I observed how alike the two men were. *They even move alike*, I thought. Dad was impressed. I learnt that my trainer was to pause the screen when the ball was stopped to make me think about how I felt and the same when the ball was rolling so that I could learn what optimal coherence felt like. By the end, I felt awake and alive, quite different from my usual state of needing total quiet and rest.

The weeks marched by, and a smart, experienced editor ploughed up my manuscript and reseeded it. Grumbling and grateful, I returned to my previous summer writing schedule. And as a reward, I received the Editors' Choice award and a professionally designed cover for free.

Summer gave way to fall.

The ADD Centre and I parted ways. They had saved my life. But exhausted with none to feed me after every session and finances worsening, I couldn't sustain brain treatments on my own anymore. I missed my brain trainers for a little while, like I missed my OT, my psychiatrist, and my psychologist. Rehab was a series of perpetual good-byes.

The big day came. iUniverse mailed me a box of my books. My spiritual mentor told me to take one out, hold it in my hand, and spend time with it to savour my accomplishment, to enjoy what I had done.

I did.

I felt nothing.

The clock started up again.

Tick. Tick. Tick.

"We have a mediation scheduled," my lawyer told me. It was for November. A late birthday present. I rested up for three days before.

In the downtown office tower, my lawyer drew me aside in an empty room before the mediation to remind me to keep my mouth shut, to let him do all the talking, and to answer their questions briefly. No extra words. I nodded. I trusted him. We gathered in the main room, Mum, my lawyer, and me on the window side of the table, the insurance representative to left of the two lawyers, one representing the two drivers I was suing who were with the same insurance company, and one representing my ex-husband because the other two drivers were countersuing him for reasons that never made sense to me. To my far right sat my ex's insurance representative who looked like she'd sucked a lemon. The soft-spoken mediator in his tailored suit and gold cufflinks sat at the head of the table between us. My eyes kept being drawn to the young, slim woman who'd spent at least an hour on her makeup and a fortune on her colourful shingled hair and spiked heels.

I thought, *This is not going to go well. She's the insurance representative of those two fucking drivers, and she has no power. The woman at the other end has more power. She doesn't have to spend hours on her appearance, but she isn't the one with the final say on settlement.* The lawyer for my ex's insurer opened by informing us my ex was the best witness she'd ever come across. I smiled smugly to myself. *Fucking drivers who ruined my life couldn't push responsibility on to my ex.*

The young woman said, "I have a train to catch at four thirty."

I sighed deep within myself. My experience was that serious mediations had no time limits. The insurance company was not serious. *This was a total waste. I'd rested for nothing.*

Blood pressure-pumped into my hands, yet peace spread through me. Lily was praying all day, asking for God's peace to be upon me. And it stayed with me as the defence offered ridiculously low amounts through the mediator. I felt pressured to accept the straitjacket of lifetime poverty so I counter-demanded high. My lawyer argued with me that I was being too ambitious. I thought he was being unrealistic. He decided to play good cop to my bad cop when he presented my counter-offers. That tickled my fancy. Maybe we'd meet at an everyone-hates-it-but-can-work middle level.

Apparently, surveillance had caught me carrying something. I thought I'd been followed.

Such a lovely feeling, I thought. *My phone is probably bugged, too.* But what was I to do? I needed to eat. With Mum away, I had no one to help me shop and carry the groceries, like the bran and fruit that felt like megatonnes to me. But the camera caught only the fact I was carrying something. Ergo, I must be OK. Did they surveil my cold showers in winter, too? The standing outside in shirt sleeves at night? Did they know this fire inside me was like having built-in pain-reducing heat packs? Did they surveil the hours of recovery? Did anyone care enough to help me?

Toward the end, my mother and my lawyer spoke with my brother through the phone. I'd surrendered my privacy a long time ago so barely cared until I received the message I was to settle. Fuck it. I had a real injury with real consequences. I couldn't even work part part-time hours for even one day. How was I ever going to earn enough to support myself again? Insurers promised to pay for medical costs, homemaking costs, and income replacement. Tort claims were to compensate for homemaking, income replacement, and pain and suffering, the latter capped at $100,000 in twentieth century dollars by the Supreme Court of Canada as if pain and suffering dollars don't go toward expensive medical treatments to alleviate the intense psychic pain but to giant TVs instead.

The mediator returned.

The highest the defence was willing to go was less than a year of salary for one person in the room. And then I learnt the government expected victims like me to be psychic, to know in advance whether a jury would award more or less than the settlement offered. If the jury ruled for less, I would have to pay all court costs for all parties, which would wipe out my award and put me into debt. I refused to settle.

I sprawled afterward on the couch in utter exhaustion.

My birthday month wasn't going well. My parents had missed my birthday because even though it had landed on a Friday, our regular night out together, they had decided to drive to my brother's to work on the invitations for the *Lifeliner* launch party that my mother had agreed to organize for me. I was in no fit state to be able to organize one, and several had felt I should have one. When I asked why no birthday dinner out, I was asked if I wanted the party. I had no answer.

I needed a therapist.

Snow howled through the air and built deep ruts on the roads mid-December. Several lost their way to the *Lifeliner* launch party, unable to see the numbers on the buildings, but it was the invites missing a numeral in the street number that lead many astray. My kin had noticed the error back on my birthday weekend but hadn't pulled out the wrong invitations to reprint and re-envelope them.

I sat at a table, greeting people I hadn't seen in years, catching up, and fighting my brain to stay engaged while it wanted to notice the clock ticking. I signed books with pens I'd bought specially for autographing, feeling like a writer, unable to believe *Lifeliner* was out sixteen years after I'd begun working on it. I overheard Dad enthusiastically talking up my book with old patients and current colleagues. Some asked him to sign it, too. As the room emptied and my brain slowed, I laboriously counted up the twenties. Not enough to pay off my credit card bill for all the copies I'd ordered from iUniverse.

Dad forwarded me with pride an email from his Thai research Fellow. She wrote, "I only intended to read a little, but the book was so unputtable down. Before I knew, it was nearly 5 a.m. and I was at Chapter 28!!"

Hope surged through me.

Fear Learnings

Chapter M

Thermoregulation

"Thermoregulation is the ability of an organism to keep its body temperature within certain boundaries, even when the surrounding temperature is very different."[19] (Wikipedia) My brain's ability to regulate my temperature and activate its cooling mechanism changed dramatically after my brain injury. I produced too much heat and could not sweat to cool down.

"Development of post-traumatic hyperthermia is one of many secondary factors that may negatively influence the outcome of patients following TBI," wrote Thompson et al in *Hyperthermia following traumatic brain injury: A critical evaluation*.[20] Yet the current evidence-based medical model doesn't acknowledge it. In 1993, Eduardo Benarroch wrote, "The central autonomic network (CAN) is an integral component of an internal regulation system through which the brain controls visceromotor, neuroendocrine, pain, and behavioral responses essential for survival...Hyperthermia and autonomic hyperactivity occur in patients with head trauma."[21]

In 2012, a brain injury expert didn't know why I was hot and told me to get on with my life. It's psychologically damaging to have to have cold showers in a Canadian winter or stand outside

---

[19] https://en.m.wikipedia.org/wiki/Thermoregulation
[20] H.J. Thompson, N.C. Tkacs, et al. *Hyperthermia following traumatic brain injury: a critical evaluation*. Neurobiol Dis. Apr 2003 12(3):163-73.
https://www.researchgate.net/publication/10763246_Hyperthermia_following_traumatic_brain_injury_A_critical_evaluation
[21] Central Autonomic Network: Functional Organization, Dysfunction, and Perspective. Mayo Clinic Proceedings. http://www.mayoclinicproceedings.org/article/S0025-6196(12)62272-1/abstract

in freezing temperatures with only a T-shirt and skirt on in a vain attempt to cool down because no one entrusted with your care is listening to you and instead instructs you not to focus on it. It's physically taxing, brain injuring, sleep depriving, and dangerous to be that hot and your body unable to cool itself down, especially in a muggy climate. Fear from not knowing what your body will do slows healing, too.

"Hyperthermia increases metabolic expenditure, glutamate release, and neutrophil activity to levels higher than those occurring in the normothermic brain-injured patient. This synergism may further compromise the injured brain," wrote Thompson et al.

My acupuncturist's needles moved the heat from my head or overheated core into my colder lower extremities. Brain biofeedback restarted my sweating ability (on and off) after about a year of treatment. I cooled myself down by frequently drinking ice water, iced coffee, iced tea; eating ice cream; sucking on ice cubes; running cold water over my head, arms, neck; or icing reddened skin then slathering on cocoa butter and melaleuca cream.

There is a second source of head heat: neurogenic fever.

"Fever has also been found to cause loss of brain function. Thompson, Pinto-Martin and Bullock, in 2003, found that patients with DA-TBI present on imaging studies were over nine times more likely to develop neurotrophic fever in patients with DA-TBI versus other forms of TBI (diffuse axonal-traumatic brain injury)," wrote Dave Siever, C.E.T., in *Diffuse Axonal Injuries, Interruptions and Treatment Using Audio-Visual Entrainment.*[22]

---

[22] Dave Siever. *Diffuse Axonal Injuries, Interruptions and Treatment Using Audio-Visual Entrainment.*
http://mindalive.com/default/assets/File/AVE%20and%20diffuse%20axonal%20injuries%20for%20publication-Final%20-%20Feb%2023%202017(2).pdf

"Diffuse axonal injury...and frontal lobe injury of any type...are independently predictive of an increased risk of development of neurogenic fever following severe TBI."[23] Neuron regrowth means the brain is healing. Yet fever from it can damage the brain. Would neuron regrowth and thus brain healing be halted if cooled?

"However, fever is not universally beneficial, particularly in cases of extreme inflammation where lowering, rather than raising body temperature has evolved as a protective mechanism. Thus, uncontrolled fever is associated with worse outcomes in patients with sepsis or neurological injuries, whereas treatments that induce hypothermia can have a clinical benefit."[24]

People with brain injury need relief. Researchers need to study this much more to both develop effective relief and ensure it doesn't slow down or halt brain healing.

Next time someone tells you to ignore it or get on with your life, ask, "If someone put a hot iron on you, would you consider it appropriate care to be told to ignore the iron and get on with your life?" And when they say no, ask them why it is for you.

For further reading, see Chapter Q.

---

[23] H.J. Thompson, J. Pinto-Martin, M.R. Bullock. *Neurogenic fever after traumatic brain injury: an epidemiological study.* J Neurol Neurosurg Psychiatry. May 2003 74(5):614-9. https://www.ncbi.nlm.nih.gov/pubmed/12700304

[24] Sharon S. Evans, Elizabeth A. Repasky, and Daniel T. Fisher. *Fever and the thermal regulation of immunity: the immune system feels the heat.* Nature reviews. Immunology 15.6 (2015): 335–349. PMC. Web. 8 June 2017. https://www.ncbi.nlm.nih.gov/pmc/articles/PMC4786079/

Chapter N

Stress

Stress can be mental, as in doing mentally taxing work; physical, as in exercise; emotional, as in those notorious family get-togethers depicted in movies; or psychological, as in having your real brain injury problems denied. Brain injury creates higher stress. For example, sensitivity to noise can be so acute after injury that the same environment that may tire a normal person out after a couple of hours is like being under a 747 taking off next to a jackhammer with a bass-thumping car nearby for a person with a brain injury.

Stress management includes gathering objective data measuring heart rate and blood pressure, as well as measures of coping and stress tests with echocardiogram to look at the health of your coronary arteries. Researchers suggest testing for autonomic nervous system dysfunction. This would include measuring heart rate variability (HRV) and busy brain with qEEG.

Pre-brain injury coping skills may no longer be present or functional even though you may find it unfathomable that they vanished in an instant. The healthcare team, social support, and the person with the injury must recognize that an injured brain is less physiologically able to cope with everyday stressors, never mind the higher stressors of illness or family breakdown.

HRV Training. "Heart rate variability (HRV) is the physiological phenomenon of variation in the time interval between heartbeats."[25] (Wikipedia) Brain injury seems to impair HRV. HRV training provides a biofeedback screen whereby you

---

[25] https://en.m.wikipedia.org/wiki/Heart_rate_variability

can watch your heart rate rise and fall in sync with your breathing and learn to deep breathe so as to improve synchronization and thus HRV.

HRV training, gamma enhancement, busy brain reductions, and low-intensity laser therapy for concussion has led to the very slow but noticeable improvement in HRV and dropping of my heart rate despite extreme stress. Emotional and heavy cognitive load stressors now rarely increase my heart rate to 130 or above.

For more on heart, blood pressure, other stress tests, HRV, and updates, go to http://wp.me/Pf8xE-16s.

Chapter O

Treat the Person

Under the standard evidence-based medical model, brain injury recovery takes years and by luck. As an adult who had had brushes with muscle injuries and illnesses, I found how long it took incomprehensible at the start and impossible to live with five years on. The level of care required to help a person with brain injury adjust to being in lifelong recovery and to process the grief of losing one's identity while striving to fulfill adult goals seems unavailable. It isn't enough to treat the brain. One must treat the person.

Losing yourself while still being alive physically is not any kind of normal grief. It needs to be acknowledged, listened to, lived with, and compassionately treated for the years that it takes to heal.

The therapist brings relief by fully engaging with the person's grief while working with their other healthcare professionals in healing brain physiology, whether through using systematic thought in psychotherapy or relating emotional difficulties to the brain trainers so as to adjust treatment.

Neuroplastic treatments accelerate regeneration significantly but don't obviate the need for informed psychological counselling of how to adjust to goals delayed and to stop that ticking clock in the person's head as they watch the world pass them by while they're relegated to endless medical appointments and begging for social engagement that accommodates their physiological damage. When neuroplastic treatments begin after years of the standard model, they may speed the person into new states of improvement that are not usually seen. Every member of the team must be aware of and help navigate the challenges accelerated healing creates. A social worker, psychologist, or psychiatrist who starts this journey with the person and stays on it for decades with them can see the improvements and believably remind the person about those improvements.

Loss of goals and dreams through the actions of others is not trivial. Suggesting that they should let them go before resolving the grief is to abandon the injured. Do not contribute to that loss by ignoring the intensive and necessary grief work, by misdiagnosing grief and damaged emotional centres as depression and medicating it, and by refusing to work as a team with the patient or client and other healthcare professionals involved in care.

For further reading, go to http://wp.me/Pf8xE-16u.

Stall

Fatigue
Weariness
Exhaustion
Tiredness.

What word can describe the unutterable slump of brain injury fatigue?

Chapter 16

The Law Settles

I realized as I spoke to a wiser man a week before my tort claim's pretrial that no one can give me what I want. They can't fix me, give me the ability to work, or to cook every day. All they can do is give me resources to compensate and cope.

"Peace, peace, peace," Lily received the night before my pretrial. I knew then it wasn't going to go well. God gives you peace when you're in the pit.

On the first Friday of June 2008, the sidewalks steamed, and heat rose from me like a smouldering volcano that air conditioning couldn't touch. I rode a cab to the courthouse in my pigeon-grey skirt and white blouse with narrow navy stripes. I couldn't button the short sleeves over my fat arms. About 9:15 a.m., I found my mother who'd gotten lost. We entered the courthouse like we were going through the secured area of an airport. My lawyer met Mum and me in the empty hallway and explained the procedure rapidly and quietly as he mopped his brow and cooled down. The escalators rode us up to our designated floor. A black-robed man led the lawyers, one for each driver, all but mine paid for by the insurance companies, through a card-controlled door in the marble-lined area. Behind the shut doors, the lawyers met with the take-no-guff judge while Mum and I remained out in the hall.

My brain tried and failed to compute this concept of me not being privy or present to conversations about my future.

My lawyer remained the good cop; I the bad cop. There was still no way I was accepting the amount the insurance company had offered in November 2007. Just because I had to wait until late spring of 2008 didn't mean my future financial needs had suddenly collapsed to less than what the poorest person lived on. My lawyer would explain he couldn't settle because, well, I was the one driving this bus. He'd shrug and say, "Hey, it's not me. It's her. I'm being cooperative here. She's the one you have to convince." He'd get the sympathy vote. I liked it.

Seats slung together in groups hugged the wall between the escalators and the big shut door. Mum and I talked, our British chatty genes keeping us occupied, as we watched people riding the escalators on our right and occasionally exiting elevators to our left near the judge's door. My eyes rested on the clean lines of the architecture. My brain liked the minimalist feel. A vision in pink and blonde rose into view on the escalator. The insurance adjuster with no power had finally showed up. We watched her walk round and round the halls in her green stilettos looking for the lawyers representing the drivers her insurance company covered. Neither of us were inclined to help her. The enemy had chosen her employment. She disappeared down the escalator and came back up following a man who let her speak to the lawyer just inside that shut door. He disappeared again, and she went to sit on the other set of seats on the other side of the escalators.

Suddenly, male voices filtered through. The lawyers emerged for a twenty-minute recess. My lawyer led us to a door on the far left side into an empty hall to confer while the other lawyers and adjuster found their own private space. He told me the judge said right off the bat to not even try to say there was no injury. When one lawyer said that they couldn't tell the difference between original and new chapters in my book, the judge asked them if they were going to call themselves as witnesses. Mum always said she preferred my post-brain injury writing, but she wasn't with the judge to tell him that. And I wasn't sure how a sixteen-thousand-word chapter was the same as a two-thousand-word one. I tuned back in to my lawyer telling me what the judge thought my case was worth. I struggled to compute the abysmal poverty the judge thought I should live in. So low, a mouse couldn't subsist on it. Was I supposed to go on welfare after a year or two? Mum figured five. I used to be good at budgeting, but that good? Then my lawyer informed me of the new rule that ensures those of us injured through no fault of our own be financially penalized: deduct CPP Disability for all time plus a $100,000 deductible. *And people think $2,000 maximum deductible for house insurance is a high figure,* I groused to myself. My mother urged me to accept, said that she or my father would support me, and said that my brother said this was the best I could get. I felt like I was back in 1993 when I'd represented myself with my husband beside me at FSCO (Financial Services Commission of Ontario), against the wishes of my family who'd told me to take what the insurance company had offered. After we'd agreed on an amount, I'd discovered I needed an extra $5,000. When I told them I was going to ask for it, every single one of them were livid. But I did. And I got it. I wasn't about to listen to them now, even though I no longer had that kind of negotiating ability. Instead, I had my lawyer, though he was getting a bit heated at my obstinate no.

The twenty minutes ticked by. He had to get back. He said he didn't want me to be beat up on all sides and badgered into settling. As he returned to meet with the judge, we stayed in the hall as emotions swamped me. I called Lily on my cell. She was appalled and calmed me down.

We returned to the main hall, and I saw the insurance rep sitting at the end of our seats. I was mad. I was mad at her company, at the lawyers, at the system, at the government, at the idea that permeated society that innocents disabled in car crashes deserve the harshest of financial treatments.

"Don't sit down until I get back from the washroom," I told Mum. She nodded. Anger powering my steps when I returned, I walked firmly and rapidly to our seats and sat down four seats away from she who represented the two drivers who had suffered nothing for the great harm they had done me. While I had met with doctors and psychologists, spent hours and days filling in questionnaires, was tested and examined, the drivers went about their ordinary days. While my lifetime OHIP record was printed out for lawyers and clerks and insurance adjusters to scrutinize line by line, claim by claim, looking for an edge to deny my injury and while every note written by every doctor I had seen and was seeing, even the ones who had nothing to do with my injury, was passed around to lawyers and IMEs, the drivers who'd hurled me into this abyss didn't have any of their medical records revealed to a stranger determined to deny their reality and increase their suffering. While I battled to get the care I needed, the drivers didn't ever have to account for their behaviour toward me, except during their own one short legal discovery years earlier.

Anger vanished. My mind blanked from fatigue. I managed to half turn to my mother and talk. The beautifully coiffed insurance rep moved back to where she'd sat originally. I smiled within myself at my one tiny, petulant act of revenge, my one useless moment of power, where I forced the insurer to move. Mum said that the woman looked worried.

The huge door opened at 12:20 p.m., and the lawyers walked out.

We left without a settlement.

My lawyer and I discussed the next phase, the trial and its preparations.

Six days later, he called me up.

"Do you have a minute?"

"Um, yes." I pushed my oatmeal aside.

"We have an offer."

"Oh."

"The more I thought about it, the more I'm excited about it." I listened as he carefully went over his reasoning, and I thought, *He's figured out how to talk to me*. He gave me all the figures, the amount that I would receive in my pocket, what I would have to win at trial to receive the same amount, what the percentages were between court costs, lawyer fees, and expenses in order to figure out what I would have to win in order to receive what I believed I needed to live for forty years without having to depend on my parents. I felt calm as I wrote it all down.

He noted one piece of bad news. He explained to me that you can't hide anything in court and that my limited support would be revealed and used against me successfully. A trial was not a good idea.

And then he slid into lawyer speak, telling me why I had to, in my perception of his words, roll over, for they had all the power. I reacted. He yelled. I yelled louder. He stopped trying to yell over me. Even though he had more puff power from having health and good lungs, I had anger and eight years of being at the unrelenting stabby end of the insurance system the Ontario government had allowed to grow like some sort of malevolent virus. I eventually wound down. He apologized for yelling and assured me he preferred clients who think instead of just going with what he says. We said our good-byes amicably.

I sank my tired, hurting body at my desk. With paper and pencil, I went through the numbers. To go to trial, I'd have to win four times more than the offer at least. A financially bleak future waved hello.

On Wednesday, June 18, I TTC'd downtown to my lawyer's office under blue skies and fluffy white clouds. I rode the long elevator up. I walked through the double glass doors of his law office and told the receptionist I was there. He strode out through one of the side doors with his assistant. It was time for me to sign the paper.

He gave me the single sheet of paper after he said his prepared spiel. I saw the numbers at the bottom and flipped out. He explained. I calmed.

He said, "This is the part where you say thank you," appending his first name.

I smiled and repeated it. Then I tried to read the entire single sheet because this was my future. Yet my brain couldn't care less. It fought my efforts to read; my lawyer knew my struggle and without me asking him like I had to with so many others, guided me through each paragraph.

A single sheet of paper.

It signalled the end of eight and a half years of fighting for justice.

I took the pen my lawyer handed me. I hesitated. I signed, my energy flowing out with the ink onto the paper. I flopped back in my chair, the pen falling from my aching fingers. I watched my lawyer as he finished the administrivia of this momentous event.

I left.

I joined Twitter.

I didn't understand it, but a shadow of my old nerdy self had wanted to join this nascent community for a while as myself, not some anonymous dude. However many months it took me to understand this world of tweets and strangers all over the world, I was going to do it as myself. And I wanted to practice my short-form writing. But I couldn't join until the insurance company was no longer scrutinizing my every word to use against me.

The effort to join drained the last of my energy.

I sat down on my couch.

I flopped over on my couch.

I lay down on my couch and stared at the wall.
For months.

Chapter 17

The Promise of Recovery

My mother dragged me to a new GP on August 4, 2009. To his delight, I handed him my list of problems, fearing memory failure. He zipped through it. The first thing he did was set me up with his fitness trainer. I phoned the trainer and explained my brain injury to him, my high heart rate and yo-yoing blood pressure, my weight and water retention, and my inability to walk more than five minutes before fatigue grabbed hold of my legs, sending my right leg into deep ache and my body into a battle with my mind to keep going.

He said, "I've seen this with the athletes I train who've had a brain injury."

Really? "I'm so tired of my weight and being unable to walk much. And I can't sleep at night." I told him about having to sleep with my head elevated and the covers off my chest and neck.

He was horrified. "We have to get you sleeping flat. You can't sleep like that."

I hadn't heard those words before. I'd like to have slept flat too, but no one else seemed fussed about how I slept. How novel.

He asked about my exercise.

"I do weights, yoga, and I row. I can't row very long. Since my injury, I've gotten up to six minutes."

"Stop the rowing."

What? "Stop it?"

"Yes, you must do less exercise."

"Less?"

He explained how my injured brain couldn't regulate my heart and I needed to not do strenuous kinds of exercise like rowing. The weights were good, but I had to dial them back from thirty minutes.

What? I heard Dad's voice in my head, "You must exercise thirty minutes at least a day."

"Let's try ten minutes three times a week."

"Ten?"

He explained. Weights only. No rowing. Three times a week.

My mind boggled. He explained again, "Your brain injury changed your exercise tolerance."

I hung up. I fell back against the back of the couch. No more self-talking through the reps. No more pep talking my way as my muscles lost their energy. No more relying on willpower. I began my new, shorter regimen. I kept the most essential free weight lifts.

It was so easy! I felt so much better! I had energy!

And one night, I carefully lowered the head of my bed a little. Would I be OK?

I was!

Heat still raged within me, but less water pooled in my head by morning.

He had me experiment with exercise times. Eight minutes three times a week was not enough to provide the beneficial energy of exercise. Twelve minutes three times a week knackered me, and I had to raise the head of my bed again.

"Stick to ten minutes three times a week," he instructed me. "And no rowing!" He emphasized that last.

Whew.

I heard again about an ABI Network funded by OHIP and was given an enormous application form to apply for acquired brain injury services. Oh-oh. Me and forms were permanent enemies since my injury. Who would help me fill them out?

My GP and Mum.

At the same time, my GP sent me for a battery of blood tests including fasting glucose. He didn't like the numbers, so he sent me for a glucose challenge test.[26] After I'd fasted fourteen hours, my mother kept me company in the lab as I had my blood taken then chugged a 75 mg bottle of the most-foul-tasting fake-sweet OJ-like liquid within a set number of minutes. I didn't usually drink anything quickly, except maybe ice water on a hot day after not drinking anything for hours.

But I did it.

We waited an hour for my blood to be taken again. And again at two hours.

"You have diabetes," my GP informed me when I saw him next.

I stared. He explained the numbers. I understood glucose. I wasn't familiar with A1C. He explained the latter was an indicator of my blood glucose over time and the marker of my real state.

"It was not very high," he said, not like some numbers he sees, but I had to drop it.

Tears suddenly appeared. I couldn't deal with a new problem. I was just starting to have showers that ended with warm water. I was just starting to sleep flat again. How could I have diabetes, too? I was overweight but not that much. I knew I had the famine gene that leads to Type 2 diabetes, but I had been so careful with my diet.

That was before my brain injury, a voice whispered in my head. Before I'd lost energy to cook and look after myself.

"You can reverse this," he said.

I don't want to deal with this! I cried inside my head as my eyes cried outside. The weight crushed me.

He explained I could take a drug or I could change my diet. He suggested I try the latter. He told me to get the low GI diet book. All I had to do was follow it.

---

[26] http://www.webmd.com/diabetes/gestational-diabetes-guide/oral-glucose-tolerance-test#1

Easier said than done with a brain demanding naps after microwaving and eating oatmeal.

"Get the book," he repeated. I'd lose the weight and the diabetes.

I walked and walked. I wasn't supposed to walk that far. But I knew of a bookstore I liked. I didn't have extra TTC tokens to spend on a stop at the bookstore on the way home. I'd deal with the fallout later.

I bought *The GI Diet Menopause Clinic* by Rick Gallop. It was the only copy of the book they had. I wasn't in menopause, but I knew brain injury meant either I did something immediately or not at all or at best, months later, when decision making met a spurt of initiation. Best to go with the impulse that was driving me for these few minutes. The diet principles would be the same. And anyway, I was aging toward that time.

I carried the heavy book home and dropped it on my kitchen table. I rang my kin. The call did not go well.

"Diabetes will kill you. If you don't start exercising and eating right, you'll die!"

I looked in the mirror. *Trust your GP. He's given you the diet. You got this. You're not going to die.*

I heaved the 347-page tome open and tried to read it.

I frowned. I recognized some of it. Memories threaded their way out of their isolated cells around damaged neurons and into my conscious mind. This was the way I used to eat, the way I cooked our meals every day. Before my brain injury.

Somehow, I had lost my way.

My lips pursed. Yeah, fatigue, confusion, weariness, sore shoulder, screaming migraines after chopping onions and celery and tomatoes, and exhaustion from putting a pot on the stove and dumping in a can of plum tomatoes left no brain space to remember how to eat this way.

I had to start all over.

Another thing to relearn and scrabble for energy to do. Along with washing clothes, cleaning the kitchen, writing, managing the garbage, reading, leaving a voice mail without panicking at what I was supposed to say and hanging up instead, decluttering my place regularly to keep my brain from overloading, organizing myself, holding phone conversations, and meeting people for coffee and not sitting there wooden.

I began.

I returned for more blood tests. I waited with trepidation for the results. My GP grinned as he entered the exam room.

"Your numbers are down," he said. "You know how many go on the diet?" he asked me rhetorically. I shook my head. "Five percent." I was one of the five percent, and he was ecstatic because my blood glucose was dropping into the normal range.

Meanwhile, I began to hear back from the ABI Network. I received letters and more forms. My brain spun, trying to distinguish between care coordinator and case management. They sounded the same to me. And why were they split up between organizations? Some of the letters asked me to apply for programs where I could spend the day making crafts and learning how to cook. It slowly dawned on me that they thought treating my brain injury was all about keeping me occupied, to make me feel OK that my life was shit. It wasn't about actually treating the psychological harm and the neurological damage so that I could earn an income and live in society.

I met the CCAC care coordinator at their offices for my assessment. The young woman, petite and upbeat, led me into a large, sunny room where two other women awaited us: her co-worker and a psychologist wearing dark, fashionable frames. I felt like I was in chains, being led into another insurance mediation, facing another firing squad. Would I ever recover from the insurance? The psychologist led the questions asking about my family. I felt detached, in neutral territory.

She moved on to emotions.

"I'm happy," I said. That Thursday before my car crash whooshed into my memory, that Thursday I laughed with my girlfriend on the phone, laughed freely with joy over following my dream, finally writing *Lifeliner*. I stopped talking. My eyes leaked. I didn't know how to stop the tears. I quirked my lips and said, "Emotions do their own thing, so there you go."

The psychologist grabbed her purse and fished a Kleenex out for me. Uncaring of possible cold germs, I took it gratefully and mopped my eyes and blew my nose.

"I used to laugh," I said, feeling no embarrassment. And then, all of a sudden, my eyes dried up, and my heart shifted into neutral. The questions continued. As my energy began to flag after an hour, I quipped: "I push too hard. It's a bad habit, I know." They laughed. Even though my brain couldn't create laughter easily or at all, I liked making others laugh. Toward the end, I told them my insurer had never assigned me a case manager and I hadn't yet heard from Cota about case management. Surprise rendered them speechless for a moment. And then my care coordinator said she would call me in a couple of days. I nodded, but I didn't really comprehend this Byzantine system of community care.

I staggered home.

A week later, the care coordinator visited me in my home because a brain injury diagnosis required two assessments. I couldn't fathom the fatigue from having to endure two because of the kind of diagnosis that sucks up all your energy. The irony didn't escape me. By the end of the first week of November, I had met the Cota intake worker for their assessment in my home, too.

And then just like that I'd qualified for a social worker, a physiotherapist, a psychologist, and an occupational therapist from CCAC and a case manager from Cota, beginning the second week of November. I jumped up and down inside my head. My lips sketched a smile on the outside.

Recovery was possible.

To read my diabetes adventures in full, go to http://wp.me/Pf8xE-16K.

Chapter 18

NaNoWriMo 2009

My mental experience and activity from the marvel of community care moved me forward. Health care came to me! After lying in bed for twelve hours while sleep stuck its tongue out at me, letting me have three, maybe five hours of rest, I could snatch an extra two since I didn't have to get up so early. Time dancing a too-early now too-late jig with my brain wouldn't make me late. No more exhausting TTC. Help came to me.

A church friend encouraged me to write with the world in November. On November 28, 2009, I thought, only two more days, two more sleeps, two more chapters until the end of 2009's National Novel Writing Month, or NaNoWriMo. I'd had so much fun, writing alone yet in a group of hundreds of thousands that I was sad to see it end. I'd achieved the impossible, seventy thousand words.

I sat back and reflected. NaNoWriMo had expanded my ability to write in terms of time and number of words. When I last wrote a book, I was able to write two thousand words in a coherent narrative, keeping it all in my head so I didn't ramble and forget what the beginning was all about at the end. I hadn't kept track of my word count since then. But I had sensed that I could write for an hour straight. After NaNoWriMo 2009, I knew I could for day after day for thirty days, though it got a tad unpleasant, physically. But fellow Wrimos encouraged, headquarters pep talks spurred me on, and the knowledge of all eyes on me kept me going. My brain finally decided it didn't need to consume quite so much energy writing for an hour. Also, after I had written fifty thousand words, I cut my writing time down to forty-five minutes most days. One day, I went nuts and wrote one hour and forty-five minutes with only a couple of brief breaks. I didn't do much the rest of the day, but even being able to write a blog post after doing that was quite something. My writing neurons had been lit and were firing brightly again. Before the injury, my mind had never shut up. I could only go to sleep by channelling my thoughts, ideas, and imagination into stories that would relax me. After the injury, my mind was the blank cave where nary a thought tread. Well, maybe a few briefly and only with external stimulation. My imagination had hid and only revealed itself on the page when I wrote. But fiction had resisted creation for nine years. I wrote my first novel's outline before November, but would I be able to make stuff up when it came to the details? NaNoWriMo 2009 taught me I could again!

Chapter 19

I Clicked Publish

A woman called. "I'm your social worker."

Oh wow! It's happening!

She arrived days later. I opened my door in the late winter of 2009 and let her in. She followed me to my kitchen, and we sat down.

She had my file. She had the notes from the care coordinator. But she still asked me a few questions. I began monosyllabically as my brain scanned her to learn her expressions and watched her lips to be able to understand her speech. But slowly, slowly, my brain let go of resources to perceive and understand and lent some to speaking. The following week in our second hour, my mouth ran away.

Nine years of pent-up grief began to spill out.

She told me about narrative therapy, how we are multiple selves and need to express those. She said, "It may be hard to find counselling. You need to write that brain injury narrative."

I wasn't sure about that. Private matters stayed private in my culture. I'd had to adjust to insurance claims ripping away my privacy and distorting my health. It had taken me almost a year to free myself from the prison of being legally stalked, of feeling eyes following me, and of hidden faces possibly eavesdropping on my phone calls, sniffing through my garbage.

My social worker insisted that it would be good for me. "Write about your brain injury on your blog. You've been kept silent for over nine years. The more you write that narrative, the more will be pulled out," she explained. "It's time to speak."

She gave me the kicker. CCAC would pay for only three visits from her. I was starting to realize OHIP had cut funding so much to community care that I couldn't get the psychologist for counselling I'd qualified for. So we had to make these visits count since I had many practical needs I needed her help with. I wouldn't be able to talk out my grief in only three sessions.

Besides which, I'd thrown off the veil of anonymity on my blog because I wanted to be heard. I wanted to be allowed to be me. It was too bad most of the male bloggers who'd followed me instantly stopped speaking to me when they learnt I wasn't male after all. But I was used to that in my pre-injury life. Even people who'd known my first name but hadn't met me in person assumed I was male because, I guess, women weren't seen as being good at the things I'd done, like statistical surveys.

Well, one thing I knew, no one I knew in real life would be reading my blog.

I sat down at my computer. With the social worker's encouraging words in my head, I started a new blog post on the website I'd set up for *Lifeliner*. Could I do this? I really wanted to. I stared at the screen. The pressure inside me demanded release. But this went against my entire upbringing.

I didn't have to spill all.

I could decide what to write and what to keep private.

My fingers hesitated over the keyboard.

Suddenly, words appeared on the screen as I wrote and wrote, the volume of grief and nine years of needing to be heard, needing to be me, whoever me was, pushing my fingers faster and faster, drowning the physical pain in my hands and the rising fatigue. Writing was my ticket to wellness. If it was in the public sphere, the only sphere that would listen for as long as I needed to "talk," then so be it.

Maybe I could help others, as the social worker had said and Glen had long, long ago. Well, only three years earlier. But in brain injury time when a day is like a year, three years is another life.

I finished.

I'd learnt to let things lie before I made a final decision.

I went for a nap.

I left my computer on. It hummed while it waited minutes, hours.

I ate. I wasn't sure. Did I really want to post this?

I went back to my computer. I rewrote.

Maybe I shouldn't do this.

I did feel better.

But this was private.

Maybe it would help another person. All this hell I'd been through, was it only for my edification? It hadn't been for my benefit, that's for sure. The blessing of studying the *Book of Job* about a good man bad things happened to and being blamed for it with my pastor, the fun of co-leading my church's Bible study group earlier in the year, and the challenge of teaching them about Job had faded. I was left again with the detritus of my life all around me, not knowing how to sweep up the fragments and chuck them in the rubbish, not knowing how to build new furnishings or unpack new books of this life I'd been thrown into against my will.

I wasn't getting a psychologist. My only other option was to find a psychiatrist familiar with brain injury because the government covered only psychiatrists because they were physicians. If I had a steady income and enough of an income...

I didn't.

What to do?

I clicked Publish.

Stall Learnings

Chapter P

Community Services

Community care should be about caring for the whole person to harness the brain's function to change its neural networks in response to mental and physical experience and activity within a web of relationships. Community care is about the professional web of relationships that encourages mental experience and activity to restore and strengthen neural networks and stop deterioration. The professional web of relationships holds the person with brain injury up as their brain changes, they deal with their grief and with an emerging new identity, and create a new life or perhaps restore their old one but in a different way. Community care should be about providing services within the home that the person with brain injury needs, for as long as they need it. It encompasses occupational therapy, physiotherapy, social work, behavioural therapy, psychologist, homecare, and medical care. It may include telemedicine to consult with physicians or participate in groups that are located in a different city or province or when the person cannot get out to their appointment. A person should not be denied healthcare and the web of relationships because they can't travel within their own city.

This web where healthy brains support injured brains helps the person keep at the stamina-challenging recovery work.

Since standard brain injury "treatment" is placebo and luck and not started immediately, too many people with brain injury lose their family and friends because our society has lost its humanity, dumping people with brain issues in the "toxic" category, making it OK to isolate them away from the healthy and happy. And so there needs to be a new way of thinking about professional relationships. They should be true relationships, not one-way, without burning out the healthcare professionals or making the person with brain injury feel like they belong nowhere. And religious leaders need to teach their flock about reaching out to the rejected and to facilitate connections so that the healthy contact and befriend the brain injured. We need to re-imagine therapy and community care so that it substitutes socially and practically for the broken web of social relationships until such time as the person can create a new web on their own years down the road.

For further reading, go to http://wp.me/Pf8xE-16w.

Hope

"What are gamma brainwaves?"
I asked.
She answered.
Because she wanted to help.

Chapter 20

Cruelty with Intent

She'd called me Sharon and showed up early. My rigid brain sent alarm signals, unable to adapt to her surprise early arrival. Angry tension stiffened my body. The CCAC OT sat across from me at my kitchen table, her fawn coat belted against me and my home as she explained how I could use a pencil to write notes about the TV show I was watching so that I could remember the characters, oblivious to how my multitasking-resistant brain couldn't take notes and watch a show at the same time. How would I search jagged charcoal scribbles anyway while a show played?

I vented like a spewing firehose to friends, Mum, and Twitter.

Three days later my care coordinator called me back. Her kind voice detonated me. I yelled while she listened, probably with her phone a few feet from her assaulted ear, about being disrespected, about how normal people treat other normal people by taking off their coats when entering their homes, about how I needed help with my scheduling, with getting things done, and how was she going to do that when she didn't understand computers, iPod Touches, or electronic calendars? And what was up with this paper and pencil method? Did that seriously work for anyone?

When my brain injury anger hiccupped to a stop, she soothed me. She didn't understand why the OT had kept her coat on. She knew a behavioural therapist who teaches clients technological stuff and would get her to see me. Even better, CCAC would fund an OT for only three sessions but still funded behavioural therapists indefinitely for brain injury. The whirling waters in my brain stilled.

A month later, on a zero-degree January day with barely any snow on the ground, a petite, capable woman walked into my home, asked me about removing her boots, liked that I had clean slippers for guests, picked her pair, removed her coat, and explained she wasn't an OT. Elizabeth followed me into my kitchen, sat down at the table, and got down to business. No more stupid assessment questions. I liked her already.

Elizabeth instructed me to open my alarm settings in my calendar app and play them. I obeyed. When the claxon shot out of my iPod Touch like a fire engine heading for a ten-alarm explosion, she pointed. "Choose that one." I did. It would be hard for my whipped, initiation-free, unmotivated brain to ignore it. She knew schedules and computers. The first OT ever! No, not an OT, a BT. She gave me homework and said that I had her for as long as I needed her to regain my functionality. I really liked her. Relief flooded me. No more staring at my calendar until finally my brain burped up some vague idea of what I was supposed to be doing. Elizabeth would help me turn my first novel into a published book, a novel my beta readers were already inspiring me to make better. I couldn't get over it. She knew scheduling and computers! As I marvelled over this, she told me she'd see me weekly and watched me as I entered my next appointment with her in my calendar.

Elizabeth was awesome. I felt safe with her.

And so when a few months later, Imeda stripped me one, I turned to her for advice. It all began because I'd made a throwaway comment on ADD to Freny. I'd studied it in university, developed a method to treat it for my undergraduate thesis, had attended a lecture with Glenda after my brain injury about girls and ADD, and learnt tons about ADD during my treatments with the ADD Centre and from people sharing their experiences with it on Twitter. Freny, showing her adolescence, challenged me. I took her up on it, remembering the kind of debates I got into at her age, the noisy arguments and counterarguments over the dinner table, the adults pulling no punches. She got upset unbeknownst to me. I was blissfully writing my first screenplay in the month of Script Frenzy with Elizabeth organizing me.

And then an email thudded into my inbox from Imeda.

On the last day of Script Frenzy.

Words popped out of his email to me like hard kernels resisting the reality of the scalding pot bottom. What I'd said to Freny really amounted to bullying. Apparently asking her to pick up a piece of litter I'd seen her drop was cause for concern. He instructed me to read my emails to her. He thought they all recognized I was drawing upon out-of-date information on ADD and typical of me to draw on experiences I had had thirty years ago as proof of the truth of something that was happening today. He talked about how he looked for opportunities to include me in events, but I chose not to accept him, put up my injury as the root of all of his insults against me, which reflected my desire to make excuses. He suggested that I marched ahead to the concept I'm perfect except for my traumatic injury; I had to get over my fear of gaining insight into my shortcomings and ignorance; I had to give up trying to control everything; and I had to learn to grow.

He stated bluntly that he preferred to work on the relationship.

My heart didn't pound like it usually did. My face didn't flush nor my throat burn. Instead his words hypnotized me. I stopped writing and reading. I sat like a lump. I stared at the screen.

A thought flickered. Would the peer-mentor that the Brain Injury Society of Toronto (BIST) had set me up with a few months earlier call for our weekly conversation about life with brain injury?

She did.

She was sick but got out of bed because she didn't want to be one more person to let me down. Gratefulness drowned me. She told me if an adolescent thought I was truly bullying her, she would stop talking to me. Instead, she was making a conscious effort to chat with me over cyberspace. I read her my email. She said that I was bang on about groups after brain injury. She told me in her best courtroom voice to forget him. Or, she challenged me, "See if he's serious by inviting him to a quiet place you can tolerate."

I objected. But the moment we hung up, I typed to my niece, apologizing, saying I never intended to traumatize her. She replied that sometimes things happen to upset her. She vented about really liking it if we didn't bring her into any grudges I and Imeda had against each other. I'd tried very hard not to do so because she was right. This wasn't her war.

Mum later said it was a pity we couldn't meet for coffee as that is where relationships started. So, exerting my will over my want, I invited him. He'd let me know when he was next in town, but first, he instructed, I had to get on with his wife before he would consider a relationship with me.

Monday broke. I told Elizabeth about my craptastic weekend. She asked me what I was supposed to be a bully for. I explained. She again asked me for examples. I had no further clue. As her questions' message slowly sank in, she hustled out to her car to get an Awareness Wheel. My mind whirled looking at the faint photocopy of a five-bladed fan with "Issue" written in the centre and "Sending a Clear and Complete Message" at the top. She explained that it was designed to strip away emotion and focus on the message. Instead of celebrating finishing my first play during Script Frenzy, we spent the session discussing my relationships, my thoughts, feelings, wants—that one stumped me as I no longer knew what I wanted from Imeda or anyone really—while she wrote in pencil all over the wheel. She suggested that Imeda and I play catch up only. She advised me to say that when our communication skills improved we would talk then. She was energized by this coffee date; I was skeptical.

Not being masochistic enough, with birthday season approaching, I emailed all to try again explaining why I couldn't handle parties.

Vashti was the only one to write back. She felt she could give me enough respect to read what I'd asked to be read. Lulled, I read her next words. I learnt that in her view I was a person who didn't give a damn about her, who wrote well, who chose carefully what I was willing to do and not do. Choice was a large part of my schedule, which as an adult she wouldn't hold against me, but the children had a much harder time with my decision. And how I went on and on about how no one understood me, on how I was the only one to accommodate my injury, yet I didn't acknowledge what she had done for me. She decided not to list all those things nor my insults she'd overlooked as they were too numerous. My neurons threw up memories about how these accommodations had cost me energy, my requests for one-on-one ignored. I couldn't stop reading, about how I'd made her kids feel bad, about how they'd invited me over to include me, and how my reasons not to visit were not held against me. I wondered why the kids couldn't visit me like I used to visit my aunts in England or my grandparents across town. She told me that once I had done something to upset someone, I should find out why they are upset, respond, and try to make amends. I was a Christian who didn't practice that philosophy. As my heart banged into my ribs, I kept reading the unending email. I read and reread about how when my mother wanted to do something with Vashti's kids but I needed her for some reason, Vashti made it easy for her to walk away from the conflict and never gave her guilt. She hated my cruelty for ignoring my mother running around for me in my blog.

A leaden bell tolled in my ventricles. Every week I couldn't wait to see Mum. I shoved through my sluggish neurons to thank her, ashamed I couldn't pay for lunch; yet, I feared the newest message she'd have been persuaded to deliver. I read on.

"What is it you want?" she wrote.

I wanted acceptance and understanding.

Vashti wanted me to consider their needs. If I didn't respect her position in her family and didn't like her protecting her family, then I was to walk away.

I flurried into distraction. I logged in to Smashwords to review my books. I strolled through Flickr, looking for photo after photo I could comment on, anything not to think, not to feel this pounding under my ribs, the turbulent volcano of grief.

Five days later, my spiritual mentor said, "Words, words. Don't allow yourself to be diminished. You are good stuff, the beloved of God." She guided me to a wise and brief reply.

Imeda didn't call when he was next in town.

I plunged into my writing.

Chapter 21

Neurodoc

I left the pituitary endocrinologist's office finished with evidence-based medicine. She'd noticed the water bloating my features and taught me about cortisol testing, but she didn't know much about the hypothalamus, that tiny brain part that controls the pituitary. The best she could offer was monitoring. Monitoring! Screw it! I'll fix myself!

Over the next two months, I tugged old knowledge out of isolated memory banks and clung to it long enough to read up about the hypothalamus, over and over. I thought about my AVE and, at the end of July, began an email conversation with Dave Siever at Mind Alive about closed head injury, the hypothalamus, cranioelectrical stimulation (CES), and AVE. My internal magma machine reminded me to push and push my brain to read, to remember, to understand, to think, and to create a regimen with my AVE and CES devices that would do for me what the doctors refused to do: get my heat down and water out of my face once and for all. By middle of August, I had Mind Alive's CES device. Three days later, I began working on what would become my hypothalamus fix (see Chapter Q). Two months later, I began my blog postings on it.

Meanwhile, I kept looking for a psychiatrist.

"I'm not taking new patients."

That was the last one on the short list Elizabeth had given me. She was the only person in my life to even find names of psychiatrists for me to call.

Months passed. A new year dawned. My eleventh anniversary. My soul cried out to express my anguish. I tweeted about it.

Two men tweeted back. They empathized and cheered me up. One raved about my blog and forwarded it to his doctor for its ADD value.

"Perceptive," he said.

Nine days later, I woke up with chilblain pain in my fingertips with matching pain on the soles of my feet. My right palm and ball of my foot were an agony of cold. The next day, heat, hurt, and itchiness plagued my palms, knuckles, some fingertips, bottoms of feet, and elbows and crawled from the base of my head down to my upper back. The next day, I returned to sleeping with my neck elevated off my pillow and sheets shoved below my shoulders. In the morning, the CES at Sleep setting cooled down my pulsing heat. Later that night, I stared at the back of my hands. I swore they were tanned. I stuck my head under the cold-water tap. Then showered again, cold spray cleaning off the gummy heat. I spread on a new layer of melaleuca cream. I began to obsess with taking my temperature: 36.3, 36.8, 38.3, 37, 38. When Elizabeth arrived for her regular appointment with me, she couldn't believe I was wearing only a tank top as the wind blew -19°C around my home under a sharp blue sky.

Obeying my spiritual mentor's instructions, I called my GP.

My GP examined the large caramelized half moon on my upper back and the patches of peeling, darkened skin all over me. He referred me urgently to a dermatologist. The next day, the Indian-trained specialist examined my skin. His residents examined my skin. With his iPhone, the resident photographed a puzzling patch for their teaching rounds. I texted Mum to calm myself before they extracted two tiny plugs of skin out of my back. Two tiny scars to add to my collection. At least I couldn't see them. I sighed.

Ten days later, I distracted myself by joining Goodreads, a website for readers that I hoped would push my Go button to choose a book and read a book month after month since I had no one to do that for me. But the excitement and hope of getting my reading back washed away when the specialist told me that Monday that the biopsies revealed nothing. He explained capillaries around fingernails should be like loops. Mine were engorged as in inflammation. I noticed my big toe was blue. At least, Mum was with me this time while the dreadful news weighed me down. No diagnosis, no help. He gave me a steroid cream for my hands. I was wearing gloves by this time to protect them and others from the sight of my palms peeling like red sedimentary shale.

After we finished talking skin, he asked, "You're not doing well, are you?"

I shook my head mutely.

"Do you need help?"

"Yes, but I cannot find a psychiatrist." I began to tell this perceptive skin doctor about my futile search.

He listened. He wasn't sure which psychiatrist would be best. I didn't know, either. I gave him two names Elizabeth had given me and silently asked God to choose.

He said, "I know the secretary at a clinic. I will speak to her."

Secretaries, the gateway to the doctor's appointment calendar.

Two months later, I discontinued the atenolol when I'd learnt blue toes were a "side effect," cheering myself up by reminding myself this time I had options, the AVE and CES gizmos I hadn't had back in 2007, and my hypothalamus fix was working. My GP sent me for heart tests to reassure himself no more atenolol was OK. My neural networks sucked up the increase in energy and directed skin cells to knit the shredded layers together until my skin was its beautiful old self.

I got an appointment with a neuropsychiatrist. On a cool, sunny June morning, he sat at one end of an office with bare desks and two chairs, looking upon me with his kind eyes. I perched at the other end with a tiny tissue box at my elbow. I began with my name and age, the date of my car crash, and the list of medications and diagnoses. The usual.

"Tell me about the accident."

I did. And soon I was yanking rough squares of tissue out of their box and spilling words and sentences.

At the end of forty-five minutes, he said, "I'll take you on."

I couldn't believe it. I had a neuropsychiatrist? Apparently, there was nothing more to discuss because he was opening the door and ushering me out. I had no idea where I was or in which direction to go. I panted to keep up with him. He pointed me to his secretary and told me to make appointments for a formal assessment. Then he would see my biweekly starting in the fall. I was hoping for monthly. Too infrequent, I guess.

Elizabeth cheered with me and said her other clients really liked him. I was in good hands. We then got down to the business of my priorities. A third novel was unfolding in my mind. A forty-year-old woman, an administrative assistant, her birthday. Boys, privileged, with nothing better to do than torture people in other times. But what year were they from? I had to figure out time travel. I had to relearn all that I used to know about physics and time and space.

My Twitter and Flickr friends helped me. They sent me links to documents and suggested books to read. I laboriously ploughed through the pages, writing notes in an app on my iPad, resisting the urge to skim, clutching on to any new information long enough to understand and to put together my ideas. My character, my emerging novel sang to my soul. But the weight of eleven years of brain injury, of dying relationships and lost identity, and my inability to compute that I had a neuropsychiatrist crushed me. My grief was swallowing me whole. I emailed the two left who sporadically emailed or called. I needed to be involved in their lives and them in mine; I needed friendship. One answered. We began fairly regular correspondence over the vast distance that separated us.

In the fall of 2011, I walked into my neuropsychiatrist's office with its stuffed bookcases and desk covered in notepads and Post-its and computer, a full trash bin underneath, and a large window with a view of the sky. A tiny box of tissues hung out behind the monitor. It moved from hiding place to hiding place each time I went, defying my neurodoc to find it. But that first time, I didn't need it.

He said, leaning forward and smiling, "I will see you for as long as you want."

Oh.

He asked, "What's on your mind today?"

I struggled to remember my goal. It had been on my mind since my social worker at TRI, ten years earlier, had told me what I needed to do before she discharged me. Since then, no one, no psychologist, no doctor, no therapist had been able to help with my goal though they all agreed it was paramount.

Maybe this man could help me disengage from my kin.

He nodded then suggested instead, "Why don't we refocus on the family?"

Uh. "I will need to see you weekly," I shot back, thinking of the emotional tsunami that would hit my decks under his plan.

"OK," he smiled.

I made a beeline to a local café afterwards. I sagged in a chair as I chewed a cookie.

Chapter 22

The Dream Was Within Reach

"Did you get me the appointments yet?" I asked right after Christmas 2011. I'd decided 2012 was my medical year, and I didn't want to dally treating my brain again.

"Not yet," my neurodoc said with a flourish of his hand. He led me to his secretary to get me into the sleep specialist for March. The next time I saw him, I confronted him over the interminable wait for the brain injury expert. He assured me that he'd get me in. When?

He first met with Mum and me mid-February 2012. The messaging from kin and kith through her had already stopped; still, I was nervous.

He relaxed in his chair, hands loosely clasped, an unthreatening persona, and asked her, "What are your thoughts about brain injury and what you see in Shireen?"

Mum replied with her thoughts about driving me in her car then segued to my reduced decisiveness and how my writing had totally changed.

He isn't zoning out like he does with me, I grumbled to myself.

He asked her in his gracious manner, "Does she exaggerate her symptoms?"

"No," Mum was positive in her reply.

I watched them in profile as they edged toward the idea of him facilitating communication between various kin and me and who to begin with.

My entire body began screaming, *No, I don't want to talk to my brother first! It should be my sister first! That'll succeed. I'm sure of it!*

"Without me," I managed to utter. They turned their heads to look at me.

Yes, I'm still here, I thought. My neurodoc's face registered that the schism was more severe than he'd thought. I couldn't say anything more. I was lucky if my brain managed to blurt out a few words while labouring to listen, absorb, process, comprehend, and think as they spoke.

Tick. Tick. Tick.

Two weeks later, I sat across from the sleep specialist as he said, "I know what your problem is."

"Oh?"

"You have physician fatigue."

I laughed. For ten years, I'd had it.

He then asked me about my sleep, my fatigue, and my pain. I didn't want to talk about pain. If I didn't think about pain, then pain left me alone. Fatigue unfortunately did not.

I said, "I don't have much pain."

"Stand up," he said.

"OK," I replied hesitantly as I stood up, puzzled.

He bent my right arm and pressed on the fibromyalgia point of my right elbow. Instant pain shot in deep, lifted my brain out of my head, and sent every neuron screaming.

"You have severe pain," he informed me.

I guess I do.

He prescribed a sleep study for the following week and told me of a drug trial he was doing with a unique structure that began with everyone being on experimental controlled-release pregabalin for eight weeks. He wanted me in it. An hour later, in a windowless room, his research associate handed me a huge consent form to read and sign. The last time I'd seen a consent form, it was a page or two. This one was...my brain refused to read it.

Outright balked.

I asked her what was in it. She gave me the gist. Hungry for lunch and grossed out at the pages of side effects, I flipped through and initialled page after page as my eyes against my will picked up words like "suicide," "asthma," "GI." After I made myself read side-eyed the most common side effects as if they were a rotting body, I signed. She vacuum-tubed blood from me, stuck on ECG leads then whipped them off when done, suddenly strapped on a watch that wasn't a watch as I was trying to put on my coat, and gave me an unmarked bottle of pills with instructions. I hurried out to meet my parents. Mum and Dad were delighted with the turn in my fortunes.

The remarkable part of my fifth sleep study in twenty years was how quiet it was. Although as usual, it was the men and me, no huge man vibrated the air, doors, walls, and floor violently with his snores. One of my sleep study mates in his silk zebra-striped pyjamas wandering back and forth, making calls, was interesting. We were given our bedtimes. While I waited, I filled in the questionnaires—so many questionnaires to fill in the land of medicine—and changed into pyjamas and robe in the bathroom where there was no camera. The camera wouldn't be turned on until I was in bed, but still.

The technician and I chatted as he measured me, wrapped belts around my chest and abdomen to track their movements, strapped tubing with nasal prongs around my face and hooked them over my ears to record my breathing pressure and temperature, and to read my brainwaves finally glued electrodes on my head and forehead with cement-like paste so that any tossing and turning wouldn't pull them off. I was glad the ECG electrodes went on my back not my chest like for the men. Modesty was already in short supply. He glued more electrodes onto my legs. And then he gathered up all the wires, plugged them into a box, and hung the whole thing over my neck. When it was time for bed, I removed the box and wires from around my neck, and he plugged the box into equipment next to the bed. I sacrificed my left forefinger to an O2 saturation monitor that was clipped and tightly taped on. Somehow, I was supposed to sleep.

Unbelievably, I was allowed to sleep in. Naturally, I woke up at 6:00 a.m. I cabbed it home to shower. The only time I wished I was bald. I had a routine I'd developed to get the cement-like electrode paste out of my hair. I had ensured my hot water tank was full and ready so that I'd have hot water to melt the paste, otherwise it would take much longer to remove. My first instinct was to massage in a large blob of shampoo, but I'd learnt not to bother. Instead, I grabbed a big bar of soap, and, while standing underneath the hot, running water, pushed the bar against the paste, like one pushes air bubbles out of wallpaper or out of a screen protector. After one blob of paste came out, I moved on to the next. Sometimes I tired pushing the same blob and moved on to another one then returned to the previous one. The paste at the back was harder to remove because it was buried in more hair. Once I thought all the paste was out (it wasn't), I massaged in a palm-full of shampoo and combed it through, tugging till paste bits flew off. I rinsed with hot water. Repeated with conditioner, this time using a fine-tooth comb. Rinsed with hot water. At last, I could commence with my usual shower routine. I soothed my scalp with cool water and swayed as I stood, pushing myself to finish.

Meanwhile, I swallowed a pill daily, dialled a phone number, answered automated questions with the keypad, and filled in a paper diary. Weekly, Mum dropped me off at the research lab to return the pill bottle and any pills left, fill in questionnaires, and receive a new bottle of anonymous pills. Nothing happened. And then as April sprung to life...

The world opened up.

"You've lost weight," my sleep specialist noted with happy surprise.

"Yes! I can walk for twenty minutes now!"

All those years of people telling me I should walk for my health, as if my brain injury hadn't stripped the automaticity from my walking, as if fatigue was no biggie, as if I was making excuses, now I could! My hip muscles began to ache more from overuse, but it was worth it.

They upped the dosage regularly. I took more Gaviscon for my poor stomach, and I upped my activity level, always feeling my accustomed level of fatigue. It didn't occur to me to keep at my same activity level and thus lessen my fatigue. I had been held back for so long by my injury, by my fatigue, by my pain that I felt like a racehorse let out of the gate. I baked cookies, puff pastries, palmiers, mushroom vol au vent, pavlova—all like I had done before my brain injury. I didn't have to actively think of each step, check and double check my actions against Post-it Notes of the recipe, or stop myself from taking the delicate pastries out of the oven too early. My brain had galloped me into a fast-moving baking impetus. It was rather weird. And startling. And amazing!

I documented the magic happening in my neurons.

> April 1: I wrote pages for Script Frenzy, a blog post, and pages for Concussion Is Brain Injury. Wow! Is it an anomaly?
>
> April 2: Baking frenzy week began with hot cross buns. No under-baking!
>
> April 2: My activity level shot up. Fatigue, however, did not drop. Bummer.
>
> April 5: Making strange mistakes, yet I dreamed up the Easter vegetarian main course and began cooking it. Successfully!

April 5: My body temperature began dropping. Although it had been slowly dropping in the previous months, this was a big shift!
April 5: The spicy Mayan Hot Chocolate at Soma did not increase my body temperature!
April 5: I acted on a thought, whether the thought was to make puff pastry or to empty the dishwasher or to write a blog post. Holy cow!
April 5: Fatigue is just friggin' weird.
April 6: I winged making icing!
April 8: I tolerated noise better—for an hour!
April 9: No long lines of pain down my arm muscles! Less pain in my lower back and hips!
April 9: I liked radio music as I did yoga. Whoa.
April 9: I read longer!
April 10: My parents told me I was coherent, together, with it, and calmer. "Don't come off that drug," they admonished me.
April 13: I read on the TTC for the first time since before my brain injury, really read. I absorbed the story, followed the plot, remembered the characters, and was engaged.
April 16: I didn't mind the sun waking me up early!
April 17: My heart rate was in the 80s!

I dared to hope that I could visit Mum and Dad at home on my own. No more waiting for a ride to go there or having to rest up a couple of days before. I could drop in! But I didn't want to say it out loud. I wasn't there yet, and what if I failed again?

"We have to drop you out of the study."

"Why?"

"Your fatigue hasn't improved."

My sleep specialist's words slowly phased into my language and comprehension centres. The study had been flawed in not measuring activity, only subjective fatigue levels. But it was too late. I couldn't go back and do less so that my fatigue looked like it was improving. I had to be tapered off.

> April 18: I laughed out loud at a small joke! I engaged more on Twitter with less effort than usual. And side effects began to let go as I went into withdrawal.
> April 27: I exercised, albeit less than two-thirds of my normal routine, on a day when I went out to appointments.

Saliva came back.
Fuzziness entered my arms, my face.
Fever chased chills chased fever around my body.
Pain lined up in rows through my shoulder and down my right arm.
Nerves on edge yet not.
The normal life I saw on the horizon slipped away.
Cranky.
Irritable.
My bowels began to work again.
I woke up, I slept, I woke up, I slept. I resumed self-talking as my initiation button shut off and wrenched activity out of my life.
What to do?
Desperation propelled my scholar brain to Google and Wikipedia, pushed my reluctant language centres to absorb and retain information on pregabalin, pressed my neural networks to relearn GABA. It seemed not much more had been discovered in the decades since I'd studied it, so why were they playing with drugs that affected it without understanding it? I shook my head. Focus. I landed on a study that talked about gamma brainwaves

stimulating the release of GABA. I read about gamma brainwaves, consciousness, and making people coherent. That's what I wanted.

I thought and pondered.

Perhaps Lynda could help me. It had been almost five years since I'd last called the ADD Centre, but they'd remember me. I hoped.

I dialled their number.

"Hi, Shireen! How are you?" Lynda's familiar voice greeted me over the phone line.

"I'm fine. I was just in a drug study." I related to her what had happened since March 2012 and asked, "What are gamma brainwaves? I don't remember hearing about them when I was seeing you."

"That's because we don't train them." Lynda launched into an explanation of what they knew. I wrote furiously in my phone notebook, hanging on with my fingernails to the research she told me about, especially about the work a Dr. Sheer had done with children with learning disabilities and how beta spindles not gamma brainwaves were associated with seizures.

"Are they connected to brain injury?"

"There was a study done on athletes." As she explained, I realized this was little understood territory, and I was starting to believe it wouldn't be possible to work with my gamma brainwaves when Lynda suggested, "Perhaps we could try enhancing them in you?"

"Could you?" Hope soared.

"We can try. Why don't you come in."

I hung up and a month later rested up to see the brain injury expert.

"I don't see or accept brain injury diagnosis based on SPECT or that all your problems are from it," the nice, smiling brain injury expert said with only my name and none of my documentation in front of him. "Easy to blame the brain injury," he asserted. I had to return in September with copies of my tests that he should already have been sent.

Two days later, on June 27, 2012, I travelled the exhausting, bouncing bus to the ADD Centre's Mississauga office. I felt more competent, more with it than the last time I'd taken the excruciatingly boring test, five years earlier. Not only were the results better than in 2007, they proved Lynda's theory: spontaneous improvement continued after stopping brain biofeedback, even premature stoppage like I'd been forced into doing. They were thrilled! I felt nothing, but I understood.

We talked about my heart. Lynda told me that US Navy research had shown a connection between brain injury and heart problems. She explained that they now included HRV training in every session; I'd forgotten all about having that in 2007.

"Why don't we try a screen?"

"Can we?" I asked excitedly.

"Yes." Andrea took over to run the screen. They both loved the perfect sine curve of my deep breathing, and Andrea was excited to be working with me on enhancing gamma brainwaves. She'd recently been researching them herself and called the training "sheer enhance," after Dr. Sheer. My muscle tension was close to the required maximum 2μV, relaxed enough so that EMG wouldn't overwhelm the small gamma brainwaves. How odd. I never felt like a relaxed person. And CZ position was best because it picked up frontal, sensory-motor, and deeper structures like the anterior cingulate, which included emotional modulation.

I slipped back into the familiar pattern of bowling a ball down a virtual alley to send virtual pins flying into the air. After three minutes, she stopped the recording, copied the stats, and began a clouds screen. I went into a hypnotic state watching the clouds part and planets appear on the screen. We wouldn't do that one again! And then the dreaded sailboat race with three boats lined up vertically in their horizontal fluorescent coloured lanes, pink, green, and yellow. Gamma was green. By the end I had a concentration headache under the CZ electrode. That was good! My brain had worked hard to produce more gamma brainwaves, and I breathed a perfect six breaths per minute.

My headache vanished when we stopped training. Andrea immediately created graphs. I suggested a sheer/EMG ratio graph. That ratio showed my brain had learnt with each screen how to create gamma brainwaves. Lynda was surprised. Andrea was excited. Happiness zinged through me, anxiety bolted, and energy flowed through my neurons.

As they scrubbed my ears and top of my head clean and I got ready to leave, I chattered, "When could I start? Can I train at the Toronto office?" "Yes," they laughed.

At the bus stop, I bounced on my toes. The bus was taking too long. I flipped open my flip phone and manually dialled Mum.

"Hello?"

"You won't guess what happened. I'm going to be doing gamma training!" Mum barely replied before I steamrollered on about what had happened, and oh, where was the bus, never mind, you won't believe I'm starting next week.

Mum edged a word into my flow. "Exciting!"

"Yes, it is!"

Welcome to happy gamma.

To read my sleep study adventures in full, go to http://wp.me/Pf8xE-16B.

For details on the gamma experiment, see Chapter R.

Chapter 23

Happy Gamma

I walked into the Toronto ADD Centre office on July 4, 2012. It was like I hadn't left, except the office had shrunk and they opened at 9:00 a.m. instead of 4:00 p.m. Back to two appointments per week, standard for new training.

My brain trainer squealed to see me. I smiled, trying hard to remember her beyond a sensed person. My memory mostly retained the trainers who had sat beside me, cleaning my ears, pasting on electrodes, setting the neurofeedback parameters, playing a game with me in between neurofeedback screens, and talking and listening as they removed the electrodes and cleaned me up.

She exclaimed over how much I'd changed: my animated face, my hair, my voice with prosody, and the partial return of my British sense of humour.

"The dryer the humour, the better," she laughed, as my subconscious threw out phrases Gatling-gun like in bursts that doubled her over, igniting my own laughter as she gasped to explain my new training. I watched her wrap the heart rate monitor around my thumb, the skin temperature one around my left pinky, and the breathing belt around my stomach. She cleaned my ears and scrubbed a spot on the top of my head. As she attached the electrodes to me, she exclaimed again how my voice goes up and down with expression. For the first time, I truly believed that my voice was alive because she was not using "articulate" to mask what my speech had been for over a decade, a monotone shadow of what it once was.

I focused on the monitor as she picked the neurofeedback screens. She set the routine for our appointments, and I couldn't wait to begin enhancing my gamma brainwaves. I sat upright during the assessment as that posture perked up the brain, and I slumped back in the chair during HRV. She chose the hardest screen first: the fluorescent sailboats neurofeedback screen. My brain screamed—ugh!—as the boat representing 3-10 Hz almost beat the gamma boat of 39-42 Hz. At least the EMG boat remained at dock. Since 2005, my EMG had almost always been low. In the next screen, a virtual ball hovered endlessly, refusing to burst into mini balls, while my brain hurt under the CZ electrode. I would have given up, but my trainer sitting next to me, the energy of her physical presence and encouraging me with "that's great!" when the ball moved a fraction, kept me going. We chatted to recharge me before she started the last three-minute neurofeedback screen where the triplane taunted me as it hung in the air every time I blinked instead of flying around its mountain island. I looked at my scores. I grinned. My gamma/EMG ratio had begun at 0.83 at my first assessment in Mississauga and was 0.85 today. By the end of three neurofeedback screens, it had risen to 0.91 in Mississauga and 0.90 today.

I collapsed in my seat on the TTC home. That night, I slept with my head elevated. I stared at my face in the mirror in the morning. Not as bad water retention from the intensive mental activity as I'd expected. I began to blog on this gamma experiment.

In the following weeks, we added HRV at the end to cool down, and she reminded me about SMIRB, a method Michael had developed decades earlier to help his patients stop ruminating. At first, I thought she'd said, "smurf," like I'd heard my other trainer say years ago.

"What?" I asked.

"Stop My Irritating Ruminations Book. SMIRB," she repeated. "Write down what's bothering you," my brain trainer instructed, "to empty your mind of that worry." After a neurofeedback screen, she started the sailboats screen with its white noise feedback, and I wrote and wrote out my worries as the computer buzzed on intermittently when my gamma brainwave rose above the threshold of 1.5μV and my EMG stayed lower than expected with me moving my hand over a page.

Tick. Tick. Tick.

My funds were dropping like a stone, but with a supporting letter in hand from my neurodoc, my amazing Cota case manager found a way to fund a new AVE unit so that I could use the SMR for Reading session while reading in addition to my regular beta 18 Hz sessions on Mondays. Maybe if AVE entrained my brainwaves to be what they were supposed to be *while* I was reading, I could read easier.

It arrived July 26. I immediately used it after my acupuncture appointment. I was feeling good after my acupuncturist had noticed that my temperature was dropping, emotion was in my voice, and I was grounded. I rested the end of that day.

But the ticking clock became noisy again as the work on *Concussion Is Brain Injury* stalled.

Mum said while washing my dishes, "Relax, it'll be concussion season when the book comes out. It'll be another opportunity and maybe better." I nodded, immovable in my chair. But I began to worry at not seeing changes in myself.

In the first week of August, I asked my brain trainer to lower the EMG threshold. My muscle tension was getting too close to that critical 2μV.

She said, "I'm being nice."

I replied, "I want it harder to keep that tension down."

She was surprised but lowered the threshold on the screen then clicked the Record button to start the neurofeedback. The challenge invigorated me. So three weeks later she dropped the gamma threshold to 1.4µV.

The changes in my gamma/EMG ratio scores were miniscule, but I began to feel my brain rewiring itself. For years I'd felt like a fractured person, a person with three boulders for a brain with fissures between each boulder preventing any contact between the three. The boulders had fused into one being while on pregabalin then had broken apart when the drug was stopped. Now my brain was whole. This time permanently. How odd! How wonderful!

September cemented the rhythm of my gamma brainwave training.

Arrive in a bad mood.

Leave in a good mood.

Arrive tired, frustrated, overwhelmed, wondering how I will do this exhausting, demanding brain training.

Leave knowing success is again and always possible.

Arrive heart beating like a bird's.

Leave with a lighter chest, slower heart rate, and easier breathing.

Arrive flat.

Crack up brain trainer.

Hear laughter erupt out of me.

Leave with a big grin.

Arrive needing but unable to talk.

Leave talking the trainer's ear off, feeling listened to, respected, and understood.

Arrive feeling alone.

Leave knowing I'm not alone, knowing I'm not hallucinating the brain injury sequelae, knowing I have real physiological problems.

Arrive effing HOT!

Leave cooler.

Arrive imprisoned within narrowed-in perception of surroundings.

Leave alert, my view of the world widened, strange new energy flickering a little stronger deep inside.

Arrive with stiff muscles and high muscle tension.

Leave with lower muscle tension.

Arrive under sunny skies that nail in migraines.

Leave under sunny skies, marvelling at all I can perceive, not caring about the plates of pain punishing my skull.

Arrive under dry skies and thunderous brow.

Leave under thundering, pouring rain, too much in a good mood to care about getting wetter than a baptized child in Lake Ontario.

In the first week of September, I said to Mum over coffee before my follow-up with the brain injury expert, "He'll be nicer to me, and I won't let loose if you come in with me." She came with.

In his sunny office as the wind blew outside, with Mum sitting beside me, he took me seriously. I persisted in getting an explanation for why I was so hot. He said that the circuits were working harder or more information was going through one circuit and so they overheated. Ergo I must pace. *Uh-huh*, I thought, rolling my eyes at his simplistic explanation and fed up with pacing as the be-all and end-all solution to brain injury. I continued to listen as he said that brain biofeedback was already helping by rewiring and creating more circuits. But he was unable to help me with my internal inferno. Time to create a rule that docs should have cold showers in winter. They'd hustle to learn about thermoregulation and fix it. At least my hypothalamus fix had helped a lot and gamma training had gotten me sweating again at times.

Afterward at lunch, Mum told me she and Dad had been talking the last couple of weeks about me pursuing a Ph.D. as my intellectual ability had soared suddenly. It would give me credibility, and I needed the stimulation. I had to admit I was getting bored. My pastor advised me. Elizabeth and my brain trainer were excited. My neurodoc said that the idea had merit.

I thought, *Oxford. Philosophy. Mind vs. Brain? Can I study that? I can't schlep to class plus do the reading and write the essays with my chronic exhaustion and lost reading ability. Can I study philosophy online?*

I checked. There was still space in Oxford's Philosophy of Mind course. Woot!

The day before the course began, as I read *November of the Soul* for my latest embryonic novel, loneliness leaked out of the pages into me. Sadness for the character caught me by surprise. Last time I felt something reading a book was...2000.

The next day I read the course's introduction, how to login, and how it worked. Brain was like, nah, not absorbing. I skipped right to the *Introduction Forum* and promptly became intimidated. My blood pressure had dropped from its insanity of the night, but I gushed anxiety as I arrived at biofeedback.

"Let's do a let's-see-what-happens when Shireen reads screen," my brain trainer suggested. My heart rate dropped, my anxiety brainwaves and EMG flew up, and I absorbed nothing. We tried to puzzle that out. Maybe my heart was remembering how reading relaxed me pre-injury while my brain freaked at the arduous work.

"What memories are coming up?" she asked.

"1981."

"Let's do two short neurofeedback screens, SMIRB for twelve minutes, another HRV, and let's try reading your course materials again, OK?" I nodded.

I wrote fiendishly in SMIRB about the huge expectations people had of my brain injury recovery, of being criticized for "failing" recovery, failing reading, failing at life, how fail fail fail played in my head as I attempted to read a course I'd chosen, a course that attracted my soul yet demanded abilities I still didn't have.

I collapsed back in my chair. She grounded me with another HRV screen, then she began neurofeedback but wouldn't let me reread that morning's material until she saw my breathing had dropped to six breaths per minute. When I read again, I finally understood it! With renewed confidence, I read silently along the course tutor's intro about her Ph.D. as my brain trainer read it out loud. Suddenly, all the words popped into my understanding. I bounced out of biofeedback, thrilled with the course, ready to write my own intro for the class.

I gradually began to understand how the course and discussion forums worked. I read on my iPad because it restricted the amount of text I could see. But mostly because I could use the select-a-word-press-Define feature, for I simply could not learn new words. Lynda told me I had to use new vocabulary in conversation. But who did I know who could talk philosophy with me? No one.

The midterm arrived. Writing the midterm essay gave me no qualms. It was remembering the new vocabulary and the concepts that scared me. Oxford didn't have any set policies on accommodating disabilities, but at the beginning of the course I'd asked my tutor for and received an extension on my essay. I put the Omniscreen on, prepped my iPad to write notes on it, opened my gargantuan philosophy textbook, started up the AVE SMR for Reading session, and began to slog through the words. I read a word's definition on my iPad, wrote a sentence, re-looked up the definition, wrote another sentence. By the end of the twenty-minute session, I was kaput. I dragged myself to my couch and napped for an hour, maybe two. The labour of it wore my brain and body out and filled my soul with doubts, but the ideas, the doing of it, filled me with meaning. I received a "Satisfactory."

Meanwhile, on October 25, my acupuncturist asked brightly if I liked the gamma biofeedback. Startled, I answered yup.

"Do you want to come back?"

I answered slowly, "Maybe in January since it's a bad month for me".

"I won't book it now," she declared. She knew I wasn't returning, for I no longer needed acupuncture. I didn't want to say good-bye to her, only the needles.

November and NaNoWriMo arrived, and so did final edits for *Concussion Is Brain Injury*. My brain began to flag. Each day became a roller coaster of inspiration to write in the morning, thrills over learning about the mind, exhaustion at the reading, and annoyance with the editing. My neurodoc helped me toil up the emotional and physical mountains of the final edits of *Concussion Is Brain Injury*. My gamma training de-stressed me.

And then Gertie and I met with my neurodoc as we wended our way through the list of people he wanted to meet. My neurodoc benignly asked me to listen to her. Like Arta, she felt she'd lost a "big sister." Words refused to exit my mouth. Thoughts juddered. Feelings absented themselves. At the end, my neurodoc said in a soft voice that she might want to join me for coffee, and that would be good. And if not, that's good, too. She did. And later that day, Gertie called me to apologize for 2003. She hadn't remembered it but had spoken to Darius. He thought he'd apologized to me. My brain's networks froze. Days later they melted down, her apology, her compassionate words knitting the raw edges of that wound closed into forgiveness. Reconciliation rebonded us.

November ended, and December arrived.

I finished my fourth novel.

I received "Excellent" on my final Philosophy of Mind essay.
I launched *Concussion Is Brain Injury* at my fiftieth birthday party.

Chapter 24

Threading New Networks

My January 15, 2013 anniversary frosted my mind and brittled my skin. My wounded heart ached over the loss of myself, my kith and kin, my marriage, my work, and my scholarly desires that fainted under the exhaustion of learning. Failure suffocated my soul. Eight days later, I embarked on the long public transit trip to the ADD Centre's Mississauga head office. Opening the familiar heavy door, it felt like nothing had changed at first. And then Lynda sat me down to do the inevitable boring test of concentration. Even though the IVA test was still a DOS program, the computer it ran on was much newer. I liked the new headphones, too. Unfortunately, they did nothing to alleviate IVA's excruciating boredom. But as I got into the test, a funny thing happened. My brain reacted to the prompts so quickly that my conscious mind couldn't keep up. I wanted to pause, but I couldn't do that mid-test. So I panted along and lifted my finger a little bit off the mouse so that my mind could be in sync with the reaction time driving my finger movement. I was absolutely convinced that my reaction time being faster than my conscious mind was resulting in errors. The same thing happened during the twenty-one-minute TOVA test. My head began to swim with boredom as my lungs faltered for breath and my eyes struggled to stay open. I craved sleep. Still, my right thumb clicked the clicker clutched in my right hand like it was in a 100 m dash. I lifted my thumb off a bit from the clicker so that my conscious mind could keep up with my reaction time. It didn't work. My reaction time sped up even more. After the single-point EEG, I sat down in

Lynda's familiar office and began talking. Her face lit up under her black geometric haircut.

"You're spontaneous!" she exclaimed. Animated was another word she used. And the third was calm. "You're calm," she said several times. She picked up the TOVA and IVA results. "Remarkable," Lynda commented.

I trudged through my appointments week after week until March 7, 2013 when Mum drove me back to the ADD Centre's head office for my first nineteen-point full-cap qEEG since 2007. The highway speed overloaded my senses and made me ill. I entered their warm office gratefully. Familiar faces greeted me excitedly over how I had changed. I was astonished at the change in Michael. The last time I'd seen him, he could barely type his hands were so gnarly. I'd never seen anyone reverse their joint issues before. I had to ask about it, but my mouth didn't speak my thoughts until it was almost too late. He and Andrea told me about low-intensity light therapy. It sounded wondrous, and I stuck it in the back of my mind until I could scrape up the funds.

I gawked at all the new technology in Michael's office. While Andrea connected the new-to-me stretchy full cap to the computer, Michael explained how they had transitioned to a more sensitive program. But, in order to compare my results to my previous ones, I'd have both the old method used on me and the new one conducted through the internet. It was as easy as plugging the full cap wires first into one box and then into another, smaller box. I forgot all about my troubles as I followed Michael's commands and watched my brainwaves stream across the screen in excited hops and dips. Then it was time for me to have the new software test me. Before she began, Andrea gave me earplugs for the sound stimulus portion and tested a startle sound. She wanted to ensure it was loud enough. I jerked at the awful, scratchy white noise. She had to figure out how to lower the volume. After a couple of decreases, the sound was loud enough to startle but not cause me to physically jump. Phew. She began the test. When it was over, as she was unplugging me, I brought up my favourite topic: reading. Looking over my results from the older equipment, Michael told me that my Wernicke's area was too overloaded with alpha. Also, there was too much dis-coherence between Wernicke's and Broca's areas.

"We're using a new treatment now," he said. "LORETA." It sounded like a woman's name: confident, tall, and attractive. "It along with tDCS of Wernicke's before gamma training may help," he said as he explained how the newest thing was working with neural networks. Michael explained tDCS was transcranial direct current stimulation. A 9 V battery would excite electrons in my brain under the stimulus sponge. Whatever networks I used during the treatment, the electricity would flow through their neurons. Then he showed me the research on LORETA. He believed that permanent effects needed more sessions than what clinicians and researchers in the area posited. That made sense to me. They really thought I could benefit.

Mum and I sat down with Lynda in her office and discussed LORETA. I asked about how I would get there. They only did the training in Mississauga, and I didn't have the stamina to take the TTC and MiWay and then do 1.5 hours of brain training and then self-talk groggily back home.

Mum said that she'd drive me.

I was less sure about that. Between cars tailgating, lane switching, sudden braking, and seeing the road come at me at a speed that made my brain faint from sensory overload, highway driving gave me the willies and hurt my neck.

"We really believe this will help you. Why not try it during the good weather when the roads will be clear of snow?"

I could do that. Twenty sessions would take me to the end of August, and the research indicated that might be enough. If not, maybe I could get a few more in before the bad weather hit.

I agreed but opined, "I really wished you offered it in Toronto, though."

She explained that they needed Michael's on-site supervision, as well as the sink facilities to clean the EEG caps.

"We can go and have cake and coffee after," Mum suggested.

"All right," I sighed. The benefits outweighed the scary commute.

They also told me about some work done in the United States about training at the left back of the brain to resolve PTSD symptoms. Although this was done on veterans who had only PTSD and not a brain injury like me, I was game to try it. The waking up of my emotions and the traumatic memories were getting to be a bit too much. We added tDCS to my single-electrode gamma training sessions, which were now moving to PZ-O1, to work on my working memory and long-term memory, as well as the PTSD, when I returned from my March staycation.

I completed the online neuropsychological test from home and took March off from all my appointments. The respite was palpably sweet, but after my first two appointments back, my first two ten-minute tDCS sessions over left frontal, the memories came springing out like some evil jack-in-the-box. That's when Mum walked in my front door. I got angry, she got ticked, she stormed out, and I howled and bawled. She came back in, looking for me. I wept on her shoulder like the universe had imploded over my head, sending Dyson Sphere plates all around me and walling me off from all humans. My PTSD had roared to life! The ADD Centre quickly re-stabilized me with gamma training over CZ again. Then we returned to PZ-O1 and put tDCS on hold. Much better.

It was time to begin LORETA in mid-April. I was nervous when I walked in to my first session with a new trainer in Mississauga. Apparently, she was even more nervous. I had a reputation for asking unusual, brain-challenging questions. When my Toronto trainer had told me this, I stared at her. I didn't think my questions were that hard or unusual. She laughed. Oh yes. Apparently, I asked things no one else thought of.

"Oh, um, well, OK. But if she can't answer, no biggie," I said. "I'm OK with 'I don't know.'"

"We told her that she can ask one of us if she can't answer your question."

"Fine by me!" I smiled.

I had filled in a form with the areas I wanted to focus on, rating them from one to ten, from least important to most important. Andrea and Michael focused only on my tens and set the training parameters based on my list. Michael had decided to work with Andrea on setting up the parameters because of my extreme reaction to the tDCS. We would be focusing on normalizing the neural networks involved in mood, pain, and working memory.

The hard part was choosing what movie to watch. Apparently, with LORETA, your brain doesn't play a looping computer game; it plays a movie. I chose Kratt Brothers *Be the Creature*, something familiar and fun and unlikely to create unwanted emotions. A good choice because when my neural networks stopped making an effort to send electrons down axons to each other, when my brainwaves lost power, or when my brain went out of phase, the image diminished to a black zero pixels but the movie kept playing. Argh! At least with a nature show, when the movie re-enlarged from pixel size to full screen, I didn't feel lost from missing part of the narrative. Five minutes later, cycle one was done. I slumped. Five more cycles. An hour later, it was over.

I inhaled my Simply Bar. I was so damn hungry. Mum got me into the car and into my favourite bakery café, where I collapsed into a chair. Glucose in the form of a sweet and caffeine in coffee revived my spent brain.

Two days later, I tweeted excitedly, "I am absolutely not going to get excited about 10min of normal reading in case it's just a blip 13 yrs aftr #braininjury wrecked my reading."

I settled into a rhythm of taking the TTC to the Toronto office for my single-electrode brain biofeedback then being driven to Mississauga later in the week for LORETA. I went from the quiet of the Toronto office to the busy client- and trainer-filled Mississauga office.

Spring coolness gave way to summer saunas.

I began to see normalcy as possible again.

I could hold a conversation. I could think. My stamina began to improve.

On August 6, 2013, we began five minutes of tDCS over Wernicke's area, behind the left ear and above it. We began at a low voltage and half the standard duration since I'm so sensitive to everything from drugs to howling wind to electrical currents and experimental gamma brain biofeedback. Michael had said that using the pathways I wanted to strengthen during tDCS would channel the stimulation along those networks. I cranked my reading networks by reading *The Antipodes of the Mind* on my Kindle Paperwhite. I'd gotten the book on the advice of my Philosophy of Mind tutor and had been chugging through it for five minutes at the end of almost every single-electrode brain biofeedback session to improve my reading, drop my heart rate, and increase my gamma brainwaves. The book was a combination of fascinating and neuron-breaking vocabulary on concepts that made my brows hurt they were so pulled together. Now we added reading with tDCS before brain biofeedback and ended with a final reading neurofeedback screen.

Before I left for home, my brain trainer reminded me, "Pay attention to any changes in your reading."

"Will do," I replied cheerfully, unbelievably wanting to read. This new desire was like a flickering candle, a small glow in the dark.

"And get back on track with your academic stuff," she added.

"OK," I agreed. I walked out. Halfway home, my stomach suddenly started to channel Garfield, shaking my legs, and getting all up in my face about feeding it NOW. I fed it fast. And then I sat outside in the summer heat to read. A busy bad bee got very interested in my iPod and me. I took my e-reader and read a couple metres away from my iPod. When I saw the bee thing had buzzed off, I returned to my seat. Rustle, rustle. A cat was staring at me. The cat walked around me and my chair like a ball swirling around a bowl, getting closer and closer to centre. Naturally the cat wanted up. On my lap. With his grubby paws. I had to teach him the command "down," which for some reason he was not too interested in learning. He meandered away for a bit. A squirrel got pissy with another squirrel. They chased each other off. I settled back into reading Grimm's familiar fairy tales when I heard a growl behind me. Cat number one wasn't taking too kindly to cat number two wandering over to say hi. Soon after, I gave up and retreated indoors, yet pleased I had read for twenty minutes in an unexpectedly distracting environment.

Hope Learnings

Chapter Q

Hypothalamus Fix

Like with much of the brain, knowledge of the hypothalamus is limited. Here I present general principles of how the hypothalamus works for those of us who aren't physiologists, with links to more details, followed by my theoretical hypothalamus fix.

The hypothalamus runs the sympathetic nervous system (fight or flight) and the pituitary gland (the bane of adolescence), among other systems. In brain injury, most focus on the latter, if they do at all, for internal-functioning problems.

According to Medline Plus,[27] the hypothalamus produces hormones that control or influence

- the pituitary and other hormonal glands to release their own hormones;
- body temperature;
- hunger;
- thirst;
- moods;
- sex drive; and
- sleep.

The hypothalamus is a small area of the brain below the larger thalamus (which controls it), just in front of and above the brain

---

[27] http://www.nlm.nih.gov/medlineplus/ency/article/002380.htm

stem and right above the pituitary stalk, which it controls.

The tiny hypothalamus determines whether or not and how much each gland or body part secretes their own hormones in order to keep your body in balance. Every endocrine or hormonal gland runs an important part of your functioning from sex to healing to rate of metabolism to stress response. It affects your sense of well-being. For instance, if the hypothalamus determines that you're too hot, it'll tell the thyroid to dial things down, and you will feel just right. The word used to describe this is homeostasis. This is where you want to be, in balance.

Scholarpedia has an extensive scientific article on the hormonal aspects of the hypothalamus.[28] The hypothalamus also controls your autonomic nervous system, which controls the autonomic—automatic, if you will—part of your metabolism, like heart rate, blood pressure, breathing (though that is also under your conscious control), and emotional arousal. The autonomic nervous system comprises the sympathetic and parasympathetic nervous systems. The former puts you into the fight or flight response when stressed, through the hypothalamus telling the pituitary gland to increase the secretions of a hormone called adrenaline or epinephrine released by one half of the tiny adrenal glands near the kidneys and through a neurochemical in the brain called noradrenaline or norepinephrine. When the stress is gone, the autonomic system will rebalance, decreasing the activity of the sympathetic system and increasing the parasympathetic system, which is the homeostatic or normal state of good functioning.

The hypothalamus receives information on how your body is functioning from many areas. The vagus nerve relates how fast your heart is beating and how bloated or not your stomach is. The reticular formation in the brain stem relates how hot or cold

---

[28] http://www.scholarpedia.org/article/Models_of_hypothalamus

your skin is and is involved in the sleep/wake cycle. The optic nerve sends signals from the back of your eyeball about how light or dark it is where you are. Certain neurons in the spaces in your brain called ventricles report whether toxins are present, toxins that can lead to throwing up. The rest of the limbic system and olfactory (your nose) system relate your level of sexual arousal and whether you need to eat or not. The hypothalamus's own receptors measure ion balance and blood temperature. It's a busy, busy brain part.

The hypothalamus is involved in the stress reaction in two ways: hormonally and through the sympathetic part of the autonomic nervous system. It takes in all the incoming information and decides if you are stressed. If it decides yes, it'll figure out which gland needs to secrete more or less of its hormones to deal with the stress and then will determine if it needs to activate the sympathetic system. When the incoming information tells it that the stress is gone, it'll send new instructions to the glands to return to homeostasis.

The hypothalamus affects heart rate, breathing, blood pressure, body temperature, water retention, emotional arousal, glucose metabolism, and so on. The chart on the following page is what I drew to describe what happens when your hypothalamus activates your stress response and deactivates it.

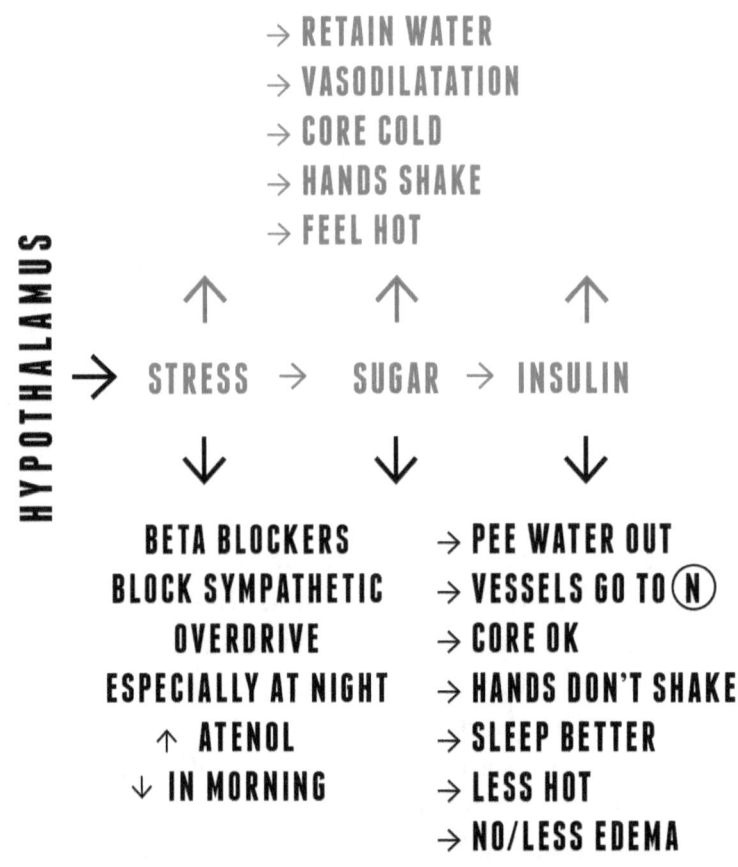

When stress increases, it releases glucose from a compound called glycogen found in your liver to provide the body with energy. The increase in blood sugar boosts insulin levels in the blood. Usually insulin facilitates the movement of glucose from the blood into muscles, but if you're insulin resistant—meaning you resist this movement of glucose into muscle cells—then the glucose will go into fat cells instead. High insulin levels are associated with sodium retention if you're insulin resistant. All this results in higher body temperature, shaking hands, a cold core as blood is shunted from digestion to muscles, your blood vessels opening up in your skin or sometimes constricting (if you're stressed due to fear like a bear attack) depending on the stress source, and water retention (the latter if insulin resistant). This prepares you to meet danger and either fight or flee. Think of the deer in the headlights that suddenly takes off.

When the hypothalamus decides stress time is over, it reduces the reaction, drops blood sugar, drops insulin levels, and you become cooler, your hands stop shaking, your core warms up to normal, your blood vessels constrict or dilate back to normal, and you pee out the excess water you'd retained. Beta blockers like atenolol somehow act to block the sympathetic stress reaction so that you don't retain water so much, your hands don't shake, your core temperature remains normal, and so on. At minimum, it reduces these effects even if unable to normalize them. But beta blockers create fatigue, an unwanted effect among others.

At the same time the hypothalamus is activating the sympathetic system, it may also tell the pituitary to secrete a hormone to act on your adrenal glands. While one half of the adrenals secretes adrenaline, the other half secretes cortisol. Cortisol is the most commonly known hormone involved in the stress reaction. When you think of how cortisol behaves, think steroids. That's why a severe stress reaction may make you bloat up with water retention like you've taken oral or injected steroids.

Chronic stress happens when this stress reaction through both the sympathetic system and cortisol doesn't switch off. This constant state of "on" can cause increased blood sugars (think diabetes), increased cholesterol (needed for synthesis of cortisol), weight gain, and mineral depletion from the bones and can increase the chance of developing diabetes, heart disease, asthma, allergies, and autoimmune diseases.

Since the hypothalamus is deep in the brain far away from the skull, it's assumed it escapes being damaged in traumatic brain injuries that don't affect the deeper structures or in which the skull is not broken. But I think that assumption is wrong. Back in 1998, a group of American researchers at Mount Sinai Medical Center conducted a study[29] to look at complaints of weight gain, body temperature, hair and skin changes, and so on. These kinds of changes reflect the stress reaction. But it's also interesting that in diffuse axonal injury, the corticothalamic loop is disrupted. This may create a negative cascade effect from thalamus to hypothalamus. Although Mount Sinai did look into the prevalence of these symptoms, not much has been done with this information other than to study those in the hospital with severe brain injuries. This doesn't help those living at home, suffering from these unpleasant symptoms or those who have closed head injuries and were never hospitalized. In Canada, these complaints remain ignored and unstudied.

There is more, much more to know about the hypothalamus, but the only other aspects I will mention are serotonin and emotions.

Serotonin is a neurotransmitter that has been implicated in depression. Low serotonin not only results in depression but also decreases satiety (in other words, you want to keep eating). Increasing serotonin lifts mood, increases satiety, and drops body temperature. Other neurotransmitters and hormones can decrease body temperature, like peptides, dopamine, estrogen, norepinephrine, and opioid peptides.

Emotions are complex. The anterior cingulate gyrus seems to be connected both to the prefrontal cortex for cognitive tasks and the hypothalamus for emotional control and seems also associated with mental flexibility and shift changing, something that is diminished or absent in people with brain injury. It connects directly to the heart, and the heart can thus influence

---

[29] http://www.brainline.org/content/2008/07/tbi-consumer-report-long-term-post-tbi-health-problems.html

the brain to increase the activity of the parasympathetic system as in HRV training.[30] As the heart rate synchronizes with the breath, the parasympathetic system increases to balance the sympathetic system, leading to calm and less stress. However, it is difficult to deep breathe 24/7. I needed something that would act directly on my brain physiology to reset its functioning back to normal.

All this gave me enough information to decide that (a) the locus of my brain injury-induced problem was in the hypothalamus and not the pituitary gland and (b) I needed to increase serotonin levels in the hypothalamus. My main focus was dropping body temperature, water retention, and hot spots on my skin (see Chapter M on thermoregulation). Any changes to heart rate, blood pressure, and shortness of breath would be a bonus. After pondering for years and discussions with Dave Siever at Mind Alive,[31] I decided to try what I call my "hypothalamus fix." (Note: I didn't think about emotional control when devising my hypothalamus fix. The question I am now asking is what role does the hypothalamus or the neural network it's located on play in emotional control and in sudden on/off brain injury rage?)

I devised a single subject research study on myself. Such a study can only point to a possible answer. It cannot and does not prove an answer is the right one.

Hypothesis

A brain injury interrupts the functioning of the network the hypothalamus is located on. The goal: to determine whether the body is responding normally and chronically to an extreme stressor(s) or if it is responding in an extreme way to stress.

---

[30] http://circ.ahajournals.org/cgi/content/full/93/5/1043
[31] http://mindalive.com/

Given that my need for atenolol increased at night and my symptoms worsened at night, a time when stress drops, I concluded that it was the latter. Furthermore, it seemed that the issue was low serotonin levels in the hypothalamus and that generally speaking, treatment needed to reset the hypothalamus to a normal, balanced state. I needed a treatment that addressed all of the symptoms, did not increase fatigue, improved well-being, and allowed me to become more functional. I decided to gauge the effectiveness of AVE and CES on hypothalamus function in myself. I called it, "hypothalamus fix."

Method

DAVID Delight Pro AVE from Mind Alive. In mid-August, 2010, I began using the AVE sub-delta session most nights at lights out when ready to sleep in order to facilitate falling asleep. I then began using it nightly at the end of August. This session emits visual pulses from 0.5 to 1 Hz and back again, along with binaural beats or pulse tones, depending on user preference, for twenty-four minutes. It is a passive session and does not entrain the brain. I kept both the auditory and visual intensities at four. Any lower on the visual intensity, and I found it had no effect. What evidence existed showed sub-delta calmed the hypothalamus.

Oasis II CES from Mind Alive. CES directs a microcurrent across the brainstem. It has three settings: Sleep at 100 Hz (short pulses), Relief at 0.5–3.0 Hz (long pulses), and micro-TENS at 0.5–3.0 Hz (short pulses). Beginning in September, I used the Sleep session every morning, right after awakening, which varied from 5:30 to 9:00 a.m., for one hour at the highest point of the low-intensity level (there are four intensity levels, each of which rises in intensity as well).

A month later I began experimenting with evening times. From mid-October on, I used the CES device nightly at 10:00 p.m. for thirty minutes at the highest point of the low-intensity level. I also upped the intensity level of the morning session to the lowest point of the second intensity level.

Results

I was looking for changes in body temperature, water retention, sleep, and skin health and a reduction in the dosage of atenolol. (I was not equipped to take any objective measurements, obviously.) Typically, I needed twice the dose of atenolol in the winter than I did in the summer. As the weather cooled, I had to increase my morning dosage from 0 or 12.5 mg to 25 mg by January. My evening dose remained consistent at 25 mg for the three years prior.

After three sub-delta AVE sessions in mid-August, I began to be cooler. By the fourth session, I began to fall asleep near the end of the session. I was falling asleep within about thirty minutes (subjectively assessed), instead of my usual one to two hours. After the sixth session, I started turning the volume down on the television (volume as a function of comprehension). By the seventh session, my speech became more animated.

I had been using the CES Sleep session alternating with the Relief session less-than-daily to two or three times a day to see what the effects were. By the start of September, I was feeling calmer after each use, and I had also begun dreaming again. The second morning I used the one-hour Sleep session consistently, the edema or water retention started to go down, as evidenced by looser rings, a thinner face, a thinner nose, and being able to feel my bones from my shoulders to my knuckles to my feet. By the third session on, I reduced the 12.5 mg morning dose of atenolol, but it still put me to sleep. Night-time sleep was becoming more consistent. By late September, my neck thinned and began to show a normal hollow at the base.

At the end of September, my acupuncturist confirmed that I was significantly less hyperthermic and my mood was elevated. For the first time in over ten years, I looked happy. She recommended reducing acupuncture frequency.

In October, I had my first hot shower in years. My skin did not erupt into red patches that swelled up and spread nor did I overheat. Having a hot shower with no need to cool my skin down was a very big deal.

There was a hiccup in my study as the outside temperature dropped and my home got cold the first week of October. My brain could not adjust body temperature to the environment very well. The optimum environmental temperature for me is about 22°C. With each degree below 20°C or above 26°C, I retain more water and become hotter, though at times I feel the outside cold (or heat). Yet because of my skin's reactivity, I could wear only loose sweatshirts and T-shirts. I also became more fatigued.

One night, the evening atenolol dose of 25 mg knocked me right out too early. I reduced my atenolol a bit and experimented with adding an evening CES Sleep session. I tried 8:00 p.m., 9:00 p.m., and 10:00 p.m. The 10 o'clock time seemed the best. Otherwise with a reduced atenolol dose, I had started to wake up again too warm and with increased water retention.

At this stage of my single-subject study, I remained cooler and had markedly less water retention. I also had less shortness of breath. This kind of shortness of breath had nothing to do with my lungs as they were clear but with my heart. I was not, however, back to normal on those three indices. I was sleeping better though still not normally. I was sweating at more normal levels. My thinking was clearer. Processing speed remained the same. I began to wear long sleeves and have the occasional hot shower. Overall my skin was less reactive to allergens or stimulations. I did not know the effects on blood pressure, heart rate, type 2 diabetes, triglycerides, or cholesterol.

Unexpected Results

Brain injury anger. Brain biofeedback reduced my constant irritability and began to reduce the severity and frequency of the brain-injury anger. Acupuncture also reduced irritability and anger. The 32-minute alpha-wave and 14 Hz beta-wave AVE sessions can temporarily calm rising irritability and anger. However, my main triggers for brain injury anger remained just as potent as ever. So I avoided them.

On October 5, 2010, I used the TTC. It was uncomfortable but uneventful. I noted it but didn't really think too much of it. The next day, I had to deal with technical phone support for a computer problem. I got angry—who doesn't—but the brain-injury anger did not rise. I did not feel edgy either. That was a first in over ten years. The hypothalamus fix was reducing my brain injury anger. I also reduced the use of my compensating strategies on the TTC from three or more to one.

Mood instability. After brain injury, mood can be fine one moment and in the dumps the next then fine or manic the next. (Antidepressants seem to be commonly given to stabilize symptoms.) I had a lack of affect interrupted occasionally by very intense moods. Brain biofeedback over time settled the wild mood swings down to regular, old instability. AVE and acupuncture helped, too. But with the hypothalamus fix, mood instability lessened in intensity markedly.

Exercise tolerance. In mid-October, I climbed a long, steep set of steps out of a ravine without having to stop. I panted like crazy, but I felt no dizziness, no shortness of breath, and no increased heat. And though I was dead tired and sleepy for the rest of the day, I suffered no worsening metabolic effects that night. Astonishing.

Despite a setback three months into my hypothalamus fix due to increased stress, my exercise tolerance continued to improve; the improvement in brain-injury anger, irritability, and mood stability remained; my skin was hardly reactive; and my regular diabetes checkup showed that it was finally under control (except for triglycerides). I also managed to make the decisions I needed to make even while I wrote almost every day. In the first two days of December, my edema started to drop. My body temperature was not quite so overheated at night. I could still take hot showers, and I still did not need to use cold water to cool my skin. Water retention varied, in direct relation to stress, as in too much exercise, difficult cognitive tasks, or emotional stuff. My neck remained thinner, and skin health remained good. But I continued to have problems. How much was exacerbated by my pre-existing hypothyroidism remained an open question. As for side effects, brief temporary dizziness is normal when using the AVE or CES as it drops blood pressure.

Gradually over the next couple of months, my pain levels increased. As my hypothalamus worked better, I was doing more (though it didn't feel like it), which put more strain on my back. The electrical stimulation of CES somehow made my muscles hurt. Or the increasing pain could have been the opposite of when my edema and body temperature increased back in early 2007 and my pain decreased. If my theory was right, the edema was due to high levels of circulating cortisol. Steroids reduce pain. I theorized that as cortisol dropped back to normal levels, as reflected in shrinking edema, the underlying pain paths could have sprung back to life. In the end though, I didn't know why I had more pain. And over the long term, pain dropped.

Meanwhile, I continued to reduce the atenolol gradually.

Cognition. On New Year's Day 2011, as I was reading Agatha Christie's *Murder in Mesopotamia*, a book I'd read often, I remembered whodunnit and some details of how the murder was done. This sudden change was a delightful shock. Then I went to the theatre and for the first time since the injury, I followed the story, stayed focused, remained engaged, remembered it, and most of all enjoyed it for its entire length. It was an operetta too, *Die Fledermaus*.

Exercise tolerance continued to improve regularly. Usually for me to increase reps or total time exercising took effort and convincing myself I could do it. But since I started the hypothalamus fix, every improvement came spontaneously. One moment, I would think I'm going to do my usual ten reps, the next I had done twelve. The exercise tolerance thing was big. It's difficult to keep a good weight and to remain fit when exercise after brain injury brings on unpleasant or even dangerous physical effects like hyperthermia, water retention, a fast heart rate that increases as soon as one begins to move, and so on. When even walking short distances can bring on unpleasant consequences, that affects your quality of life, too.

I moved my one-hour evening CES session to half an hour after I took the evening atenolol, about the time the medication's fatigue side effects usually kicked in. It didn't seem to entirely get rid of the drug's fatiguing effects, but sometimes it reduced the length of time it lasted. However, it was much easier to do the CES session over the supper news hour. Overall, I was feeling better.

Late 2012, I continued to use the sub-delta AVE session nightly at lights out and use the CES Sleep session for one hour first thing in the morning before I got up and again for one hour at 5:00 p.m.

I adjusted my weight-loss regimen in early 2011. Water retention is a serious impediment to losing weight. Water increases one's weight and masks fat gain as well as fat loss. But after I lost a substantial portion of the water, my runaway appetite began to lose steam, enough so that eating fewer calories didn't leave me feeling very, very hungry. Emotional eating was part of that, but people with a brain injury will eat whatever's in front of them and never feel satiated. It's an odd combination of perception that doesn't see what's actually there and this beast taking over so that you can't stop. I guess that could stem partly from a lack of impulse control, which infects every aspect of life and is pretty typical for a person with a brain injury, in addition to possible low serotonin in the hypothalamus.

As of mid-2012, I weighed my food three or four days out of seven, as a way to reinforce and retrain myself to know how much I should eat each day. To be honest, it's tedious and tiring having to weigh food every single day. I'd like not to have to do it anymore. But it works.

As of 2017, I continue my hypothalamus fix but have moved the evening CES Sleep back to about 9:00 p.m. To improve the hypothalamus fix, I've added SMR/Beta L13.5/R18 AVE most days to restore healthy functioning of the corticothalamic loop. I also sometimes follow CES Sleep with one-hour of CES Relief because the hypothalamus fix, gamma brainwave training, and low-intensity light therapy have increased my walking to the point that my hip and back are overworked. But it's good physically, mentally, and emotionally to walk.

For updates and to read the original posts, go to http://wp.me/Pf8xE-16y.

Chapter R

Gamma

Introduction

GABA, or *gamma*-Aminobutyric acid, is the chief inhibitory neurotransmitter in the human central nervous system, i.e., the brain and spinal cord.[32] To recap Chapter 22, experimental controlled-release pregabalin, a GABA analogue, had several temporary effects on me:

- calmer
- presented as being alive
- normalizing body temperature regulation
- healthy skin without heat eruptions that moved around and increased on contact with anything
- able to drink or eat spices without increasing my body temperature to uncomfortable levels that would create eruptions on my skin
- eliminated water retention
- reversed initiation deficit so that I got things done
- increased activity even though fatigue didn't abate
- increased alertness even though body was tired

---

[32] https://en.m.wikipedia.org/wiki/Gamma-Aminobutyric_acid

- reduced need to nap in the afternoon and/or afternoon sleepiness
- normalized appetite, i.e., the constant hunger was turned off
- increased exercise tolerance
- increased reading time
- ability to read in a distracting environment
- wrote more blog posts or worked on book drafts more often
- reduced fibromyalgia pain
- increased tolerance to noise
- tolerated noise when doing an activity, e.g., being able to listen to the radio or music while doing yoga
- improved intellectual capacity (this had the side effect of boredom, but boredom drives one to find stimulating activities)
- ability to laugh at normal levels of stimulus
- engaged more with people
- removal of a barrier between me and the world
- coherent as a person

The question was how to increase GABA to achieve these effects permanently without the unwanted effects of experimental controlled-release pregabalin.

Turns out, gamma brainwaves are associated with GABA, and brain injury may reduce gamma activity.

Gamma brainwaves around 40 Hz are called a "binding rhythm." Gamma-producing neuronal clusters bring together cognitive processes so as to produce a higher-order cognitive act coherently. They bind different aspects of a cognitive event together or bind different neural networks together. Gamma brainwave production is associated with coherent thought and harmonic brain activity and with glial cells. Glial cells wrap around axons, increasing the speed of transmission of electricity down the axon through the myelin sheath and bringing nutrition to the cell while removing waste products.

I theorize that gamma brainwaves represent the web that holds together brain functions—outputs of neural networks—and that stimulating gamma-producing networks induces self-repair. But much remains unknown about them or GABA because of lack of basic scientific research.

However, I think it's safer working with brainwaves through brain biofeedback than with a drug that induces a not-well-understood neurotransmitter and may have side effects like suicidal thoughts.

Also, drugs bathe the entire brain. Their dosages are determined based on aggregate data though hopefully fine-tuned for each individual to mitigate unwanted effects. In contrast, brain biofeedback targets a specific individualized location and brainwave frequencies after individual qEEG assessment. Initial individualized parameters can be adjusted immediately during treatment.

Hypothesis

Brain biofeedback stimulates neural networks thereby increasing brainwave power at chosen frequencies in different parts of the brain in order to repair and normalize brain functions. In discussions with Dr. Lynda Thompson of the ADD Centre, we hypothesized brain biofeedback to stimulate the networks that produce gamma brainwaves would both enhance gamma activity and increase release of GABA between the related neurons and thus reproduce the effects I had experienced.

There were three caveats:

1. Muscle tension (EMG), as reflected in increases of 52-58 Hz amplitude, had to remain below 2 µV so as not to interfere with gamma feedback data (see Chapter I: EMG).

2. The standard of twenty to forty sessions to begin to see results may not apply. It may take longer.

3. We did not know the optimum ratio of gamma to EMG. Muscle tension increases amplitudes of higher frequencies like gamma, so keeping the ratio a bit higher ensures training true gamma of 39–41 Hz, not just measuring a small increase in muscle tension and so creating a false increase in EEG amplitudes, that is, muscle artifact.

Relationship of Gamma to EMG

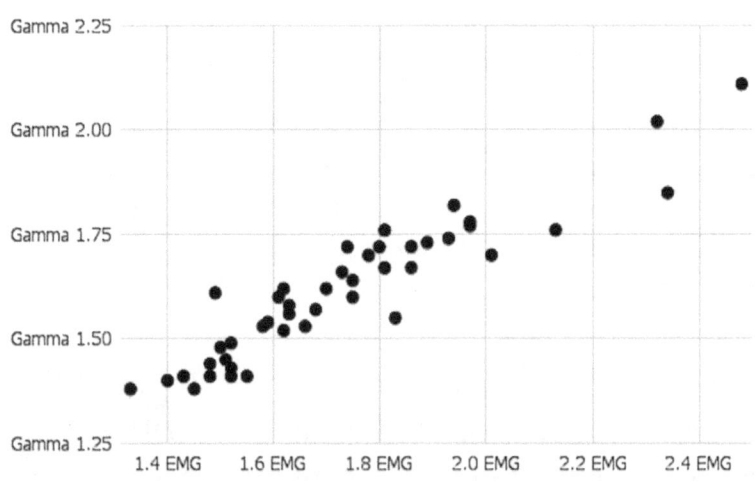

After 20 Gamma Training Sessions, Relationship of Gamma to EMG

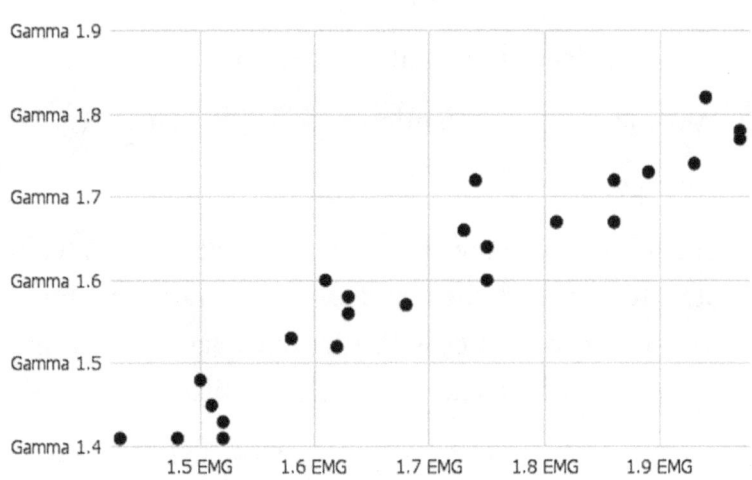

Since glial cells, specifically microglia, are associated with gamma brainwaves, perhaps enhancing gamma would also increase the number of glial cells and so stimulate repair of my injured brain beyond normalizing brainwave activity in certain locations.

Method

Single-electrode brain biofeedback in the standard CZ location twice a week. Tapered withdrawal from gabapentin prior to starting. Switched from ad hoc to scheduled use of audiovisual entrainment (AVE) during the week.

The ADD Centre conducted baseline assessments beforehand:

- ACQ (ADD Centre Questionnaire), the Wender Utah Rating Scale (for retrospective ratings of ADHD symptoms in childhood), the Adult ADHD Self-Report Scale Symptom Checklist (from the World Health Organization), the Burns Anxiety Inventory, and the Burns Depression Inventory

- IVA to test visual and auditory attention

- TOVA to test visual attention

- Draw-a-person task

- Three-minute baseline single-electrode EEG at CZ with heart rate, breathing belt, and skin temperature monitors while I watched a timer with eyes open, jaw relaxed, and body still in order to minimize EMG artifact

Being tied to 52–58 Hz, if 40 Hz goes up more than 52–58 or does not go down as much, then we can successfully measure 40 Hz. I had a measurable 39–40 Hz of 1.02 µV and 40–41 Hz of 1.

HRV training enhances and makes brain biofeedback easier. We preceded the neurofeedback screens with five minutes HRV.

To enhance 40 Hz, we bracketed the feedback parameters from 39–42 Hz and, as in standard brain biofeedback, set feedback parameters to inhibit excessive delta, theta, and EMG. We began with three three-minute neurofeedback screens in which visual and auditory feedback played only when, through my brain, I increased my gamma brainwaves' power above a set threshold and decreased delta-theta and EMG below their set thresholds. I chose the visual feedback: bowling ball and clouds. They chose the third screen: sailboats in fluorescent colours that most clients do not like. Each sailboat represented one of the brainwaves we were training. The idea was to have the gamma boat beat the delta-theta and EMG boats. In subsequent training, we used the sailboats screen with its white noise auditory feedback (meant to sound like the wind), a screen with a ball that broke into small balls, and lastly a triplane that flew around a mountain. I chose the musical auditory feedback for the latter two.

CZ was chosen because it picks up the frontal cortex, the sensory-motor cortex, and deeper structures through the corticothalamic loop of the anterior cingulate (see Chapter Q). EMG also least affects it. The initial protocol was

1. enhance 39–42 Hz;

2. inhibit 3–9 Hz; and

3. inhibit 52–58 Hz.

My first results showed my brain learnt with each three-minute screen. I developed a concentration headache underneath the CZ electrode that lasted an hour or two and mild dizziness that lasted about four hours. But these effects dissipated as my brain got used to twice-weekly training again.

The interesting immediate effect after the first training session was how giddy I felt. Perhaps after twelve years of having no effect, any normal production of an emotion would feel extreme. I talked and talked, though my body was tired, and was driven to begin writing on public transit after training even though the dizziness and nausea increased as I wrote. I could not stop. Once home, I was driven to write down every detail of the day. About an hour after initial training, everything in my visual field was in focus with a colour clarity that popped. In addition, my perception of the world, i.e., my open awareness, expanded. Another hour later for about an hour, my body temperature dropped and I felt cold, unusual for me. And best of all, no anxiety. The feeling of stress dropped significantly.

Training

The ADD Centre reviewed my assessment results and fine-tuned the brain biofeedback parameters so that neurostimulation would enhance gamma brainwaves while meeting my individual need to inhibit delta-theta-alpha.

Training method

1. Have single-electrode brain biofeedback at CZ twice a week for forty-four sessions.

2. Begin with two minutes eyes closed then three minutes eyes open HRV, setting the breathing rate to six breaths per minute since this seemed optimal to produce gamma brainwaves.

3. Enhance 39–42 Hz.

4. Inhibit 3–10 Hz as my alpha at 10 Hz was spiking and so needed to be included along with delta-theta.

5. Inhibit 52–58 Hz, which reflects EMG.
6. End with two minutes of eyes open HRV.
7. Eat a nutrition bar with usable sugars at the end of the hour and drink water throughout to replenish and hydrate the brain.

Data

Date	Gamma/EMG	Gamma µV	EMG µV
27/06/2012	0.826291	1.76	2.13
4/7/2012	0.845771	1.7	2.01
10/7/2012	0.850806	2.11	2.48
11/7/2012	0.952941	1.62	1.7
17/7/2012	0.909677	1.41	1.55
18/07/2012	0.972973	1.44	1.48
25/07/2012	0.955056	1.7	1.78
27/07/2012	1.080537	1.61	1.49
31/07/2012	0.972376	1.76	1.81
01/08/2012	0.790598	1.85	2.34
07/08/2012	0.846995	1.55	1.83
08/08/2012	1.037594	1.38	1.33
15/08/2012	0.951724	1.38	1.45
21/08/2012	0.955556	1.72	1.8
28/08/2012	0.980263	1.49	1.52
04/09/2012	0.870690	2.02	2.32
05/09/2012	0.921687	1.53	1.66
10/09/2012	1.000000	1.62	1.62
12/09/2012	1.000000	1.4	1.4
18/09/2012	0.968553	1.54	1.59
19/09/2012	0.897849	1.67	1.86
25/09/2012	0.934524	1.57	1.68
26/09/2012	0.922652	1.67	1.81
02/10/2012	0.959538	1.66	1.73
03/10/2012	0.937143	1.64	1.75
09/10/2012	0.968354	1.53	1.58
10/10/2012	0.993789	1.6	1.61
17/10/2012	0.914286	1.6	1.75
24/10/2012	0.915344	1.73	1.89
30/10/2012	0.927632	1.41	1.52
06/11/2012	0.924731	1.72	1.86
07/11/2012	0.986667	1.48	1.5
13/11/2012	0.969325	1.58	1.63
20/11/2012	0.938272	1.52	1.62
21/11/2012	0.938144	1.82	1.94
27/11/2012	0.903553	1.78	1.97
28/11/2012	0.957055	1.56	1.63
04/12/2012	0.988506	1.72	1.74
05/12/2012	0.986014	1.41	1.43
12/12/2012	0.901554	1.74	1.93
18/12/2012	0.960265	1.45	1.51
19/12/2012	0.940789	1.43	1.52
15/01/2013	0.952703	1.41	1.48
16/01/2013	0.898477	1.77	1.97

Results after Forty-Four Sessions

Assessment included
- single-electrode EEG;
- IVA;
- TOVA;
- draw-a-person task;
- full cap EEG;
- evoke potentials; and
- online neurocognitive test battery.

For the purposes of this chapter, I will compare only the tests we did before and after.

IVA

Full Scale Response Control Quotient: 136 to 122 (in 2012, auditory stamina was inordinately high) (July 2006: 106; August 2005: 93)

Auditory Response Control Quotient: 132 to 127 (July 2006: 109; August 2005: 93)

Visual Response Control Quotient: 131 to 111 (July 2006: 101; August 2005: 95)

Full Scale Attention Quotient: 121 to 122 (July 2006: 106; August 2005: 50)

Auditory Response Control Quotient: 123 to 127 (July 2006: 105; August 2005: 47)

Visual Response Control Quotient: 116 to 115 (July 2006: 106; August 2005: 64)

Balance Quotient: Remained slightly auditory dominant (July 2006: No Bias; August 2005: Auditory Dominant at extreme end)

Readiness Quotient: Auditory at 124 to 97, with 97 at no bias, and Visual from 111 to 97. (July 2006: Auditory 107, Visual 91; August 2005: Auditory 81, Visual 108)

Comprehension no change with both auditory and visual at WNL (within normal limits) (Same in 2006 and 2005)

Persistence no change in auditory at WNL and visual from 92 to 111 (WNL) (WNL in 2006; 2005: visual at 99, auditory at 75)

Sensory/Motor dropped in auditory from 302 ms to 224 ms; visual from 250 ms to 219 ms. (July 2006: Auditory 285 ms, Visual 314 ms; August 2005: Auditory 556 ms, Visual 530 ms)

Sustained Auditory Attention Quotient: from 121 to 118

Sustained Visual Attention Quotient: from 118 to 115

Auditory correct responses: 124 to 125/125 (July 2006: 124/125; August 2005: 98/125)

Visual correct responses: perfect (July 2006 125/125; August 2005: 109/125)

TOVA

My ADHD score increased from 2.17 to 3.72, both WNL. The scores being in the positive range reflected better attention than most women of the same age.

2012: 58th percentile in the total standard score of RT variability, and 99th in response time.

2013: 88th percentile in the total standard score of RT variability, and 99th in response time with more consistency across all four quarters.

Single-Electrode EEG Gamma Brainwave Ranges

39–40 Hz increased from 1.02 µV to 1.15

40–41 Hz remained at 1

41–42 Hz increased from 0.97 to 1.1 µV

Functional Changes

The changes included
- the feeling of being whole and no longer fragmented;
- improvement in intellectual capacity;
- improved stamina but not yet stabilized;
- increased exercise time up to half-an-hour four times per week with no adverse effects;

- increased walking time from five to ten minutes to twenty minutes one day a week;
- walked up an escalator;
- recovery time shortened but not yet stabilized;
- animated, not hyper but alive with an underlay of calm;
- calm;
- induced stress reduction that lasted longer as the weeks went by;
- reduced anger;
- reduced negativity;
- not as overwhelmed;
- uplift in emotion;
- immediately after training, "happy gamma," i.e., increased energy and talked more with animation;
- improved sleep from an average of 5.98 hours in June 2012 to 7.06 in February 2013;
- walking became automated, no more conscious direction required;
- spontaneous: I didn't need to wait for questions to prompt me to keep talking;
- responding in real time during conversation because self-talked much less or not required to begin conversing;

- I wasn't thinking while I was talking because I was saying what I wanted to say;
- I didn't forget what I wanted to say; and
- I got things done faster although I didn't feel I was going faster.

Daily Average Hours During and After Gamma Training

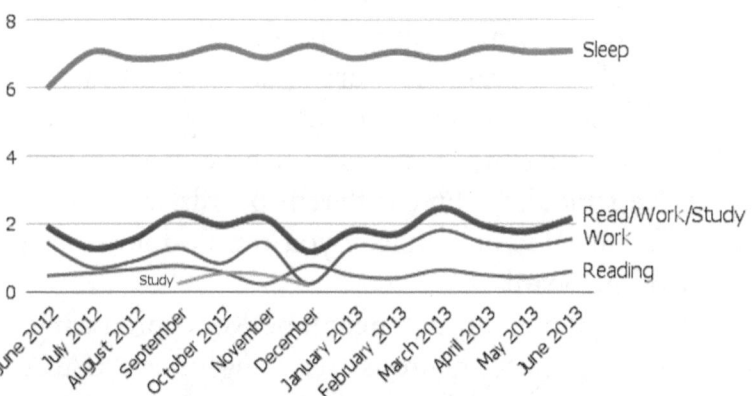

Conclusion

Gamma brainwave enhancement seems to improve cognitive, emotional, and physical states. A home routine to induce relaxation may keep EMG down. Initial results suggest aiming for a gamma/EMG (39–41 Hz/52–58 Hz) ratio of 1.0 or above.

In 2013, it was too early to say if the effects were permanent after forty-four training sessions. In 2017, I can affirm that the sense of wholeness, reduced anger, intellectual increase, speech fluency, and physical effects has remained. Extreme stress unfortunately derailed brain recovery; thus, long-term results on emotion and stress reduction under normal conditions could not be determined. However, gamma training became critical to coping under conditions of extreme stress.

Discussion

I experienced a brain without much gamma brainwave activity and a brain with it turned on quickly. The contrast gave me some thoughts.

You don't normally go through life feeling like you're fractured. I'm not talking multiple personality, but rather like different parts of your brain are working at different rates and at different levels and you yourself are not working as one biological unit. It's a strange feeling. Personalities have, well, personality. But this is like straddling three different boards with each board rising at different rates until finally you can no longer keep one foot on any of the boards.

Then all of a sudden, through neural networks producing more gamma brainwaves and neurons releasing more GABA, the boards plank together and fuse so that you cannot even see the cracks in between them. Now you're standing on a solid platform even though all your difficulties are not resolved. I have felt like one coherent biological unit since the forty-four sessions of gamma brainwave training.

Neuronal clusters that produce gamma brainwaves and GABA are the web that links all the rest of the networks and stimulates the other brainwaves, is what it felt like to me. When gamma activity increased, all the other brainwaves did as well. For example, alpha is open awareness. My awareness widened to such an extent right after each training that it was like receiving a new set of perception goggles. This went beyond the normal improvement in visual acuity after any kind of neurostimulation; my improved sensory and cognitive perception had a direct line into my processing centres. I could see and perceive the traffic in a way that I could understand all of it in real time. I could see people, buildings, and colours all at once in a way that didn't overload my brain. Normally, sensory information coming at me in that way would overload my processing, but it didn't. It left me in awe.

I think that accounts partly for the de-stressing effects of gamma. When your emotions work well, when your thoughts are clear, when your perceptions both sensory and mentally are freer flowing, it is much easier to perceive the problem, understand the problem, process the problem, and have emotions to guide cognitions to resolve the problem. That increases a sense of competence and drops worry.

I was thinking about the happy gamma effect. Where does happiness come from? Why when I've been enhanced in the exact same place with other brainwaves known to induce relaxed, calm attention or better ability to think, did that happy effect not happen but it does immediately with gamma? With gamma, you can literally drag yourself in, sunk under the demands of a world that doesn't accommodate brain injury, and skip on out after training, feeling high on life.

Research on diffuse axonal injury shows that neurons that previously fired together delink, networks become noisy, and so structures along networks no longer sync. It takes a long time to regrow axons and the networks that they used to be a part of so that one far off structure of the brain once again fires in response to or in anticipation of another. But gamma brainwaves seem to restore that connection instantly. While training, one feels "let go," like you're flowing as one excellently running biological being where the body harmonizes with the brain. It's a happy feeling. Gamma brainwaves are like a carrier wave that stimulates and synchronizes neurons in other networks to produce alpha and beta brainwaves and also facilitates communication between far-apart neurons and structures that have delinked. Perhaps neuronal clusters that produce gamma brainwaves feed a foundational web over and through the entire brain. Stimulating them re-fires the web so that, like a flame seeking open routes along a wired grid, gamma-producing clusters turn threads back on and reconnect structures through alternative pathways that injury had sliced apart.

In this case, gamma-producing clusters are much more than consciousness. They tie the mind to the brain. They support all neural networks and allow for the full expression of the mind through the biological human. This may explain the results of Whitham et al in a 2008 study[33] showing mental activity affects gamma solely through EMG. When the web is healthy as in normal subjects and all the threads are active, stimulating any one of those threads won't make a difference. An active thread is an active thread. Adding more threads to a complete web won't make the web stronger or better either. But when injury turns off a thread, things fall through and so stimulating can turn a thread back on, showing up as increased gamma beyond EMG alone. The questions are: which neuronal clusters produce gamma? Can training gamma first, potentiate training of the other brainwaves to accelerate and enhance their production after brain injury either through single-electrode brain biofeedback or nineteen-point network LORETA feedback? Even though in theory I don't believe so, whether non-brain injured people can benefit can only be determined with good quality research.

Since EMG must be below 2 µV yet most cannot achieve low muscle tension, is there a way to passively induce gamma

---

[33] Emma M. Whitham, Trent Lewis, et al. *Thinking activates EMG in scalp electrical recordings.* Clin Neurophys 119 (2008): 1166-1175. http://www.clinph-journal.com/article/S1388-2457(08)00045-X/pdf

brainwaves through a technology like AVE? Could we use that to prep the brain for active brain biofeedback of the other brainwaves?

Conversely, could SMR/Beta AVE and/or low-intensity light therapy be used to drop EMG just prior to gamma brain biofeedback?

Would gamma training before difficult physical or occupational therapy not only make therapy easier as it restores automaticity but also increase its effectiveness by firing along network pathways around the injured neurons to effect easy movement and improve balance? I believe so.

Brain biofeedback is exhausting. But gamma brainwave enhancement uniquely gave me energy that overcame the exhaustion of the work despite the fact that training gamma is probably more difficult than any other brainwave because of the intense need to keep EMG low. So how does gamma generate enough energy not only to feed the requirements of the work but also pep one up? Is it the web effect and/or because it acts like controlled-release pregabalin and increases GABA?

Normally brain biofeedback takes a while to show effects. Even after training has begun to show changes, the immediate effects aren't seen for a day I'm told. In me, gamma enhancement shows up immediately. Perhaps that's my plastic brain that allows that. But it is interesting that gamma training has the most intense and the quickest effect of all the brainwaves I've had trained. The very first time the effect was obvious within the hour, not true for other brainwaves in me even after months and years of training. I had my first gamma training after almost five years off from any biofeedback training. I had continued using AVE and CES (cranioelectrical stimulation), yes, but again I don't believe that accounts for the immediate and dramatic effect after training gamma the first time. Perhaps I still had higher levels of GABA from the gabapentin in me, which could account for the effect. As training progressed, the dramatic improvement diminished as my baseline gamma brainwaves increased. However, the immediate effect after training remained stronger for gamma than any other brainwave in me.

I believe that brain injury rehab must include gamma brainwave training and in the earliest stages. The question is how?

For further reading and updates, go to http://wp.me/Pf8xE-16D. *Also see Chapters 22 and 23.*

Shock

Sewing the mouth.
Releasing the torments.

Chapter 25

Alone in the City

Only a few LORETA sessions left, I thought in late July 2013. *Then maybe I'll continue until October, really cement in this training,* I considered as I climbed into Mum's car and we drove off. Highway driving had become tolerable. It had been a good day. I had read the subtitles during LORETA to see if we could activate my reading network. As usual, the movie resisted staying full size, but my scores had soared, a sense of well-being had grown in me, and hope sprang alive in my breast. Mum's phone rang through into her car's speakers, interrupting my chatty happiness. She answered it.

"I was looking at a property," a strange man's voice spoke into the air between us.

My heart began to pound. I said nothing as I listened to real estate talk. Eight months earlier, Mum had promised me they weren't planning to move. The conversation ended. I was silent. All my life, my mother and my mother's family taught us one never broke one's promises. Or commitments.

People make promises all the time, I thought, *saying they will do this or that, but when it comes to the point, when it's time for promises to be kept, people don't. This is why Jesus says to toss oaths and simply focus on yes being yes.* My brain's networks threaded new connections as the LORETA effect continued in me, the bad news stimulating neuronal activity in a mood-threatening dimension. I watched the highway unfold in front of me as we followed its straights and curves and the multi-hued grey cars in front of us.

We sat down in the café, and she told me. They were moving out of Toronto into the country.

Normalcy vanished. My new life wasn't anything like I had asked or imagined, as we recite like sheep in church as if it can only be good.

The rule of every good thing must be outbalanced by shit strikes again, I griped to myself. Any thought of returning to the days when I used to visit my parents' home, the home I grew up in, vanished into the vat of losses my brain injury kept filling up. How did I get here, where I went from having many people I could call on to none? How did I end up being a person people didn't want to spend time with? I feel like a duty. How was it only healthcare people wanted to talk to me or looked forward to seeing me? It was like God was playing a game of what would it take. How much more isolation will it take to force her to choose expensive academic studies and non-earning writing over her kin?

I sat unmoving the next day in my neurodoc's office as I held my purse against my stomach. My childhood stomach aches had returned.

"I feel unwell."

"You don't look well."

I couldn't speak.

"What's happened?"

He waited. He was good at waiting. He leaned back, eyes on me, face benign.

I looked at him, but my mouth refused to open. I was not going to say those words, my subconscious had decided. The feeling of watching kith and kin spiral away and being unable to do anything about it, deluged me. The feeling of people leaving when I was in great need was not much different than when they left because I seemed much better and they could take off safely from that which had caused them anxiety. Me. But the changes in my brain weren't stable yet! The rewiring was suddenly going in the wrong direction.

I sent my eyes roaming around his office, the books and piles of brochures on depression and anxiety and the computer monitor blanking out on his other side. The second hand in the utilitarian clock above my head ticked its black hand around its white face. Tick. Tick. Tick. Tick. Tick.

"They're moving."

He waited.

"I will be alone in the city."

The ticking in my head stopped.

Thirteen days later, on a humid day, during LORETA training, my beta one spiked off the charts in Brodmann area 30. My emotions had connected with memory. It didn't last long, but the good news of my brain's default and emotion networks beginning to reset countered briefly the shock that kept reverberating my neurons.

Weeks later, my socked feet dragged across my kitchen's cork floor, whispering the words banging from one side of my brain to the other, the words my neurodoc had spoken to me while advocating on my behalf to my mother: be flexible, both give, and look at the positive opportunity of vacations.

"You get to go skeet shooting," he crowed, ignoring my disinterest, my weak shoulder, and my sensitivity to sudden noise. "You have a lot of anger from the past," he stated, while not talking about the practical support I needed. "You can write in your parents' new home," he cheered, seeming to think I could write anywhere, ignoring how writing bled my brain power and how my books sprout out of my fingers only into my computer at home. He spoke to me as if I was simply being closed-minded; he seemed to wave aside as if not true how the continual neural changes in my brain demanded external rocks of structure and routine. He nodded at my mother's complaint that I didn't accept Imeda's out-of-the blue offer to photograph magnificent terrain outside of the city and left it to me to defend on my own my fatigue, my migraines, and the unanswerable question of who would care for me while I lay beached on the couch after such a trip.

Where was the advocacy?

He'd boasted once how he'd bluntly explained reality to other mothers who hadn't understood his patient's health needs. I'd believed him. I'd believed my neurodoc was on my side as he claimed. I'd believed he understood how exhaustion is my constant companion, how the desperation to see normalcy pushed my engine past the empty tank, and how I wanted so much to at least be able to visit my parents under my own steam and spontaneously. I'd believed he had empathy for me, his patient, or at least more for me than my parents, his professional and social peers. I'd believed that he would speak for me while shock shut down my thoughts and tied my lips. Calmly, firmly, non-threateningly, he would say the words I would if I could, and he would ask why hadn't they discussed their concerns with me as they would have before my brain injury? But I didn't hear him utter the questions I needed to hear: How did you imagine Shireen would cope? How do you think she felt that you didn't discuss the ramifications on her before you made the final decision? How could we ensure Shireen is not left alone in the city while meeting your worries? I'd believed that somehow he could turn this horrible news around.

Those unspoken questions locked in my brain said, "The reward for fighting to get help, to make yourself better, is punishment."

You get left.

Tiredly, he said, "Don't give up."

I stared out the window, counting the days until I could see my spiritual mentor. Under the wide-awake stars, the barriers to tweeting out my real feelings tumbled down. No one would be awake to read them. I forgot my Twitter followers live in different time zones.

"The light at the end of the tunnel is turned off until further notice," I wrote, channelling a sign my ex and I had printed out when we were young and dollars scarce in the 1990s' recession. Blackness wreathed my fingers as I typed on my iPod Touch from my flat bed. "Vanity, vanity. All is vanity, for the sun sets on everyone," I finished writing, channelling Ecclesiastes. I retweeted, "Loneliness is the leprosy of the modern world."

A kind Nova Scotian woman, a fellow writer and editor, read my tweet and direct messaged me, "Are you all right? Virtual hugs are coming your way. Can I help?"

We spoke. She put me in touch with another woman with a brain injury, someone further along in the journey than I was. That woman joined Twitter, tweeted and emailed me, until finally, in wonder, I answered and gave her my phone number. We spoke for an hour and a half, at the end of which I had a coach, someone who could help me heal. I sat back in awe. And then my Cambridge friend from Flickr messaged me, concerned.

Spiritual energy surged into me. I was able to finish the #ABIchat page on my website. Richard, @MyABI_byRH, a young man from across the pond, had inspired me to launch #ABIchat. I could still start the weekly Twitter chat to help him and others cope with this awful, awful injury. But I wasn't able to write for my blog or the *Huffington Post* anymore.

Three days later, my coach directed me to the positive psychology questionnaires at authentichappiness.org, run by the University of Pennsylvania. She wanted me to discover my top five strengths. I did it. My top strengths were creativity, ingenuity, and originality. I felt no emotion. While on the website, I spotted one for optimism and hope. It had few but strange questions. I was rated optimistic.

Cool, I thought, *I'm more positive than my neurodoc thinks I am. He can't dispute this objective evidence.*

He questioned its validity.

"I wouldn't be here if I wasn't optimistic," I pointed out. I added that he was the one who had extolled positive psychology. He admitted that, smiling readily. He read out loud the only low score of optimism I had for good events persevering, and I suddenly understood what that meant. He agreed I had a right to be angry about my situation but felt he had advocated for me.

"I'd like to try again," he said positively. I doubted it was worth it. He nodded as I vented that they didn't understand my fatigue. He encouraged me to take another course and that I had nothing to lose to ask my parents for the course fees. He said, "I hope I've given you back some of the motivation that I killed in the last session." I didn't know.

September crawled in. At last I was sitting in my spiritual mentor's warm, yellow-painted office, her candle lit on the small coffee table between our embracing armchairs.

I poured out my heartache, my shock, and my desire to fire my neurodoc's fat ass. I was in the middle of a staycation as I'd put it to him, but really I'd once again missed the timing of booking a new set of appointments with his secretary. Too bad I hadn't missed it by more.

My mentor had walked with me in my journey for ten years, seen me at my lowest, seen the hope dawn only a few short months ago, and encouraged me when I'd been ready to quit before, as I seemed to do every few years. She said, "As I listen to you, I see waves. There's a trough, and then right after, a wave comes to rise you up. Every seven waves, the seventh is bigger."

She asked, as she had asked me before, "Why is your neurodoc not focusing on you?"

I didn't know. I'd followed all his ideas and focused on my relationships and his advice so that he couldn't say I hadn't tried. I remembered her words from long ago. My mind travelled back twelve years and travelled forward through all the people who had left me. So much had not changed! My parents were finishing now the leaving that had begun ten years ago. But then I had to be fair. My relationship with my mother was better and made so by my neurodoc.

Unlike my neurodoc, my spiritual mentor empathized with me over the bad news and didn't press upon me the idea of how great this move would be. She said, "Don't look for God's will but walk on. I'll pray for you. Look to your passion, to what you enjoy. Look for what lifts you up. Look for the waves." She urged me to give my neurodoc a chance since he'd helped me until now. "Think carefully, Shireen," she encouraged me.

Because I trusted her, I kept my appointment with him in mid-September, but I was not courageous. I feared confrontation. My brain didn't work quickly enough to counter points. I'd thought through everything over and over so that I'd remember what my mentor had said and what I felt. My emotions had a habit of disappearing in the face of difficult conversations, taking thoughts with them. I needed to rely on my memory so that I could advocate for myself. But what if my memory failed like it had too often?

But the gamma enhancement training had improved my memory. There were even early signs my photographic memory was returning. I could do this.

I sat down in my accustomed chair, and my neurodoc asked, "How are you doing?"

"Fine."

"How was your staycation?"

"Good."

He looked at me with his smiling, pleasant expression and asked me specific questions about my new coach and the Oxford course on metaphysics I'd decided to take and had just begun. I was forced to answer with more than one word and to admit I'd followed his advice to ask Mum for the course money, and she, as she so often did, found a way to help me.

"Good! What did you think?"

I muttered my response.

"What was that?"

"Nothing."

His expression slipped a bit, revealing the effort he was putting in to get me to talk. I felt mildly sorry for him, but I was a tightly lidded cauldron boiling at his pathetic advocacy, at his betrayal by not standing by my side.

He leaned back and asked, "What's bothering you?"

I stared at him.

He said, "I'm good at reading people."

I looked away, thinking it doesn't take a genius to see my rage. I watched myself not saying a word, surprised at being so silent. It felt like my conscious mind was waiting for my subconscious to supply the words I needed.

I looked up at him and asked, "What do you think is bothering me?"

He shrugged.

I asked again.

He said, "I could hypothesize, but I want you to tell me."

"How honest?"

"Very." He folded his arms and crossed his legs.

I said, "You're in a protective posture."

He deliberately unfolded his arms, but then he kept moving, adjusting his position, his smile firmly fixed on his face. I kept my eyes on his and his posture. He clasped his hands around his upright crossed knee as he kept looking away and back at me.

Good enough, I thought. He may hear what I have to say and what I promised my spiritual mentor I would say.

My heart thumping, my anger driving me, I spoke, the intensity of my emotion rumbling my voice, empowering my thoughts.

"You ill-served me," I said. I grilled him on his memory of all the things I'd shared about my fatigue and my difficulties. I pushed him on his inability to understand my exhaustion. Out of the recesses, I heard myself challenge him on the blinders of being a white male toward what it's like being a minority of a minority woman. He objected. But now that my subconscious was in control driving my voice, I wasn't letting go. All my frustrations poured out. My own neurodoc couldn't understand the problem of another deciding for me what I could or could not do or what my interests should encompass. He couldn't understand that brain injury had taken away every vestige of control over myself, my relationships, and my life.

Choosing where to go and when for optional trips was within my control at last, even if still not for appointments like with him. I could see him only on a certain day of the week. And I had to make it work within my schedule. If he saw me late and had to leave early, I had no choice. I had to accept my appointment being much shorter than the forty-five minutes I was entitled to. Was he trying to force me to speak up? I couldn't tell, and I didn't feel it was fair that with my broken brain and trashed self-confidence, I had to advocate for even my appointment duration.

I asked him again and again, "Why is it OK for me to lose days in order to visit someone, but it's not OK for you or for anyone else to lose days? Why is it OK for me to rest up two days before and recover four days after a social event but not any of you? Why is it OK for me to lose all that time, to not be able to work on my books or study for my course or do any of my personal priorities for the sake of people who wouldn't do the same for me?"

I saw light dawn in his eyes when I asked him, "When you're asking me to put my energy to my course, why are you now telling me I should use my energy to visit my family?"

I began to feel strong.

"You didn't even try to advocate for me with Mum."

"She's not my patient. I can't change her mind."

"After all you told me how you were with others, you didn't even try."

He began to understand why I thought he had ill-served me. He brought up my file, chose a date to try again with my mother, and wrote down my points that I wanted his advocacy for. I asked, "Why am I supposed to be the only flexible one when I'm the one with the brain injury?" He nodded and added it to his list. Feeling emboldened, I said, "You're deferential to my father." He acknowledged that he might be in his subconscious.

I sighed. I usually chose physicians who didn't know Dad. But I had had no choice because so few treat brain injury, even in Canada's biggest city. I took his non-denial and hoped for the best.

He said, "I hope you will give me a second chance."

I nodded.

I stood up to leave and opened the door.

He looked up at me and asked, "Are you feeling better? I hope you are."

"Yes."

He smiled widely. "Good."

Chapter 26

Not a Reader

December 10, 2013. 1:16 a.m. I shivered underneath my fleecy pyjamas and bed covers deep into my chest. My pulse was not there. Then there. Then it stopped underneath my listening fingertips. Time spooked. I moved and began deep breathing. Warmth returned with my steady pulse. The doctors had missed that special sign in my sleep study. And because he'd given me a phone number he didn't check daily but had allowed me to believe he did, my neurodoc didn't return my call until long after fear had fled under the busyness of the day. So I didn't tell him. And I left for my appointments.

I stepped onto the subway platform as it hit me: I was not a reader.

I was no longer the Shireen who travelled to her parents, who visited kith and kin, who baked the birthday cakes, who hosted parties and cooked multi-course dinners, who wrote for two hours straight and jumped up after to make omelettes and pizzas, whose self-discipline trampled tasks into submission, and who held appointments, phone numbers, faces, names, facts in her head and linked them up effortlessly to create new concepts. I was not the Shireen who leapt from book to book, read newspapers over breakfast, e-newsletters before work, mass paperbacks over lunch, marketing-course material in the afternoon, research any time of day, a mystery novel as a snack, and pages of a literary novel after preparing supper before my husband got home. Now, initiation deficit delayed my next book choice for weeks. Every lunchtime, I self-talked myself to open up the easy-to-read mystery novel, reminding myself that I enjoyed the act of reading even though flow eluded me, characters swanned in and out of memory, plots got lost in my neurons, and mysteries I'd read two, three, four times remained mysterious. Sure, I was reading to the end of a sentence then to the end of a paragraph before stopping to go do whatever my brain had decided I had to do right then and there. *That was good*, I cheerlead myself. But as my booted foot touched down on the terrazzo floor that freezing December morning, I admitted that books had become Venus volcanoes, endless scrabbling up to the last page. Within hours of relishing my success, they imploded into a Mariana Trench of not remembering the plot, the non-regular characters, or even if I had read it before.

I was not a reader.
I wasn't getting the help I needed.
I didn't have what it took to rehab myself.
I was alone in the yoke of daily life.
I felt sick.

I confessed it in my blog post for myself. I had worked on my reading for thirteen years with barely any change. New vocabulary in the philosophy course continued to dodge my memory banks. My healthcare team said if I could read as long as the average person, that was good enough. Writing demanded hours of reading per day. Napping after just twenty minutes and recalling barely any of it was not average. My neurodoc deferred to experts, except there were none. He'd chased a supposed one for a year, at the end of which he abashedly handed me a Post-it Note with the aphasia website address I'd found on my own long before.

Secretly, I hoped someone in my real life would read my confession and do something. Encourage me. Ask me how they could help. Maybe call my neurodoc and say, "Hey, did you know she's struggling here? Do something!" Or he'd notice himself. But nope.

Ice rained down from angry clouds, encasing the city, creating pools of powerless darkness, and landing me on a relative's couch, alone on Christmas Day. While the oldest generations opened presents and feasted at their adult children's home, I stared fixedly at *The Holiday Fireplace* on TV. I was so depleted from protecting my frozen home from the days-long blackout on my own, I couldn't move. I absorbed my stupidity in trying to hold on to my Christmas beliefs with my meagre reserves while my kin in their wealth rigidly stuck to their plans. While other families celebrated the unifying thrill of moving Christmas to the weekend when the power returned, mine did not.

No more, I excoriated myself and walked away from the idea of Christmas with them. My neurodoc let me avoid talk of the ice storm as I ran into 2014. I looked to him as a haven from all the forces knocking me down and told him in our first appointment of the new year, "I don't know how to get myself out of this state of shock. I don't want to treat myself anymore. I have to put so much effort into everything."

"All right. All right," he said as if calming down a child.

"I've fallen down. I can't be strong anymore. I need to lean on someone." I had no one. But he had the smarts and the education to take over from me coordinating my home treatments and healthcare, even though, like other physicians I'd met, he had little to no knowledge of the latest discoveries of the brain. I asked him. But he didn't want to learn what I knew of electrophysiology, and he didn't want to coordinate my healthcare. My GP couldn't, and anyway I was so fearful of hearing more bad health news (my diabetes had returned) that I was avoiding him. I began to deteriorate.

In early February, during tDCS of Wernicke's area, I chatted with my brain trainer instead of reading. I couldn't go through the motions anymore of trying to read when it wasn't working. I stopped doing the FutureLearn course I'd begun on December 4, 2013. I couldn't resolve on my own how to pursue a Ph.D. with my limited cognitive reading skills and low funds and Cota help to find resources do so was dwindling. My books sat on my shelves, silent testaments to the person I used to be. I let go. I didn't notice my studies fade behind me in the chaos of new emotions and disturbing flashbacks.

After one month of activating the conversation network during tDCS, I finally experienced conversation again, not just one-on-one but in a small group in a quiet setting, too. I didn't have to "warm up." I didn't have to listen for a while then drag out of my blank mind what I wanted say. I plunged right into the conversation—I heard and generated related thoughts in real time—rather like a normal person. Lynda explained that the Wernicke's area integrates language to understand what you hear and read. Expression is in the frontal and Broca's area. You need to understand what you hear so that you know what you want to say, otherwise your talk is unrelated to what others are saying.

November 2014 loomed. I had nothing. No novel idea. No human to gear me up. All I had was my new identity as a writer who wrote during NaNoWriMo. With no research done, what could I write?

A character said hello in my mind.

Another showed up.

And another.

And another.

I began writing the last chapter of my Twitter novel on the first day of November for NaNoWriMo.

The logistics of it overwhelmed me. The characters spoke in my mind and created their identities in the Twitter world, but I didn't like the ending I had begun with. My original idea didn't pan out in the way I had envisioned. So much needed to occur off Twitter, not just in the tweets between characters. Yet for about an hour a day, I escaped my life and lived in one welcome part of my new identity.

At the end of each new chapter, fatigue chained my hands and led me to the couch as my writing self shouted louder and louder, "Stephen King is right. You need to read to write."

I told myself, *Your writing has leapt beyond your reading. You're going to lose your writing if you don't read. You can't even complete a novel in thirty days anymore!*

Fear, anger, and grief shot off the pressure valve and spewed all over my neurodoc. "You have to help me relearn to read!" I cried over the phone four days after I'd repeated to his face that I needed reading rehab. His only answer had been not to give up looking for help. It usually took my brain two days to process emotions and conversations.

"I'm not an expert," he replied now.

"Neither are the reading experts if all they can come up with are fucking aphasia websites. I need to work with the person I see every week. I need someone to read to me, not just me reading on my own," I yelled. "You have no preconceived notions of what reading is, how to measure it, or what to do to treat it. You know nothing about reading rehab. That's why you'll ponder what will actually work. And work with the ADD Centre, too. It's a team effort, you, me, and them."

Getting healthcare people to work as a team was like herding cats glued to their own beds. I didn't have the strength.

"I won't do literature searches."

"Everyone I know who has a brain injury has similar problems with reading and no one has solutions. You'd need an upside-down periscope to find something that obscure in the literature!"

"All right," he said. "I'll think about what I can do in the new year." But he wasn't going to work with others. I'd have to consult experts on my own.

Tick. Tick. Tick.

One by one, in early 2015, my neurodoc handed me articles from *Wall Street Journal* to *Toronto Sun* and some poetry too and asked me to read them aloud the way I read silently.

No one had done that before.

He accurately observed my reading problems in action. His diagnostic energy encouraged me to research it on my own.

Long ago as a student in psychology, I had been a guinea pig for a reading experiment. They had told me from tracking my eyes that I was a fast reader, the kind whose eyes read partial words and jumped lines. Maybe my eyes were reading like a fast reader, but my brain needed to track whole word to whole word in order. Perhaps I could sign up as a guinea pig for an eye tracking experiment in exchange for finding out how I read.

I emailed several psychologists at the University of Toronto in any area remotely related to reading. I found a young one. What set him apart was curiosity, intelligence, lateral thinking, and most of all a desire to help someone.

That last made a difference to me.

I met him in his office near the end of February 2015. I rested up and prepared over and over what I wanted to talk about so that I'd remember. There in his office, in that hour or so with him, I wanted to be a normal non-brain-injured human being talking about an intellectual puzzle that happened to be mine.

I left his office over an hour after I'd arrived, my mind buzzing with new knowledge, my soul energized by being treated as an equal, my brain challenged to keep up with a level of intellectual thought that it hadn't had to in a very long time, my ideas valued, and eye tracking on the horizon.

Tick. Tick. Tick.

I flew to England during March break to visit my oldest aunt and an older cousin I'd never met before and to escape my brain injury. Except you can never escape brain injury. I arrived in England to discover that however I wanted to communicate was fine with everyone. I could text if I wanted to, phone if I wanted to, or email if I wanted to. I didn't have to pretzel my way around other people's preferred twentieth century communications. Instead, they in their normal lives, busy work, and relationships said, "Let us know what works best for you, and it's all right."

All right?

I almost wept.

I got on the tube trepidatiously. An old, convoluted system with narrow passageways and erratic stairs, the tube seemed perfect to siphon my energy. I got off at my stop, following the multiple Way Out signs with their visible arrows, with the same amount of energy as I'd gotten on. This never happened on the TTC, the Toronto Transit Commission, Toronto's excuse for a public transit system, whose idea of accessibility is to not put stop request buttons next to every priority seat reserved for the disabled in the new European-style streetcars. English society embraced accommodating me with a smile. I soared home having been welcomed, accepted, supported, and rejuvenated and landed back to being lectured on my perceived closed-mindedness, to being forced to self-drive my reading, and to struggling with the inaccessible TTC and city, like Toronto's garbage system where I had to remember and figure out which piece of garbage went in which of three bins while the bins hogged narrow sidewalks, challenging my precarious balance. I fought not to end up on the road in the path of careless drivers. I cried.

"Are you going to move?" my brain trainer, neurodoc, and peer mentor all asked me as I related my adventures, my memory of being accepted lifting my face with joy.

"No," I said, "I'm not moving. God has brought me to Toronto, and this is where I need to be. And I am, first and foremost, Canadian, anyway."

And then I received the most unexpected message through Facebook from Glenda. I hardly ever went on Facebook. I'd had to prune back my social media because shock and traumas had stretched out their vacuum hoses to the little energy plants in my neurons. Stunned, I let her know she could email me, and she wrote back that an old friend had suicided. I attended the memorial on a cool spring day with white clouds puffing across the arc of blue sky. The clock whirled back to when we were close, as if our relationship hadn't fractured.

We met for lunch and coffee two weeks after that. I wasn't sure I'd be able to eat. But I'd grown up with Glenda. Surely, my brain could multitask eating and talking since I knew her face, I knew her expressions, and her gestures. My brain didn't have to consciously watch, process, and interpret all that so that I could respond. Surely, it would be automatic with her like it was with my mother. My speech pathologist had said back in 2001, "With social conversation, it doesn't matter if you miss stuff, they won't notice." But Glenda deserved my full focus. I ate sporadically, and we talked for over two hours. I wanted to know how she was doing and what life had brought her. I could see healing in her eyes.

The fourth time we met, I ordered coffee and water only. I needed to resolve the way we had parted in 2006, and I wasn't about to attempt multitasking and fail at both eating and resolving. I needed to find out if she'd heard me say, "You call me at the end of the three months." And I needed an apology.

My brain trainer had said, "You will do it because I know you." But my heart hammered, and I feared the confrontation of asking. Brain injury wallops your cognition. Conflict becomes a minefield of unspoken thoughts and imponderable English. Before you get to the other side, you're blown off course and then detonated right out.

I hedged by asking Glenda why she thought we separated. She indicated that I'd hurt her, yet soon I understood she hadn't understood the depth of my social isolation, my difficulty in maintaining human connection when we didn't speak regularly, and the reasons for my request to talk three times a week as my spiritual mentor and I had discussed I should ask for. I explained. She listened intently. The others in the café became irrelevant. Water became immaterial.

Suddenly, I heard her say, "I apologize for hurting you."

The wound I'd tamped down, avoided speaking its existence, leaked out. The energy of her remorse and my unspoken forgiveness sewed its edges together. We hugged in parting on the warm concrete sidewalk under the sun.

Tick. Tick. Tick.

Several months later, I got my eye tracking information. I was right. My eyes tracked like a fast reader, and my brain worked too slowly to interpret. When I'd read out loud as my neurodoc had instructed me to do, using my finger to guide me, my eye tracking slowed to the speed of my brain. Reading whole words sequentially meant I could recall.

My neurodoc assigned me readings to get around my indecisiveness. But he didn't regularly check up on me or bother sharing his thoughts or observations except the odd time desperation lashed me to ask him and I received brief answers. *I can do this*, I recited to myself as I laboured over my daily homework and failed to coordinate the big picture of my reading rehab. He continued to drop my reading priority in favour of what he considered other priorities despite the brain biofeedback showing reading profoundly pepped my brain and relaxed my heartbeats.

The psychology prof remained the one bright spot for me. Over the year, in sporadic meetings, I learnt more and more through his generosity of spirit and intellectual curiosity about my reading issue.

But PTSD and a healing brain flared emotions that halted me; initiation deficit bulged. I was blogging, straining to stay positive, trying to see small changes as good. I no longer had to nap for two hours, only one hour, then not at all after reading. But my recall didn't budge. My inability to learn didn't budge. My inability to see the big picture didn't budge.

I gave up.

Again.

And this time, I didn't care about the effect on my writing. My coach and I had parted ways. I'd lost another new friend. Kin was scattered outside of Toronto—given the exigencies of my injury, far enough way to be on the other side of Canada. My parents saw me less and less. At the beginning of this journey, Mum and I visited three times a week and Dad weekly on and off. By 2015, I saw my father not at all and my mother once a week and spoke to her only on that day. Grief built a wasp's nest in me.

I stopped baking. Another loss in the vast valley of losses. What did it matter if my writing exited, too?

Shock Learnings

Flashbacks torment.

Re-emerging emotions breed uncontrollable chaos.

Shireen Jeejeebhoy

Misdiagnosing diffuse axonal injury as psychiatric or characterological destroys.

Social isolation vanishes a mind.

Flashbacks

Flashbacks cry out for immediate comfort by trusted, reliable family, friends, and neurodocs. Flashbacks demand hourly, daily, weekly reliable shoring up of the person's defences.

Re-emerging emotions demand expert, gentle, and kind guidance to relearn them and (re)attach them to memories.

Family and friends socially isolating and healthcare professionals not keeping contact when the person can't get to the office, fragment and crush the soul, bolt in grief permanently.

You turn a person into the scariest kind of all, the one who has nothing left to lose.

Grief

Depression is an affect, a mood disorder, a label physicians put on people with brain injury as if it is the same state as those with the mental illness of depression.

It is easier to say that this looks like depression or it must be a mood disorder, than to think that this person has a brain injury, neurons are dead, neural networks are offline, emotional centres are damaged, and cognition or movement disrupted.

Depression diagnosis denies the effect of a complex injury on affect.

Depression diagnosis denies the effect of people's reactions to brain injury.

Depression diagnosis ignores that rejection and abandonment create PTSD, slice apart social bonds that tie human beings together in relationships of trust not to harm one another, and leave us on our own to cope with our injury and manage daily life with a broken brain.

Depression diagnosis relieves physicians of the responsibility to research and treat injured neurons.

Characterological diagnosis denies the reality and pain of managing the simplest of activities with a brain that cannot problem solve, decide, feel emotions normally, think clearly, and perceive and process in real time.

Labelling incomprehensible behaviour toxic relieves our friends and family of providing daily emotional, social, and cognitive support they would normally give a person they profess to love when in distress.

Baffling or absent emotional states relieve people from taking initiative to help us function and participate in society.

Depression diagnosis allows psychiatrists to replace the needed several-times-a-week support with a pill and monthly monitoring.

Depression, characterological, and negative-attitude diagnosis denies our deep, intense grief over the death of our selves.

Misdiagnosis grants everyone the right to abandon us in our suffering.

For updates, go to http://wp.me/Pf8xE-185.

Now What?

The future lay impenetrably ahead
As the present wound incomprehensibly
Around me.

Chapter 27

Labyrinthine Recovery

I hesitated. December 2015 rain chilled me and, as I stepped onto the cedar-fragrant path of the labyrinth, fear filled me. My legs resisted as I walked forward into that fear, and Jesus joined me in the labyrinth, speaking to me all the way through, except when he fell silent. His silence spoke to me too. Even when I could not hear him, his message in my mind said, "Keep walking. You are not alone."

In 2014, the first time I'd walked the labyrinth's narrow, cedar mulch path between borders of stones, the centre with its rock of solitude and meditation seemingly walled off, I hadn't known what to expect. It'd looked ordinary to me, small. Yet the moment I'd stepped onto the mulch, God had begun to speak to me. I was not alone.

"The journey is long," I'd heard. "You're doubling back over and over to the beginning."

Now in 2015, under December clouds, the rain drizzling my feet on the giving mulch, I hastened my steps toward the centre through the labyrinth's circuitous path. I felt the centre represented my purpose in life. But the path turned me back.

"You're turned back because the centre was a sham," I heard. I was not in the truth of rehab. My old goals were shams not built on the truth.

I stopped walking right next to where the labyrinth entrance was. I was back at the beginning of my injury. I felt I couldn't go on.

"You're to have patience," I heard. "Faith. It's a long path, long and arduous." I moved through the rain, the centre seeming miles away yet I could see it. I just couldn't reach it.

And then I did.

The centre was God's love. God was holding my dreams in his hands. As I walked the back half of the labyrinth, God's love flowed out from the centre and fed the entire network, my life, my past, and future. The soil of my purpose was always under my feet.

"You take it with you wherever you go," God said. When I thought I was heading to the end, the path again turned back. I wanted to shortcut it, to get in out of the cold wet, and to dry my sodden shoes. But God said, "Don't shortcut it, else you will shortcut the fruit." I sighed and tramped on. I turned the corner, and this time the end was for real. I exited the labyrinth with joy as I heard God say, "Don't give up because what you want is there when you're ready to give up."

Tick. Tick. Tick.

Six months later, I stepped out my door, Dad's cane in one hand, earbuds jammed in my ears both to protect me from the noise and to hear my neurodoc's voice leading me on my walk as I recovered from eye surgery. The measles had probably half blinded me when I was three, yet the unthinkable had happened: my vision had been improving since my brain injury. Somehow the injury and my treatments were restoring sight to my blind eye. I'd had eye surgery to stabilize those changes and make the eyes work together again. The surgeon in his understated way had tried to warn me about the vision changes coming. None of my healthcare team had discussed post-surgery with him.

The silos kept their boundaries, and I suffered for it.

At first, I didn't see the suffering coming as I froze in wonder at seeing details in bricks, the nuances of the fluttery wings of a sparrow, the intense greens of trees leafing out in May 2016, and the depth of grooves and ridges of a wood carving. The sheer length of how far I could see halted my steps as I stared and stared at vanishing points far away. Faces changed, and my brain glommed on to features to process microexpressions, colour nuances, and lines now visible to me. Some people looked very different than they had before my surgery. I realized it was because they kept a part of themselves hidden and my new vision could see it.

My injured brain struggled to integrate this photonic surge of new information. I walked like a drunk, one foot stomping down hard to catch my balance, my opposite hand gripping the cane so as not to lurch right over. Dizziness spun my head; nausea rose up in answer. My auditory system didn't like my vision reclaiming its space in my visual cortex, and the two began to duke it out. Just like in 2000 and 2001, evidence-based medicine had no answer for me. At least this time, it didn't pretend to. Earbuds and a cane became my friends to dial down the world's volume that the surgery had suddenly increased and to give me stability in this heaving visual world.

I'd anticipated fatigue for six weeks, not months. But like in 2001, I was back at the beginning, the recovery excruciatingly long, consuming, and arduous. My surgeon spent time explaining to me over the phone that my brain had to remap the whole world with my dramatic vision change. My old vision hadn't fed information efficiently to my brain. Now much more information was going in, and my brain wasn't used to it. Once it was, I'd have more efficient perception and proprioception. He stated that my neuro team could help me. My eye surgeon paused only briefly when I told him they hadn't thought about this or prepared me or had anything to say on how to adapt, before he considered the cognitive aspects, helped me understand what was happening in my brain and why I'd suddenly lurch, and gave me some advice. I had to practice using my eyes in walking, reading, using the computer, etc. Practice would get me back to independence.

Movement, of myself, people, dogs, or cars would be the last thing my brain would adapt to.

I had no one to practice with. In my home, I could hang on to my walls. Outside...

I rang Meditech. They suggested using my personal low-intensity light concussion protocol on my neck every other day. It helped.

A week after my surgery, my neurodoc decided he had to get me out of my confinement before my muscles deteriorated. He'd call me on my cell and guide me. He couldn't catch me if I fell, but I was determined not to. He could tell when I was trying to quicken my steps from ten times slower than normal to five times slower and caution me to slow down. He ensured I was inside my front door at the end of my walk before hanging up.

By the third week of May, we were in a rhythm. He'd begin by asking, "Did you receive any calls from your mother?"

"No."

"Did you receive any?"

"You know I don't receive any calls. You need to remember that! Asking only keeps putting it back into my mind."

"Fair enough. What did you do on the weekend?"

"Binge watched TV."

"How's your vision?"

"Yesterday, it wasn't clear. But it's clear again today."

"How's peripheral?"

"I'm practicing when I wake up to see the ceiling and ensure I still see one-eighty degrees panorama."

"How's walking around your home?"

"I'm back to normal in parts I've been walking in daily but still dizzy in other areas."

"Where do you want to walk?"

I told him. A really short walk that would have taken me two minutes there and back before my surgery now quailed me at its sheer length. I stepped out my door, and he reminded me to narrate my movements.

I did and told him Dad had offered me his cane. It made me feel older, vulnerable, but it was better than the umbrella I'd been using.

"How do you feel about that?"

"It's a little too tall, but I don't know how to adjust it. And it being Dad's...whatever. I have to use it." *And however fractious our relationship, he always wants me to get better. He gave me his cane. Things will get better between us again, like always.* The effort I expended to walk and talk finally vapourized the emotions my neurodoc had stirred up when he asked if anyone had called me.

"How are you with distractions? Are those children?"

"No, just birds making a racket."

The lilac I passed threw its heady scent into my nostrils and parked my feet. My neurodoc fell silent. I was alone. I asked him to talk to me; I needed to hear conversation, feel like a human being not the receiving end of duty.

He said, "You're risking disuse atrophy. I'm thinking about how to prevent it. I need to somehow call you even for short walks."

I muttered, "My hips hurt."

"I'm not surprised."

I was back inside after twenty-eight minutes, exhausted, dizzy, and nauseated. My neurodoc hung up, and I began to carefully extricate myself from my jacket and stagger to the kitchen for a glass of water, my hand on my walls.

Meanwhile, my former peer mentor had put me in touch with the CNIB (formerly Canadian National Institute for the Blind). They sent me an orientation mobility trainer to begin training me the first week of June. I had no idea what to expect. Why did I need to learn how to orient myself on a sidewalk, cross a street, or walk toward people? This seemed bizarre to me, even though I was still in the midst of relearning many things that the brain injury had slayed. I soon learnt why.

He guided me so that my brain could fire signals down neurons to move my feet. He kept me safe from cars and people while my head refused to turn and my brain could see so clearly yet not understand much. After our first training, I tried not to cry for those early years when after brain injury I had no one to help me, to ensure I didn't fall over or be hit as my overwhelmed brain struggled to navigate sidewalks. My CNIB guide also chattered up a storm. He explained the Pokémon Go craze to me and discussed the merits of different apps. I had thirsted to talk to someone unafraid and knowledgeable of smartphones and texting and apps for so long that I drank up his words. Unbeknownst to me, his chatter was psychological care. He'd noticed my anxiety dropped when he chatted and I walked more steadily along the sidewalk next to traffic that shrieked danger into my too-sensitive ears and confused vision centre.

But he couldn't help me with reading. After the surgery, text looked sharper and clearer than I'd ever seen, yet my brain refused to read anything wider than my iPhone screen. My eyeballs moving back and forth spun my head. My surgeon recommended a higher resolution monitor. I had to practice eye tracking and reading, and again I needed to yell for it.

It took months. In late July 2016, my neurodoc said, "I'll read with you two times a week. I have to get you back to sessions. I have to look at the global picture. I know it's frustrating."

"It's goal destroying," I said into my iPhone as I watched Mum hustling after her dog to stoop and scoop in the dog park. I hung up, opened the gate under the hazy blue sky in the humid air, and weaved cautiously between the dogs eager to hit the beach.

I caught up to Mum as her dog sailed ahead, ears flapping in the breeze of her speed. I plodded along beside Mum, leaning on my cane, seeing so clearly water, trees, soil, and dogs.

No, don't look at dogs, I reminded myself. Too dizzying with their wagging bodies! That morning after two and a half hours of sleep it had hit me: I still wanted to read. My profound loss. My biggest goal. But my neurodoc wasn't hearing me.

As Mum concentrated to stick with my tortoise speed, I kept my eyes briefly on her dog's leggy, muscled form trotting to the beach so as to teach my brain to perceive visual movement while learning to perceive the paw-printed sand under my shoes more efficiently. Dizziness assailed. I rested my gaze on the lake. The still water lapped gentle waves onto the main beach. The crowd of dogs disappeared into the rest of the park, and I collapsed on a bench as Mum's dog sniffed along the sandy shore. The Carolinian trees whispered overhead.

Grief erupted out of me, and I confessed, "I need my reading back. I'm not getting the help I need. Two times a week of reading practice is not enough. It'll never be enough practice to get back my reading. I have to update *Concussion Is Brain Injury* and have to read it to remind me what I wrote. My writing has disappeared too after the surgery. It's the general anesthesia effect. It'll wear off, I'm told, but will it? How will I ever be able to update my book when I can't remember what I wrote and can't read it on my own? I'm losing this opportunity, too. So many opportunities to improve my reading lost because my healthcare team won't ramp up the support at critical times. My writing is way ahead of my reading, but I didn't relearn to write on my own. I can't relearn to read on my own. My neurodoc tells me not to be a perfectionist, but I'm supposed to surmount my initiation deficit and relearn to read with only two times a week support. I can't do this anymore!" I cried.

Mum agreed that two times a week was not enough. She asked me how much I read. I couldn't remember. The eye surgery had fractured my memory. It would come back. I was told that, too. I'd forgotten what I read and how much I read before the surgery. I could only recall reading the wordless graphic novel the psychology prof had given me. For twelve weeks, I hadn't read the graphic novel nor practiced reading. She suggested we call my neurodoc and have him coordinate my reading.

Through Mum's car's speakers, he listened then agreed to test my current ability, but he wasn't going to assist me with reading *Concussion Is Brain Injury*. He wanted to continue with the articles to have variety in my reading. Mum scheduled reading in to her BlackBerry to read my book with me three times a week. My neurodoc chose two days a week with me. I doubted he'd remember. I doubted he'd retain the structure I craved. And would Mum lose steam after a month or three like had happened so many times before with others?

She didn't.

We began the first week of August. After my neurodoc assessed I could read three paragraphs comfortably out loud before recalling, he suggested they'd read three paragraphs to me, then I would read three to them while my finger kept pace with the words being read. Mum got me to recall after she read the first three paragraphs and again after I read the next three paragraphs, then we discussed it. She understood that just because I could read words out loud didn't mean I could recall them. I passed the message on to my neurodoc, and he managed to keep that structure most of the time.

Mum's new commitment to my reading kept me at it, no matter how despondent the sluggish progress made me. The text was so clear to my eyes. It was unfathomable and amazing and so physically easy to read unlike any time I could remember. Yet I struggled and flagged from the cognitive effort. Slowly over the months, I graduated to an e-reader to an iPad to my new computer monitor. I read more and more with less and less energy drain. I began to trust that this time practice was making a difference. I returned to weekly gamma brainwave training at CZ, and the ADD Centre enrolled me in Cogmed to improve my working memory and so maybe my reading. In 2016 and 2017, Cogmed taught me the double effectiveness of working to the edge of my ability and fatigue: more neurons got busy healing, and the extreme exhaustion submerged my emotions from my consciousness. I decided to read Dave Siever's article on AVE and diffuse axonal injury with Mum, and my neurodoc was game to read *Concussion* with me so that I could read both and return to writing. He wanted me to earn an income, whatever it took. When Mum and I had finished the article, I added the AVE SMR/Beta session at first three days a week, then up to six days a week. Like my brain injury compatriots who'd suffered from the failure of medicine, my grief and PTSD wouldn't be treated and healed, but my attention, sharpness, and thinking speed soared. Although I remained on the edge of overwhelmed, my anxiety and agitation plummeted. Maybe, just maybe, if my initiation deficit and cognitive motivation healed enough to restart and maintain coordinating the big picture of my reading rehab and to fill in the gaps on my own, my reading would return, too. Books and I would cozy up again in the embracing chair in the warmth of my kitchen.

Chapter 28

You're Not Alone

Recovering from brain injury is like being a long-haul trucker driving an overloaded forty metre long triple road train loaded up with gold-containing ore, starting at the far eastern tip of Newfoundland with the seeming destination being the far western edge of the Yukon. Being a person with a brain injury is like being that trucker who climbs into the familiar cab with a companion to drive a familiar journey, until they reach Newfoundland's ferry docks. An old ferry belching black exhaust awaits, not the familiar smooth, modern craft. Concerned but unaware, the trucker and companion leave the truck in the hold and go up on deck to gaze upon the familiar white-capped waves splashing up against the hull. Halfway across Cabot Strait to Nova Scotia, a vesuvian wave rises up and steams toward the two who remain oblivious to the approaching menace until it breaks over them, drowning them in alien detritus before sucking back out to sea. What the heck happened to the predictable, easy journey?

Experts race to clean the trucker off. The trucker cannot see the companion, but experts assure, "Follow our map of rest, and you can return to normal with your companion." Map programmed into the truck's GPS and back on asphalt, not seeing the stains left behind by the detritus, optimism flows back, just like after one's brain injury diagnosis when you believe the journey will be mere weeks.

The blacktop whistles underneath. As the trucker banks on a gentle corner, the last trailer in the triple yaws and almost topples off the road. The trucker wrestles with the steering wheel, knuckles white, palms red where fingers dig in, just like the brain-injured person struggles to gain control over their brain, their life. With relief, the trucker straightens the train and is soon rolling out of New Brunswick and crossing Québec. Recovery regained, the trucker like the person with brain injury soon forgets about those unexpected struggles. It's smooth sailing now.

Ontario goes on forever; recovery goes on forever. The trucker's eyelids droop. The trucker wants to stop, just like the brain-injured person wants to get off the rehab train and return to the familiar normal life they had before the injury. But the clock is ticking. The experts had set a clock to reach Kluane National Park and Reserve in the Yukon, similar to the time frame doctors give for brain injury recovery. Every time the trucker stops—one stops rehab—the deadline ticks down faster. Panic sets in.

Suddenly, the trucker is crossing the Ontario-Manitoba border, buses and cars zooming to their jobs. Suddenly recovery doesn't seem so hard. Normalcy seems attainable. The trucker flies through the Prairie Provinces and angles northwest up the Alaska Highway. Traffic vanishes from the bereft scenery just like friends who don't understand brain injury disappear. The trucker marvels at the open blacktop. You shoulder on, believing your recovery once attained will bring your friends back.

The trucker enters the barrenness of the Yukon and bounces along into Kluane, gravel chips and tar bits chinking the windshield. The trucker was warned about that, about how that would signal the closing down of the time clock. The trucker accelerates, desperate to get to the destination, to full health, before the clock ticks off the final second.

Suddenly, there it is: the weigh station. The trucker stops with a hiss of the brakes and a flurry of dust. The trucker steps out of the cab. The lonely silence slams into their chest, a silence too many with brain injury feel and live with day in, day out, with no one to gab happily with over the tiny and major recovery successes. The trucker draws in breath, walks around the cab, and peers at the digital readout on the weigh scale.

It says, "Wrong load." It says, "You're carrying granite, not gold." It says, "Wrong destination."

Disbelief rocks the trucker. The trucker runs to the back trailer of the triple and tears it open. Glassy quartz winks out between granite boulders. The weigh station is telling a different story from the experts' map, just like when you discover the injury you thought you had is not the one you have. The recovery you want is not the recovery the experts extolled. You want health, work, meaning. They want...?

The trucker bends over and upchucks. The trucker scans for help, for guidance from the experts, for a sign. But not even an eagle screeches against the burning sun in the Yukon's thin air. Like the trucker, the brain injured are alone, confused, uncomprehending in their recovery. Rehab has discharged them, declaring them good to go.

The trucker hauls themself back into the cab and decides nothing for it but to return to that misdirecting expert. But the GPS's pixels flash on and off. The trucker smacks it. Meaningless lines flash chaotically. Then suddenly it shows the way. With great effort, the trucker turns the triple around on the two-lane highway and heads east. That's where Newfoundland is, right? It's like when you try to return to the expert who gave the initial prescription for brain-injury recovery.

A narrow bridge appears. A sign reads, "Dawson City." The trucker blinks. The bridge is north of Kluane, not east. It's like when recovery suddenly veers away. The trucker decides to follow the healthy sun instead of the experts. The trucker makes a painstaking U-turn south to the Alaska Highway.

The triple eats up thousands of paved kilometres. The GPS conks out completely, like effective guidance from the medical community vanishes. The trucker buys a paper map. Slashing rain and roiling skies obscure the sun. The windshield cracks; the tires run bald.

Suddenly the trucker is in Ottawa. The trucker pulls through a gleaming chain-link gate into a new expert's place, who like a psychologist or psychiatrist in a cutting-edge clinic has the latest knowledge and the latest technical equipment. The trucker is happy to know at last that they're not alone, that help is just a phone call away, that the expert will direct them well. The expert's team removes one of the trailers, decreasing the haul of the semi, and provides a new GPS and a cell phone in case of emergencies. The new medical expert promises unceasing efforts to alleviate the effects of the brain injury and to provide support. The trucker grins thanks. Like after a bout of treatment that regenerates neurons, the trucker skips into the cab and roars out of there with new life.

The trucker stumbles across new experts and talks to one then another, thinking the experts must know each other or have some sort of loose network, and will talk to each other to pool their knowledge and show the trucker the way back east. But the experts don't, just like how GPs, community care, and specialists don't. Still, the experts take pity and give out scraps of old maps to the trucker. Sometimes, they take out some of the remaining granite boulders, to ease the effects of brain injury. One day, the last boulder in the last trailer is removed, and the trucker is able to unhook it. The truck becomes a turnpike double and becomes easier to drive.

The trucker looks for another kind of map maker and in between takes pit stops and a sixteen-hour nap. Recovery from a brain injury is exhausting. One after another, map makers shrug, saying "don't know," dandruff falling lazily from their full heads of hair onto cotton-clad shoulders. Never mind. They're busy.

And then the trucker overhears the name of a narrow road and follows it to find a new map maker, who says, "Your home destination no longer exists, but you can journey to a better one." The trucker has been gone so long that the original destination is lost in their subconscious. Driving to Alberta, maybe to Nunavut, maybe to the far northern reaches of Vancouver Island sounds exciting. The new expert hasn't exactly specified the end goal, but the trucker has confidence in the expert and cannot wait to find out what this unknown destination—this new state of health—is like. For a moment, the sun glows, warming the cab, lighting the way.

One day the paper map falls to crumbs under the booted foot that is glued to the accelerator. A hurricane whips across, spinning the truck around, throwing rocks and mud and silt into an impenetrable wall between the truck and home. The trucker is lost. The only certainty is that they can't leave the semi. Brain injury never leaves. Ever.

The trucker sees the sign Welcome to Ontario. The sky clouds over. Lazy snowflakes, huge and fat, fall down to cover the asphalt and hide the white and yellow lines. The trucker grumbles at the Ontario government, which refuses to widen the main highway, refuses to pay what's needed to keep the lanes clean and clear of snow. The trucker screams at another reckless driver passing on a solid yellow who upon seeing the truck barrelling down on him swerves back into his lane causing mayhem. The road to wellness is a dangerous, frustrating one.

The trucker unhooks the old CB, calls for help, and hits the road again. No answer. The trucker tries again. Over and over, the expert with the old ways doesn't answer. The new map maker has no answer. The road is no longer one of hope but instead a monotonous, seamed, cut-up blacktop, while the sun turns each day into a sultry harlot guide of false promises. The trucker turns off the paved highway onto one of southern Ontario's many gravel roads. The trucker is used to the load, the injury, now. The trucker brakes and watches the plume of dust rise up in an obscuring cloud and then dissipate around the cab.

The trucker steps down onto the slippery gravel. Like the brain-injured person, the trucker has no plans. The trucker leans against the semi's engine, unheeding of its heat, head hanging, yearning to quit. Tired of staring at the gravel, the trucker lifts their eyes and sees amongst the bare branches across the road a message pad, its pages lifting in a brief waft of air. The trucker steps over to grasp it and flips it open. Someone has been there before. Others with the same injury have blindly travelled this same route. Someone is willing to say, "You're not alone."

You are not alone.

Now What? Learnings

Chapter S

Social Isolation

Social isolation is a real thing. One researcher opined that it's more unhealthy than smoking. It deteriorates brain function and seems to increase inflammation in the body.[34] Why after initially rallying around and asserting they'd be there in sickness, do people leave then blame the person with brain injury for their own social isolation? Why, when they asserted the person was a good friend, a loved sibling, a valued co-worker?

The person they knew has changed fundamentally, and the injury lies invisible behind an intact skull. Superficial feel-good stories peddle the myth of swift recovery. They make the person look like they're not trying hard enough. Only education counters this misperception, yet few seem to read the books, talk to the therapists, or come along to the appointments. And so the myths that it's behavioural, a bad attitude, toxic, or depression persist and provide permission to leave while ascribing fault to the person left.

Remedy to Social Isolation

Through education and practical support, the healthcare team facilitates the person's social network to stick with them. The network can adapt in several ways.

---

[34] http://www.businessinsider.de/how-social-isolation-affects-your-health-2016-1

- Be willing to learn about brain injury, to accept and adapt to the person and their TBI snafus, and to initiate social interactions.

- Embrace caring. Don't relegate it to day programs or nursing homes.

- Organize family, friends, neighbours, workmates, etc. so that no one person is overwhelmed with meeting the social needs of the person and they aren't left alone for days at a time hearing the silence hum in their ears until they're ready to fall to the floor and curl up.

- Design a social life for the person that they can physiologically handle. A weekly one-hour coffee date in the same quietest café. Regularly scheduled phone calls from a rotating list of friends. Lunch dates after the hardest medical appointment: the hour with their psychiatrist. A slow fifteen-minute walk in their neighbourhood.

- Ask them how to help with their hobbies. Assist in creating new ones. Don't get upset if they say no to your suggestions. Focus on them not your ideas.

- Don't expect the person to travel to you. That becomes feasible when their health has improved enough that instead of days to recover they may need one night of sitting stock still in front of the TV as their brain slowly regains resources to do more than pump their heart and move their lungs. So do not ask them. They want to please because they see their social life slipping away. They fear the silence so profound they can hear atoms move. They'll agree to anything no matter the functional cost until the day they realize keeping the pre-injury status quo prevents them from meeting their own goals.

- Connections improve all our health. When we deny our social biology, we deny ourselves and worsen our health.

So what can we with brain injury do since no one can force another human being to want to be with us?

- Join social media: Twitter, Facebook, and/or another, whichever makes you feel good.
- Twitter's 140 characters do not overwhelm our injured cognitions.
- Twitter is more naturally suited to conversations that can ebb and flow in time and draw in others.
- Search #braininjury to find others like you.
- Check out who brain injury associations follow. If you like their feed and they look like they know how to converse, follow and reply to something they said.
- Put Twitter or preferred social media app on your smartphone. It's easier to read and tweet, especially in bed or on the couch when you want company. Socializing makes you feel better and gets you going.
- Discuss with your therapist or other trusted individual safety precautions before meeting people in real life.

- Go out as your health improves.
- Find a coffee shop near you and try and go there regularly perhaps before or after an appointment to avoid initiation deficit preventing you.
- Stick with the one where the barista remembers you. Those few seconds of small talk where someone recognizes you will lessen a little the effects of social isolation.
- Visit the library and talk books with the librarian.
- Sit near others. This is purely to meet your biological need to be near other people, not to improve your reading. If your reading is good enough to read a book there, then bonus.
- Enroll in an online course to learn and talk to others when you can in the virtual classroom. Ask your healthcare professional to help you find good ones for you. As your health improves, try ones that include essays but allow for extensions. Ensure it has no deadlines.
- Join a local Bible or scriptures study group, a quiet one that won't overload your senses. They will get to know you and you them. It won't be so difficult to remember faces. If you have trouble with names, perhaps the leader will be willing to get everyone to wear name tags. If you have difficulty overcoming your fatigue, initiation deficit, and injury to your prefrontal cortex, ask your healthcare

professional to find a group and arrange with the leader to drive you there.

As you can see, these suggestions are in increasing order of difficulty. As you master one and improve brain-wise, you can try the next one. If it doesn't work out, stick to what has been working for you and try again in a few months or a year or two. Ignore the people who tell you what you should be doing. Don't let their unrealistic expectations become yours and then lead you to crashing in exhaustion for months.

Be sociable within the boundaries of your injury.

Chapter T

When to Treat

All concussions should be diagnosed and treated immediately, even ones that seem to reconcile on their own, because cognitive change happens. I theorize the brain's function is to change its neural networks in response to mental and physical experience and activity within a web of relationships. Networks power structure and function. Concussions injure neurons in networks, and that's why all concussions should be healed not learned to live with.

At the May 2017 conference, Thompson said there are six networks:

- motor
- affect
- executive
- salience
- default
- placebo

The placebo network is "remembered wellness." Research shows that within forty-eight hours of a traumatic brain injury, especially diffuse axonal injury (DAI), biochemical processes further damage axons.[35] Inflammation from microglial activation

---

[35] https://en.m.wikipedia.org/wiki/Diffuse_axonal_injury

continues for up to eighteen years;[36] neurogenic fever can also damage the brain. Research with solitary confinement of prisoners points to how social isolation contributes to brain damage.[37] The mental experience of unlinking social bonds would lead to negative changes in the affect network, I'd theorize. Every brain is unique; every injury as well. Doidge said at the conference that you can't have thousands of studies proving one treatment works.

The brain produces microvolts of energy, and so it probably doesn't take volts of energy or 2 or 3 teslas of magnetic flux density to effect a healing change on such a delicate instrument as our brain. Doidge and Thompson stated in the conference they believe that treatment includes resynchronizing the noisy brain, getting other neurons to take over, and multimodal therapies with counselling.

I write this chapter as a thought experiment **not** a prescription. Perhaps this **theoretical program** could form the foundation for a study or for critical thinking about the current standard of treatment. I suggest the neuroplastic treatments I'm familiar with or have related in this book; however, using the same principles I outline, other neuroplastic treatments such as what Doidge wrote about may be more effective for some individuals.

Theory

I hypothesize effective treatment determines where the damage is, begins immediately, harnesses the brain's basic function, includes brains supporting brains, and is tailored to each individual. One person, such as a neuropsychiatrist or clinical

---

[36] Johnson et al., Brain 2013. From Dr. Lynda Thompson's slide.
[37] PBS *Frontline*. 22 April 22 2014. http://www.pbs.org/wgbh/frontline/article/what-does-solitary-confinement-do-to-your-mind/

psychologist, must coordinate the entire assessment and treatment. The clinician must understand both neuroscience and emotional health and be the primary therapist, too, in order to monitor closely the roller coaster ride of brain injury and healing. The clinician must also see and treat the patient as an equal member of the team. The patient must have a sense of control and value and is more likely to participate in treatment if part of the team.

Assessment

A roadside or rink-side concussion test is key. Perhaps a portable HRV test, with an immediate electronic referral to a specialist for that day or the next as apparently concussion affects HRV.[38] Or if no specialist available, educate GPs so that they can do the necessary full assessment and direct initial passive treatment while waiting for a specialist. The full assessment must be done within hours of the injury.

Location. Identify where the blockages are in the brain and the affected networks, using qEEG, SPECT, and/or DTI. (Diagnostic labels and the DSM do **not** point the way to treatment.)

Cell. Blood and urine analysis, including for hormones and all the fatiguing factors like iron, B12, calcium, magnesium, and Vitamin D deficiencies.

Functional. Night and day sleep study, heart measures like Holter and twenty-four-hour blood pressure, balance, eye and ear exams including eye tracking, reading, musculoskeletal, respiratory, digestive, etc.

---

[38] M. Paniccia, V. Lee, T. Taha, et al *Heart rate variability: exploring age, sex & concussion symptoms in youth athletes.* Br J Sports Med 2017. 51:A41.
http://bjsm.bmj.com/content/51/11/A41.1

Passive Treatment

The idea of resting the brain is problematic because unlike an ankle which rests on a stool so that it doesn't bear any weight, there's no such thing as lifting the brain so that it doesn't run your body. You'd be dead. Worse in diaschisis, the brain learns a circuit isn't working so it stops using it. Doidge called that "learned nonuse." It leads to continuing damage. Rest **as treatment** exacerbates nonuse. However, there's no doubt that the brain requires more energy to do the same tasks and additional energy to repair,[39] and so rest for energy management is essential.

Cell health. To return health to cells, consider vitamin therapy, nutritious food on small plates to prevent overeating, regular glasses of water, and omega-3 supplements (I prefer the vegetarian one as I found fish oils too "pushy"). Hyperbaric therapy may help if used immediately after injury. Early research shows that individualized low-intensity light therapy on the cervical spine, including the brain stem and cerebellum, "facilitates ATP production providing the necessary energy for healing and repair of tissues." It may also alleviate inflammation and pain and may promote neuron regeneration.[40] My hypothalamus fix may promote sleep and reduce the effects of thermoregulation dysfunction (see Chapter Q).

Medical team leader. Choose a therapist who has the neuroscience education and the practical experience to manage the complexity of brain injury and can commit to years-long support. This relationship is crucial to healing. They coordinate treatment and help the person cope with affect changes,

---

[39] https://www.scientificamerican.com/article/why-does-the-brain-need-s/
[40] Fred Kahn, M.D. *Concussion - A Therapeutic Solution and the Presentation of Two Classic Case Profiles.* https://bioflexlaser.com/2015/07/01/concussion-a-therapeutic-solution/

traumatic experiences, and situations that cause chaotic emotions to malfunction.

Deep breathing. Guided deep breathing, preferably with computer feedback, by a trained healthcare professional and practiced daily with a family member or friend engenders calm. However, it is work, and so one might begin with a minimum of two minutes. Learn and practice.

Education. Understanding the injury helps everyone deal with it appropriately, accommodate the sudden changes in the injured person, and watch for and report on new symptoms or problems. This is ongoing.

Social. Injured brains need the support of healthy ones. Internal chaos demands external routine and structure for mental, psychological, and emotional stability. Like a very young child who goes to school and plays but is not expected to cook and coordinate activities for themself, so the same holds true for the person. All their brain energy is being used to heal the brain and to run the body. To facilitate that supportive web, the healthcare team coordinates systematic and structured social support (see Chapter S). The person also has input into their treatments and activities in order to retain a sense of dignity and being an adult. This is important to preventing loss of self-esteem. Set up early family sessions that include friends to educate and ensure support, as well as support the caregivers.

The web of relationships includes regular, frequent medical and therapeutic support to reassure, treat, educate, provide practical help, and compensate for memory loss by reminding the person that they have been injured and are being treated. The doctor-patient relationship has been shown to be critical to successful treatment. Trust and commitment to the long haul by the professional is the bedrock of that relationship.

Structure and routine. Unpredictability requires cognitions that the person may not have and demands energy the person won't have. Introduce smartphones, calendar apps, and tablet computers and gradually teach how to use them for daily life and work (see Chapter D).

Exercise. Precisely calibrate exercise with mental activity to avoid increasing heat, water retention, and heart rate. Find a physical trainer familiar with changes to the heart to tailor a program that conserves energy and doesn't exacerbate autonomic nervous system dysfunction. Perhaps begin with weights and movements that use little brain energy, three times a week for ten minutes per time. Monitor the effect for a week, and experiment with less time and more time, monitoring the effect each time for a week. The injured brain has limited energy. Every activity, whether mental or physical, consumes energy. If mental activity eats all the brain's energy, then physical activity will strain the brain and cause unpleasant effects like increasing heat. And vice versa. For example, I didn't exercise on the days I went for brain biofeedback. On the days I exercised, I didn't go for treatments.

Include acupuncture, physiotherapy, low-intensity light therapy, and/or massage therapy for physical injuries. Seatbelt injuries can cause chronic pain and weakness if not treated. Acupuncture by an acupuncturist familiar with brain injury may help alleviate the symptoms.

No alcohol, nicotine, pop, or recreational drugs. Coffee and 70 percent dark chocolate is good (see my e-book *A Nibble of Chocolate*[41]).

Neurostimulation. Begin gentler forms of stimulating the neurons to prevent or begin to reverse delinking of neurons and to restore the corticothalamic loop. These include AVE—

---

[41] https://www.smashwords.com/books/view/58672

SMR/Beta L13.5/R18 has been shown to restore the loop in those with DAI—CES, low-intensity light therapy, and systematic thought. The person won't be able to do the latter on their own. They will need a guide to remind them of what they're supposed to be thinking about. For example, the person would speak a rhyme out loud while walking or narrate travel before heading out and while travelling, too. If the person is on their own, have them text check-ins, for example, "I'm at the bus stop at the corner of..." or "I'm on the bus sitting in the first single seat." Reply to reinforce the web of relationships in brain function.

Reading program. See Chapter U.

Rest. After treatment or cognitive homework, sit in nature for a couple of hours or more, whether the backyard, a parkette, beach, ravine, or near a city tree. Have a treat and favourite non-pop beverage. Do nothing but nap, eat, watch the scenery, or at most write poetry on your smartphone.

Passive-Active Treatment

Levels of fatigue vary from person to person. If some of the above is fatiguing or not tolerated well at first, it may be delayed to the beginning of the passive-active stage.

HRV. Graduate from learning and practicing to using deep breathing automatically in stressful situations while managing fatigue from it.

AVE. Begin to use the principle of activating the networks one wants to heal by using the Tru-Vu Omniscreen Viewhole so that the person can read, write, or work on the computer while using either SMR for Reading session or SMR/Beta.

Stress management. Teach stress management principles; use HRV, AVE, CES, and deep breathing to manage; and include the social support network so that both the person and their network can learn which kinds of stress can damage healing and how to avoid them.

tDCS. This therapy follows the principle of small voltages to effect large changes in the delicate brain while engaging the networks one wants to work on. Under the principle of brains support brains, tDCS is conducted by a trained person who sits in close proximity so as to watch the person for any sign of working too hard and to participate in activating the desired network.

Exercise. Under the guidance of a trainer familiar with brain injury and sticking with a routine that gives energy, increase weight and repetitions, and walking distance and time, gradually, always monitoring for a week the effects of any changes before incorporating them permanently. Change one thing at a time. Months may elapse between changes.

Guided social outings. These can be done under conditions that support the injured brain while providing an escape from the medical regime and home environment. Quiet places with familiar faces not judging the inevitable social TBI snafus. Gentle walks in natural areas with benches or perhaps the social support can carry a portable seat for frequent rest breaks. Maintain the web of relationships in a way the person can manage so that the web doesn't break and the person doesn't deteriorate from too much or too little social engagement.

Advocacy. Set up educational seminars for every group the person belongs to, e.g., church, workplace, volunteering, community, etc.

Reassessment

Since each brain is individual, it's important to reassess both for healing and signs of cascading damage, repeating all the tests above. These diagnostic measures will form the basis of the active treatment protocols.

Active Treatment

I theorize that once cells have begun to heal and neurostimulation has gently begun, active treatment to work the brain to its edge of ability will stimulate regrowth, restore power to the brain, and lead to neuromodulation and neurorelaxation, two stages of Doidge's neuroplasticity model.[42] However, due to the extreme exhaustion this will bring on, the person will continue to need reliable social support for daily living, a calm, warm environment in which to recuperate between treatments, immediate glucose-rich snack after the intense mental activity, nutritious meals otherwise, company to help them keep up with their exercise routines, and support from both their healthcare team and social network to ensure adherence to homework when fatigue, initiation deficit, and memory failure get in the way. Without such support, the person will require inordinate amounts of willpower and be fighting the odds to persist when results may not be seen for weeks or months. It's shown that willpower consumes energy, thus its excessive use will work against healing the brain.[43] Also scale back any increases in work or social routine because at this stage, you want the energy to go to healing the brain. Building on the above treatments, add in

---

[42] Norman Doidge, M.D. *The Brain's Way of Healing*. New York: Penguin Books, 2015, 2016. Pages 108-113.
[43] MT Gailliot, et al. *Self-control Relies on Glucose as a Limited Energy Source: Willpower Is More Than a Metaphor*. Journal of Personality and Social Psychology 2007, Vol. 92, No. 2, 325–336 https://www.researchgate.net/profile/Lauren_Brewer/publication/6524614_Self-Control_Relies_on_Glucose_as_a_Limited_Energy_Source_Willpower_Is_More_Than_a_Metaphor/links/5537d8370cf247b8587c7349.pdf

ones that require the person to actively train their brain. You may try adding these in earlier if the person is capable.

Brain biofeedback. Begin with single-electrode brain biofeedback, twice a week for forty sessions, to train attention and problem-solving beta brainwaves. Use AVE SMR 14 Hz or SMR/Beta L13.5/R18 the morning of the brain training with eyes closed. If achieving good EMG is difficult, try acupuncture the morning of or home low-intensity light therapy on the neck and shoulders the night before. Using it one hour before bedtime will aid in falling asleep as well.

Brain biofeedback is hard work and requires encouragement, but my results prove it's worth it, as seen in the graphic on the following page.

Concussion Is Brain Injury

IVA Auditory Response Times
2005 Before Brain Biofeedback
2006 After Initial Standard Training
2013 After Initial Gamma Training

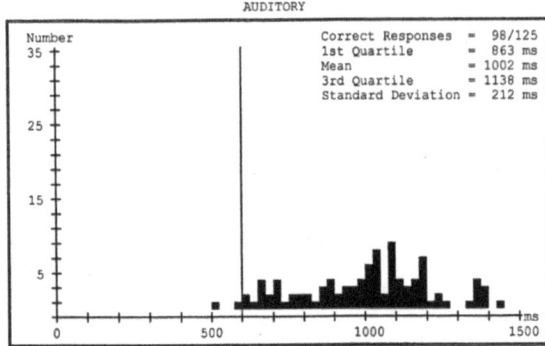

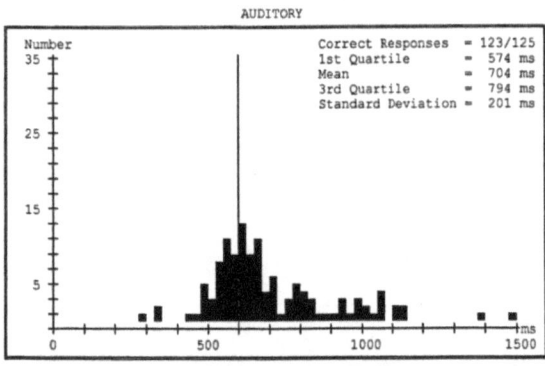

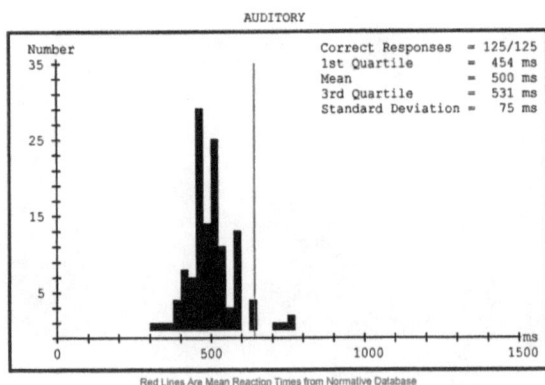

Experimental chronotherapy. Establish sleep and wake schedules so that the person is extremely sleepy before they retire to bed and must wake up at the same time every morning, once the person can use alarms or discipline to stick to the schedule. Using AVE SMR for Sleep immediately after doing the hypothalamus fix sub-delta AVE may help. Melatonin may be initiated to treat delayed onset of sleep.

After forty sessions brain biofeedback, reassess with IVA, TOVA, qEEG, evoke potentials, and online neuropsychological test. Transition to once-weekly training either with new protocols or the original one.

LORETA. Once the person's brain has learnt how to do brain biofeedback, they can begin once-weekly LORETA with a minimum of two days rest before or after single-electrode brain biofeedback with or without tDCS.

Intensive Treatment

By this time, the person should be able to (partially) exercise on cognitive work days and to reduce EMG to enable more advanced brain training. TV time will begin to drop naturally with healing.

Therapy. If brain injury wasn't diagnosed and treated immediately, social bonds probably broke, in which case, treatment should also include trauma and grief therapy with the understanding that it's a combination of grief and physiological degeneration not a mood disorder. In addition, reconnecting recovering emotions with memories will need to be done on pace and in concert with brain biofeedback.

Goals and behavioural therapy. Begin to establish short-term goals for work and play. Set the person up for success. Talking about future goals earlier than this stage leads to inevitable failure. Don't look at the long term yet, though. Bring in a behavioural therapist assistant under the guidance of a behavioural therapist to help the person create, organize, initiate, and stick to goals. Celebrate each step and goal achieved, no matter how small.

Gamma brainwave training. Start after brain biofeedback is familiar and EMG is below 2.0µV (see Chapter R).

Cogmed. This intensive and exhausting program improves working memory after brain biofeedback improves attention.

Exercise. As automaticity returns, begin walking further to de-stress and improve physical health.

Maintenance

Once treatment ends, maintain the good changes within the web of relationships and catch any deterioration early. Like with other major injuries, when brain injury is treated immediately and effectively, there may be less psychological trauma. However, restoration to the original may still not be possible, and we still do not understand spontaneous recovery or long-term ramifications, such as sudden onset of seeming "depression" (untreated grief) or dementia.

Therapist. Maintaining regular contact allows picking up of regressions, sending for reassessment, topping up of treatments, and preventing brain-injury-created stressful situations.

Behavioural therapist assistant. Some aspects of brain function may take years to return, especially the ability to sustain work. Along with the judicious use of technology assistants, the assistant can keep the person on track with their life and work goals and help them maintain exercise and stress-reduction regimes to prevent re-injury.

Medicare should cover the above and the reading rehab in Chapter U. It's good for government and the economy to have people working not living on social assistance, falling into trouble, and attending day programs. It's good for society and a country to have healthy communities that support people from affliction to thriving.

For updated thoughts and further reading, go to http://wp.me/Pf8xE-16G.

Chapter U

Reading Rehab

Reading is more than deciphering letters and words. When people with brain injury talk about reading, they mean the kind of reading they learnt through high school where you learn to read in a state of flow, process, understand, interpret, and integrate complex stories without images to assist comprehension. Reading requires the eyes to send in bits of visual information together and in focus; the back of the brain to combine those bits into words into phrases and send them to the language centre to be interpreted, which sends those interpretations to the frontal cortex to be synthesized, add in emotions and memories, and integrate with the existing knowledge base. In real time. It requires relaxed, focused attention, short and long-term memory, the ability to build up the picture of what you're reading, the ability to acquire and retain new vocabulary, and the prefrontal cortex functions of organization and decision making. It requires eyes and brain to work at the same speed.

The information age and knowledge economy require one to read successfully. And reading is just plain fun.

I present here a **theoretical framework** for a reading rehab program to restore reading. This is **not** a prescription. I **theorize** that practicing at the edge of ability,[44] using systematic thought, and treating the injured areas will stimulate the brain to change its neural networks back to reading. Dr. Norman Doidge writes

---

[44] Practicing at the edge of ability comes from the Cogmed program model. http://www.cogmed.com/how-it-works

that systematic thought "is a potent way to stimulate neurons."[45] However, this framework may lead to neurogenic fever from creating new neurons, emotional stress, and extreme exhaustion such that social support will be critical to alleviating the responsibilities of daily living and ensuring healthy eating. Also, CES Sleep, rest, and ice water, as well as emotional therapy, may help to cool one down and mitigate stress that could counter any healing.

This program is separated out of my "When to Treat" chapter because of the complexity of reading. But the assessments listed in that chapter should be done first to pinpoint the cognitions and reading-related networks that need treatment. I believe that reading rehabilitation must begin quickly in order to avoid frustration, the resulting fear and anxiety, and what Dr. Norman Doidge calls, "learned nonuse," i.e., the brain changing its networks toward not reading. I base my theoretical program on how we teach children to read: instructed in school and practiced in school and at home daily. The longer the delay in starting or by doing it in fits and starts, the more likely the brain will deactivate the reading networks and the harder to restore. When a person tells you they want to read, partner with them. And show them through consistent, long-term effort that you believe them and will not give up on restoring to them such a complex skill.

Reading coach. The program begins with finding a reading coach, who will coordinate the reading rehab. The most important qualifications for such a coach are commitment, reliability, initiative, and problem-solving ability. This coach will assess, coordinate the rehab, be a safe listener for venting over the dramatic change in reading ability, cheerlead, and guide the

---

[45] Norman Doidge, M.D. *The Brain's Way of Healing*. New York: Penguin Books, 2015, 2016. Page 109.

structured reading routine for years. The reading coach will check in at least weekly and practice with the person over the phone or, better, through videoconference, possibly several times a week. The coach is like a child's teacher, and the person with the brain injury is like the foster kid who has no self-discipline to do the work on their own and no parent to help. If there's social support, they can practice the person's reading with them five days per week. Just as with children, practice is critical to relearning the skill. The coach will coordinate the practice schedule.

If it's difficult to find a coach or social support is lacking, then perhaps you, as the injured person, striving to incorporate as much as you can of what I theorize below may help. But whether or not it does, doing something for yourself when others cannot or will not support you, is like a gift to yourself that says you're valuable.

I've broken the program down into five sections:

1. assessment
2. passive-active treatment
3. active treatment and rehabilitation
4. intensive treatment
5. maintenance

Assessment

Assess damage. Determine levels of
- alertness;
- processing speed;
- initiation;

- organization;
- decision making;
- visuospatial and auditory working memory;
- selective and sustained attention (Chapter K);
- distractibility;
- memory;
- building up the big picture;
- integration of new concepts into old knowledge;
- vocabulary acquisition; and
- retaining new knowledge and concepts.

Assess how the person actually reads. The reading coach will begin with having the person describe what reading is like: how they see the words, how they read sentences, when they forget, and what distracts them. Select a variety of reading material from tabloid papers to magazines to poetry and different modalities for each including paper, smartphone, e-reader, and tablet computer. Have the person read out loud the way they do silently each type of reading material and modality until fatigue begins. Reading until fatigued will show the true stamina for each kind of reading. Time what they read and in which order. Calculate speed, percent recalled, repetitions, when they slow down, at what point they stop, total paragraphs read, and length of rest between readings and have them report back how long they napped afterward and how long till they returned to their normal level of fatigue and functioning. The following week test long-term recall.

Based on this data, choose the easiest material and modality for reading rehab. Graduate to the other materials and modalities over time. Retain the materials for reassessment so that you can compare apples to apples.

Reading strategies. Teach reading strategies and assess which ones work best by observing each strategy in action as the person reads a simple article. Strategies include but are not limited to

- pacing;
- highlighting key words or phrases;
- writing notes in the margins;
- writing a summary of each paragraph in a notebook;
- covering up text;
- reading out loud;
- using a finger to keep eyes on each word in sequential order; and
- adjusting the size of text on a smartphone, tablet, or e-reader.

Retain strategies that work both agree work. Ignore all the rest. Use stickers, treats, and daily rewards of the person's choosing in order to facilitate success.

Vision. Work with surgeons to correct eye tracking issues. Ensure reading glasses have the correct prescription. Choose a smartphone and/or tablet with the highest resolution possible. If the text is blurry or not quite in focus, the brain will have to work harder, thus leading to headaches and fatigue.

Social support. Assess the level of social support to help the person practice, persist, overcome initiation deficit and emotional turmoil, and balance rest with reading. The less social support, the more healthcare professionals and the reading coach will have to do.

Passive-Active Treatment in Phase with Passive of "When to Treat" Chapter

Guide the person to set up a quiet reading area with few visual distractions. A view of trees or plants may be calming.

Choose what to read. Keeping in mind impaired decision making and initiation and guided by the person's likes and work requirements, the coach chooses the reading material. Text reading engages the areas involved in reading. Graphic novels engage areas involved in understanding concepts, a critical part of reading that may be missed while words remain difficult to absorb and process. Review factors for how to choose reading material.

Factors for Reading

- length of book/article
- new material or already read
- complexity
- media type
- interest level
- current energy level

The text should be short, for example, a newspaper article. Determine the number of paragraphs or graphic novel pages that can be safely read without strain and cut that in half as a daily homework. Articles do not need to be finished; a new one can be chosen for each day. Cutting out the decision making will free up energy for the act of reading and ensure consistent practice.

Practice daily. Daily practice reinforces the brain changing its dynamic structure back to reading. Set up a reading schedule in the person's smartphone with alarms for prep and reading practice, preferably with a nagging feature. Choose the most alert time of day.

Prepare. Begin with using the AVE SMR or the SMR/Beta L13.5/R18 session, lying back, eyes closed, and deep breathing. Drink water. After awakening, continue to deep breathe for ten minutes until the coach or social support calls. The reading coach may have to remind until the person can act on the reminder alarms on their own.

Practice. The coach or social support calls to reduce the mental load. At this stage, the act of reading is more important than the ability to recall and follow. Start with five minutes. If that's too long, begin with one minute per day. The coach reads out loud slowly half the homework while the person reads along silently and with a finger to guide word to word. Then the person will read out loud the other half of the homework. The person deep breathes for a minute between each paragraph.

The person reads the graphic wordless novel on their own, preparing in the same way, with the coach reminding and rewarding when done.

Post. Discuss how it went. The person drinks water, eats immediately something nutritious with glucose to feed the brain, and rests until back to usual self. That may be a two-hour nap or three hours in front of the TV. Do not try to get up prematurely.

For two weeks, track how many days practiced, how long, when fatigue hit, what activities done before and after, and length of rest. Adjust the practice accordingly so that it doesn't lead to overfatigue and frustration. Weekly, discuss progress: what's frustrating, what's working, it's OK if there's none, and so on. This check-in precedes daily practice. Emotions such as grief over losing a critical skill and/or fear from repeated failures may begin to appear and paralyze the person. Gentle, compassionate support allows them to stick with practice and carries them through the frustrations created by the difficulty and exhaustion.

Once the person is stabilized and starting to find it easy, increase the amount each reads by one paragraph so that the practice is always on the edge of the person's ability.

Self-guided practice. The coach will assist in setting up a Twitter news feed that caters to the person's interests. Since systematic reading is what stimulates neurons, set up a schedule to scroll through Twitter and read each tweet. Tweets are short enough to be read easily and introduce a low level of decision making. Set alarms to begin and to end. This keeps reading in their métier, is pleasurable, and increases their social life.

Active Treatment

This phase begins after forty to sixty sessions of brain biofeedback have been completed, depending on the person's individual reading difficulties. Re-assess following the procedure above, and include the results from the "When to Treat" assessments.

Brain biofeedback practice. After twenty sessions or when begin to see changes, the brain trainer will work with the reading coach on choosing text to include for five minutes of reading during brain biofeedback after at least two neurofeedback screens, increasing to ten minutes over the months. During these five minutes, the computer will record heart rate, breathing rate, skin temperature, and brainwaves and provide auditory feedback only, perhaps pink noise. The brain trainer may turn off the screen to reduce visual distraction. The brain trainer will inform the coach of any changes, especially in delta-theta waves, busy brain, heart rate, and breathing rate. If heart rate increases and brain tires overly, the reading coach, brain trainer, and person may have a conference meeting during one of the biofeedback sessions to discuss how to reverse that.

tDCS over Wernicke's area may help. Begin with one to five minutes at minimal power and increase over many months to ten minutes at normal power once per week. During tDCS begin with conversation on what was read during practice with the coach. When the person achieves significant conversational improvement, switch to reading out loud text chosen by the coach, using a finger to guide reading one word at a time. Brain biofeedback reading can count as that day's reading practice.

Practice. The goal of this stage is to read without needing to rest afterward while continuing to practice on the edge of ability, following the principles above. Add in one minute of the coach reading rhyming poetry at the start while the person listens with their AVE going. This can be increased over time to five minutes. Monitor fatigue closely. Ensure there is at least one hour downtime between reading and exercise.

Transition to graphic novels with text and introduce recall. After the coach reads their paragraphs, the person will recall, deep breathe for one minute, then read their paragraphs, followed by recalling what they've read. The coach prompts what is not recalled and may introduce gridding or another note taking strategy if recall is poor. If much of the material is forgotten, then reread the forgotten paragraphs and re-recall. Finish with briefly discussing what was read. This should be more on the lines of a natural discussion than a question-and-answer session.

When the person can read and recall eight paragraphs of an article each, the person summarizes in a journal through handwriting what was read. The coach will end the call with a reminder to do that and at the next practice will ask how that went and discuss introducing books into reading practice.

Transition to a light novel. At this point change from tracking paragraphs to pages. Begin with reading one page each then increase the page numbers by fractions, e.g., from one page to one and a quarter pages.

At the same time, the coach will help the person join Goodreads. It's like a Fitbit for readers. Goodreads tracks reading progress and encourages setting an annual reading goal. At this point, ignore the last. After each practice session, update Goodreads reading progress. The coach may have to remind the person to do this. Once finished a novel, immediately write a review on Goodreads before they forget what the book was about. Initially, the coach will assist. In the review, mention likes and dislikes, favourite character, and favourite plot point. Don't just write "good" or "so-so." By thinking about specific details, it will strengthen the regenerating reading networks. Ticking off the Finish button in Goodreads reinforces progress. Every three to four months, reread novels and again track them on Goodreads. Notice any stamina or speed improvements. Every month, review Goodreads stats and compare their first reviews to current ones to see how summarizing, comprehension, and writing are progressing.

Heal emotional centres. Without emotion, it's "neurobiologically impossible to build memories, engage complex thoughts, or make meaningful decisions."[46] In addition, when "emotionally invested in the learning or finds it intrinsically motivating, dopamine is also present. And dopamine helps strengthen neural networks." Alongside the brain trainer and therapist, rebuild emotional centres by choosing novels associated with good memories from a time when the person had affect and asking questions to tease out

---

[46] *Why Emotions Are Integral to Learning.* By MindShift, 31 May 2016. https://ww2.kqed.org/mindshift/2016/05/31/why-emotions-are-integral-to-learning/

remembered emotions. Close friends or family who share memories of those novels may be able to trigger forgotten memories and thus pull out the emotions.

Self-guided practice. Begin to read any articles linked in tweets.

Vocabulary building. Choose one unknown word from the novel, define and use it in a discussion. Test recall the following week and build up over time to at least three new words per week.

Intensive Treatment

This phase begins after Cogmed and, perhaps, gamma brainwave training.

Goals. Set daily duration and recall goals, discussion goals, long-term recall goals, vocabulary goals, and learning goals.

Decision making. Using the Factors for Reading list, gently guide the person to choose for themselves the next novel to read, and start this discussion about fifty pages before the end of the current novel. If they can't decide within a week of completing a novel, the coach will step in and actively work with them to decide.

Self-guided practice. Begin reading novel pages on their own once a week for four weeks, then twice a week for a couple of months, then three times a week for three months, and so on. The coach continually reinforces that they're not going anywhere, that the person isn't suddenly going to have to do it all on their own, and that weekly check-ins will continue no matter what. Find a person they can continue to work on their vocabulary building with regularly as the coaching sessions lessen.

Grief and regression. If reading is treated assertively almost immediately after injury, the issues of grief, fear, abandonment, and being overwhelmed may not occur. In which case, transitioning to on-their-own reading may happen quicker. If regression occurs, immediately add back in one or more days of reading with the coach.

Cognitive vacations. They say that after two weeks of no exercise, you lose conditioning. Apply the same principle to reading rehab. Cognitive vacations are good, but you don't want to lose the momentum, especially since memory issues may complicate the person's ability to resume the routine.

Introduce tests of learning. Can the person integrate the new information and retain it for a month? Can the person change old knowledge in the face of new knowledge and retain that learning? If any problems, work with the lead healthcare practitioner to figure out what is blocking learning and reading. If there's no social support, then relearning to read may be quite difficult, in which case, try to look for substitutes.

Maintenance

Schedule for success. Use electronic alarms to ensure a systematic reading schedule, preparing and practicing as outlined above. Transition coach check-ins from weekly to three times a month to every other week to monthly. The week of the check-in, email challenging material with new vocabulary. During check-in, the person recalls the text and uses new vocabulary. At the point of this writing, I recommend the secure Signal texting app by Open Whisper Systems[47] to keep in touch for any issues that may arise. Retaining momentum is critical. As well, motivation and emotional and social stress may continue to be long-term complications of brain injury. A person may do well for quite awhile and then suddenly stop all reading. That's when the monthly check-ins and access to secure texting allow the coach to

---

[47] https://whispersystems.org

temporarily compensate through reminders and practicing with the person until they are no longer overwhelmed and can gradually return to routine. The coach can also determine if something else is going on to impede the reading and notify the lead healthcare professional.

For updated thoughts and further reading, go to http://wp.me/Pf8xE-16I.

www.ingramcontent.com/pod-product-compliance
Lightning Source LLC
LaVergne TN
LVHW041617060526
838200LV00040B/1318